Pro Windows 8.1 Development with XAML and C#

Jesse Liberty

Philip Japikse

Jon Galloway

Apress·

Pro Windows 8.1 Development with XAML and C#

ISBN-13 (pbk): 978-1-4302-4047-1

ISBN-13 (electronic): 978-1-4302-4048-8

President and Publisher: Paul Manning
Lead Editor: Jim DeWolf and Ewan Buckingham
Technical Reviewer: Todd Meister and Dan Maharry
Editorial Board: Steve Anglin, Mark Beckner, Ewan Buckingham, Gary Cornell, Louise Corrigan, Jim DeWolf,
    Jonathan Gennick, Jonathan Hassell, Robert Hutchinson, Michelle Lowman, James Markham,
    Matthew Moodie, Jeff Olson, Jeffrey Pepper, Douglas Pundick, Ben Renow-Clarke, Dominic Shakeshaft,
    Gwenan Spearing, Matt Wade, Steve Weiss
Coordinating Editor: Christine Ricketts
Copy Editor: Jana Weinstein
Compositor: SPi Global
Indexer: SPi Global
Artist: SPi Global
Cover Designer: Anna Ishchenko

Distributed to the book trade worldwide by Springer Science+Business Media New York, 233 Spring Street, 6th Floor, New York, NY 10013. Phone 1-800-SPRINGER, fax (201) 348-4505, e-mail orders-ny@springer-sbm.com, or visit www.springeronline.com. Apress Media, LLC is a California LLC and the sole member (owner) is Springer Science + Business Media Finance Inc (SSBM Finance Inc). SSBM Finance Inc is a Delaware corporation.

For information on translations, please e-mail rights@apress.com, or visit www.apress.com.

Apress and friends of ED books may be purchased in bulk for academic, corporate, or promotional use. eBook versions and licenses are also available for most titles. For more information, reference our Special Bulk Sales–eBook Licensing web page at www.apress.com/bulk-sales.

Any source code or other supplementary material referenced by the author in this text is available to readers at www.apress.com. For detailed information about how to locate your book's source code, go to www.apress.com/source-code/.

*For my wife Amy and my wonderful children, Conner, Logan, and Skylar. All I do - I do for you.
Just keep being awesome. Love, Dad*

*This book is dedicated to my two amazing daughters, Rachel and Robin, my wife, Stacey,
and my indomitable mother, Edythe Levine.*

*To my wife, Rachel, my daughters, Rosemary, Esther, and Ellie,
and to you for reading this book! Enjoy!*

Contents at a Glance

Contents

About the Authors

Jesse Liberty is a master consultant for Falafel Software, a Microsoft MVP, a Telerik MVP, and an author, and he creates courses for Pluralsight. Jesse hosts the popular *Yet Another Podcast*, and his blog is considered required reading. He was a senior evangelist for Microsoft, an XAML evangelist for Telerik, a distinguished software engineer at AT&T, a software architect for PBS, and the vice president of Information Technology at Citibank. Jesse can be followed on Twitter at @JesseLiberty.

 **Philip Japikse** is an international speaker, Microsoft MVP, ASPInsider, MCSD, CSM, and CSP, and a passionate member of the developer community. Phil Japikse has been working with .NET since the first betas, developing software for over 30 years, and heavily involved in the agile community since 2005. Phil is the Principal Architect for InterKnowlogy (www.InterKnowlogy.com), helping an amazing team create high-impact software experiences. Phil serves as the Lead Director for the Cincinnati .NET User's Group and the Cincinnati Software Architect Group, co-hosts the Hallway Conversations podcast (www.hallwayconversations.com), founded the Cincinnati Day of Agile, and volunteers for the National Ski Patrol. Phil is a frequent speaker all over the world, from user groups and meet-ups to large-scale professional conferences. You can follow Phil on Twitter via www.twitter.com/skimedic and read his blog at www.skimedic.com/blog.

Jon Galloway is a Senior Technical Evangelist for Microsoft. He's been developing applications on Microsoft technologies for 17 years on desktop and the web, from scrappy startups to large financial companies. Along the way, he's contributed to several open source projects, started the Herding Code podcast, and helped build some of the top keynote demo apps for Microsoft conferences over the past five years. He travels worldwide, speaking at conferences, Microsoft Web Camps, and developer events. Jon tweets as @jongalloway and blogs at http://weblogs.asp.net/jgalloway.

About the Technical Reviewers

Todd Meister has been working in the IT industry for over 20 years. He's been a technical editor on over 75 book titles on topics ranging from SQL Server to .NET Framework. Besides doing technical editing, he is the senior IT architect at Ball State University in Muncie, Indiana. He lives in central Indiana with his wife, Kimberly, and their five shrewd children.

Dan Maharry is a UK-based professional technical author with over a dozen books to his name and many more as technical reviewer and editor for a variety of publishers including Wrox, Apress, Microsoft Press, and O'Reilly Media. He's also a .NET developer, with past stints for the dotCoop TLD registry and various web development houses under his belt. He contributes code and documentation to various open-source projects and tries to blog and speak to user groups about cool stuff from time to time. He listens to a lot of new music as he does these activities.

Acknowledgments

Wow. Writing a book of this magnitude is a *huge* effort, and the authors are only a part of the whole process. My involvement with this book started much longer ago than I care to admit, and I would have never made it this far without an army of awesome folks from Apress helping me every step of the way. I can't even begin to thank them enough, but I'll try. Dan Maharry and Todd Meister were tireless in making sure the code samples were clear and concise, and more importantly, actually worked! I couldn't have asked for better tech reviewers! Thank you for keeping me sharp, making sure I got the code in the right places, and didn't leave anything out that would confuse (or frustrate) the readers. Ewan Buckingham and Jim DeWolf started this process with me, and kept me moving forward. Chris Nelson has seemingly dedicated every waking moment to making sure the book is the best possible it can be. Thank you for constantly reminding me that what's clear in my head isn't always as clear to someone else! Chris made sure that we had consistency throughout the book as well as that the message was clear and concise. Jana Weinstein then went over everything with a fine-tooth comb and significantly helped me to improve the copy. And finally, Christine Ricketts gets a big high five for kicking me in the butt when necessary. It's not a fun job, I'm sure, but a most valuable one! Without this all-star team collaborating with me on this, we never would have made it to press, and you wouldn't be reading this.

I also want to thank Jesse Liberty and Jon Galloway for trusting me to finish what they started, and giving me the opportunity to work with such an awesome team at Apress.

And of course, my family deserves a huge high-five for putting up with me constantly hacking on new code and then writing it up. And for keeping me motivated! Conner's constant "Where are you in the book?" would remind me that I needed to get back to work, and then I'd knock out another section of a chapter or another review. Thanks to Logan and Skylar for being patient with me. Now that we are done, we have a lot more time for XBOX!

—Philip Japikse

Jesse Liberty would like to acknowledge the amazing people at APress who made this possible, his extraordinary co-authors Jon and Phil, and the folks at Microsoft who have built one of the great operating systems of our generation.

CHAPTER 1

■ ■ ■

Getting Started

Windows 8.1 development with C# and XAML carries a lot of similarities with developing Windows Presentation Foundation (WPF) applications. Well, they both use XAML and C#. And many of your existing skills with user interfaces (UIs) and program code can be leveraged for Windows 8.1 apps. But there are a lot of differences, as well. Windows 8.1 apps are touch-centric (but also support mouse and keyboard interactions). There are specific design guidelines, quite contrary to WPF development. The isolation level for Windows 8.1 apps is much higher than WPF, presenting a new level of safety and security, as well as unique challenges when working with data. Apps are deployed through a central store (as opposed to click-once deployment or Microsoft Installer packages).

Not a WPF developer? No worries! This book will take you through everything you need to know to build Windows 8.1 apps.

Background

Microsoft released the latest revision of its Windows operating system, Windows 8.0, on October 26, 2012. This release was groundbreaking for several reasons, but at the top of the list were the dual interfaces of Windows 8 and support for ARM devices.

Dual User Interfaces

The original release of Windows 8.0 introduced two UIs—the desktop for Intel-based hardware and the tiled interface (formerly called Metro) not only for Intel-based hardware, but also ARM-based hardware, a first for Windows.

The desktop UI, simply put, is a better version of Windows 7. The install is much smaller (I regained 6 GB of hard disk space when I upgraded), it's even more secure, and it runs faster on the same hardware that was supported by Windows 7.

The tiled UI was completely reimagined for Windows 8.0. Although the same type of tiled interface had previously been used in the Windows Phone operating system, this was the first time that a non-phone-based version of Windows had a major change in many, many years.

ARM Support

ARM-based processors (created by ARM Holdings, a British Company) have dominated the tablet market. What was very clearly missing from that market was an offering from Microsoft—at least from Microsoft's point of view. But also for Windows users. The introduction of the Microsoft Surface RT brought a Windows-based offering in the tablet space, allowing users to sync their desktop/laptop, phone, and tablet. And Microsoft Office runs on the Surface RT!

Acceptance

How did this dramatic change go over in the first year? If you listen to the press and the analysts, terrible. Not with the operating system itself, but with the response from the masses. From "Where is my Start menu?" to "How do I print?," there were outcries about moved cheese and change. Were they legitimate complaints? It depends on your point of view, but the quick release of Windows 8.1 bringing back the Start button and addressing some of the most common complaints certainly adds credence to those people who weren't happy with the original version.

Interestingly enough, in looking at the numbers from several different sites, Windows 8 adoption in the first year rivals that of XP adoption in its first year. And if you are old enough to remember the Windows 95 revolution and the outcry at that release, this is same old same old. Things change, people freak out, and then after the initial shock, they settle down and start using the new software.

Fast-Release Cycle

Less than one year after the release of Windows 8, Microsoft released Windows 8.1 on October 17, 2013. Much more than a service pack, this release addressed many of the issues that people were complaining about, such as the return of the Start button and the ability to boot straight to desktop mode. Made freely available through the Microsoft Store, the install rate for Windows 8.1 has been extremely high.

The Microsoft Store

How many times have you had to do tech support for a family member because he clicked on some random pop-up on the Internet, or installed some software that a friend told him about? The main mechanism for getting apps is from the Microsoft Store. Having that one central place to get apps for Windows 8/8.1 helps prevent rogue software from getting installed, increasing the security and reliability of the device. It also provides a centralized location for developers to place their app for others to find. For more information about submitting your app to the Microsoft Store, please see Chapter 12.

What's New in Windows 8.1

There are a lot of changes between Windows 8.0 and Windows 8.1. At the top of each chapter in this book, look for the "What's New in Windows 8.1" sidebar to get a high-level overview of the changes in Windows 8.1 concerning the chapter's topic. The chapters themselves are dedicated to using Visual Studio 2013 and Windows 8.1, with detailed information is included in the body of each chapter.

Windows Design Guidelines

In order to get your apps accepted into the store, you must make sure they meet the seven traits of a great app and also follow the five Microsoft design principles. There are additional technical requirements that will be discussed in Chapter 11.

Let's look at the seven traits of a great app first. To achieve greatness, it must:

- Be fast and fluid
- Size beautifully
- Use the right contracts
- Invest in a great tile

- Feel like it is connected and alive
- Roam to the cloud
- Embrace modern app design principles

Being Fast and Fluid

Modern apps can be run on a variety of devices with a wide range of capabilities. While Microsoft has set minimum standards for all hardware that carries the Windows 8 logo, it's important for the success of your app (as well as the success of Windows 8) that your app doesn't perform poorly or cause the hardware to perform poorly. You will see as you work your way through this book that in order to develop Windows 8.1 applications, you must use asynchronous programming to ensure a responsive UI. Additionally, the very design of the Windows 8.1 process lifetime management cycle ensures that background apps don't drain the battery or use up precious system resources.

Use the async pattern liberally. If your app is taking a long time to load or to run, people will uninstall it. Or, worse yet, they will write a scathing review and *then* uninstall it.

Sizing Beautifully

Windows 8 devices come in a variety of sizes and screen resolutions. Apps can be run in a landscape or portrait view as well as resized to share the screen with other apps. Your app needs to able to adjust to different layouts and sizes, not only in appearance but also in usability. For example, if you have a screen showing a lot of data in a grid, when your app gets pinned to one side or the other, that grid should turn into a list.

Using the Right Contracts

Windows 8 introduces a completely new way to interact with the operating system and other applications. Contracts include Search, Share, Settings. By leveraging these contracts, you expose additional capabilities into your app in a manner that is very familiar to your users.

Investing in a Great Tile

Tiles are the entry point into your applications. A live tile can draw users into an app and increase the interest and time spent using it. Too-many updates can lead them to turn off updates, or worse yet, uninstall your app.

Secondary tiles are a great way for users to pin specific information to their Start screen to enable quick access to items of their interest.

Feeling like It Is Connected and Alive

Users are a vital component to Windows 8 apps. It is important to make sure that your app is connected to the world so that it can receive real-time information. Whether that information is the latest stock prices or information on sales figures for your company, stale data doesn't compel users to keep using your app. They already know what yesterday's weather was. The current forecast is much more interesting.

Roaming to the Cloud

Windows 8 allows the user the capability to share data between devices. Not only can application settings be synced but so can the application data. Imagine the surprise for a user who enters some data into your app at work and then picks up another Windows 8 device at home, starts your app, and the data is right there.

It is important to leverage the cloud whenever possible to make transitioning from one device to another as seamless as possible.

Embracing the Modern App Design Principles

In addition to the traits just mentioned, your app must meet the modern app design principles. Microsoft's full list can be found here: `http://go.microsoft.com/fwlink/p/?linkid=258743`. A brief summary of the five principles follows:

- *Show pride in craftsmanship*: This is fairly simple. Pardon the vernacular, but just don't build crappy software. Build software that you would be willing to list on your resume. If you're making an app in order to make money, you will want people to use it, to "like" it on social media, to show it off to their friends. These things are important unless you have a huge marketing budget, but even then that will only get first-time users. Once word gets out that the app isn't very good (and remember there is a rating system in the Microsoft Store), your app is done.

  So, make sure it works. Consider hiring a graphic designer if you're not design inclined. Let users test it (consider friends and family). Get feedback. Fix the problems—whether the problems are bugs or user-experience issues.

- *Be fast and fluid*: Microsoft is serious about this one, having listed it here and in the traits for a great app. In addition to the traits previously listed, design for touch and intuitive interaction. Be responsive to user interaction, and make a UI that is immersive and compelling.

- *Be authentically digital*: Take full advantage the capabilities of the device. Use bold colors, beautiful typography, and animations. Of course, use all of the effects (especially motion) with purpose. Just because you can add flaming arrows shooting across the screen doesn't mean you should!

- *Do more with less*: Chrome may look great on a motorcycle, but in software, it just distracts users from what they care about, which is the data. Instead of buttons and tabs, leverage the app bar and nav bar. Take advantage of the charms and contracts to reduce even more chrome.

  Focus the functionality of your app. Don't try to solve all problems. Just solve one or two really well. Be focused on that solution, and do your best to immerse your users in their data, not the app.

- *Win as one*: Work with the Windows 8 paradigm. Leverage common touch gestures and familiar mouse and keyboard themes so your users can leverage what they already know. Work with other apps through contracts so that your app can become bigger than just the sum of its parts.

UX Guidelines

There are many more guidelines suggested by Microsoft. For the full guidelines, see `http://msdn.microsoft.com/en-us/library/windows/apps/hh465424.aspx`. If you would like a downloadable PDF of the same guidelines, you can download it here: `http://go.microsoft.com/fwlink/p/?linkid=258743`.

Tooling

While you can certainly remain in Visual Studio the entire time you are developing your app, leveraging a combination of the available tooling provides the best experience. For developing Windows 8 applications, the two main tools you will use are Visual Studio 2013 and Blend for Visual Studio 2013.

Visual Studio 2013

In November of 2013, Microsoft released Visual Studio 2013. Among the changes in the latest version of Visual Studio is support for creating Windows 8.1 apps. This is a mandatory upgrade, as Visual Studio 2012 will not support building apps for Windows 8.1.

Versions

If you are reading this book, then you are probably very familiar with Visual Studio. In this section, I'll talk about the different versions of Visual Studio 2013 available to you and some of the differences between them. If you aren't very familiar with Visual Studio, don't worry. As we move through the chapters of this book, the relevant features will be discussed in greater detail.

Visual Studio Express

Visual Studio Express 2013 is now separated by the target platform. Although I haven't seen any official communication as to why, I think it was just too big to keep it in one free download, and people who were new to Visual Studio were getting lost in all of the features.

The available versions are:

- *Visual Studio 2013 Express for Web*: for ASP.NET developers

- *Visual Studio 2013 Express for Windows*: for Windows 8.1 app developers

- *Visual Studio 2013 Express for Windows Desktop*: for Windows Client application developers using Windows Presentation Foundation (WPF) or WinForms

For the purposes of this book (and creating Windows 8.1 apps), you will need Visual Studio Express 2013 for Windows.

Visual Studio with MSDN

There are essentially three paid versions of Visual Studio 2013 for developers: Professional, Premium, and Ultimate. All of them are part of MSDN and provide everything you need for developing Windows 8.1 apps plus a whole lot more. Note that there is also a fourth version, Visual Studio for Test Professional, but it doesn't apply to building Windows 8.1 apps, so we don't discuss it here. For all of the nitty-gritty details of what's in each version, see the documentation on the Visual Studio site here: www.visualstudio.com/products/compare-visual-studio-products-vs.

The Windows 8.1 Simulator

All versions of Visual Studio come with the ability to run your Windows 8.1 app in a simulator. This is essentially a remote desktop session to your PC with the added ability to change orientation, form factor, gesture support and to simulate many factors of a tablet (even if you are developing on a nontouch device). This is one of the reasons that you must be working in a Windows 8.1 environment to develop Windows 8.1 apps.

Creating Your First Windows 8.1 App

To create a Windows 8.1 app, create a new project in Visual Studio 2013 by selecting File ➤ New ➤ Project. In the left rail, you will see all of the installed templates for your Visual Studio installation (your mileage may vary based on version you installed and what third-part products you use). Select Installed ➤ Templates ➤ Visual C#➤ Windows Store, and you will be presented with the dialog shown in Figure 1-1.

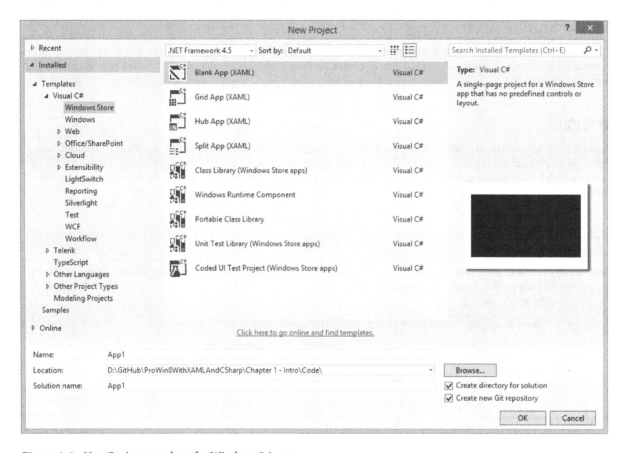

Figure 1-1. *New Project templates for Windows 8.1 apps*

In Chapter 4, we will go into great detail for all of the project templates, so for now, just select Blank App (XAML). In fact, this will be the starting template for *most* of our projects in this book, and is the template I typically start with when I develop Windows 8.1 apps. You can leave the project name as the default App1.

After you create your project, take a look at the Default Solution folder (shown in Figure 1-2). The Blank App template actually does a lot for us. In addition to creating the project and bringing in the appropriate references, it supplies us with several assets, the App.xaml file, and MainPage.xaml. The Assets folder contains the images for the splash screen and the default tiles (more on that later in this book), and if you are familiar with WPF, the App.xaml and MainPage.xaml files should be very familiar. Again, we will spend a lot of time in the book on those files.

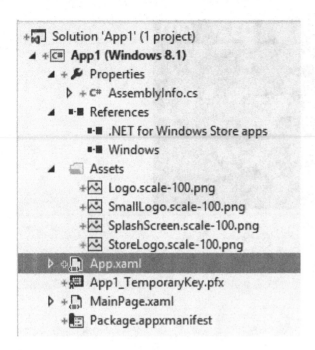

Figure 1-2. Default Solution Explorer files

To run the app, you can press F5 (to start with debugging), Ctl-F5 (to start without debugging), click on Debug in the menu (to be presented with the same options), or click the toolbar item with the green arrow (as shown in Figure 1-3).

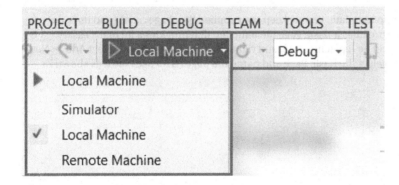

Figure 1-3. Run toolbar utility

By default, Visual Studio will run your app on the local machine in Debug configuration. Go ahead and click on the green arrow (or press F5) to run the app. We would expect to see a completely blank screen, but instead we are presented with some changing numbers (they change as you move the mouse around the screen) in the top corners of the screen, as shown in Figure 1-4. The frame rate counters show you, from left to right, the UI frame rate (frames per second), the App CPU usage of UI thread, the system composition frames per second, and system UI thread CPU usage. If you run the app without debugging, you will not see the numbers in the corner. This is because all of the Visual Studio–supplied templates enable the frame rate counter display while running in debug mode.

Figure 1-4. *Debugging with FrameRateCounter*

Turning this off is very simple—you just open `App.xaml.cs`, and in the `OnLaunched` event handler, comment out this line of code:

```
this.DebugSettings.EnableFrameRateCounter = true;
```

so that it looks like this:

```
//this.DebugSettings.EnableFrameRateCounter = true;
```

Now, when you run you app in debug mode, the numbers are no longer displayed.

Adding a Basic Page

Even though I typically start with the Blank App template, I rarely keep the supplied `MainPage.xaml` (and its code behind file `MainPage.xaml.cs`). Visual Studio provides a Basic Page file template that provides a lot of necessary functionality. Delete the `MainPage.xaml` (we will be replacing this), and right-click your project and select Add ➤ New Item. From the Add New Item—App 1 dialog, select the Basic Page and name the page `MainPage.xaml`, as shown in Figure 1-5.

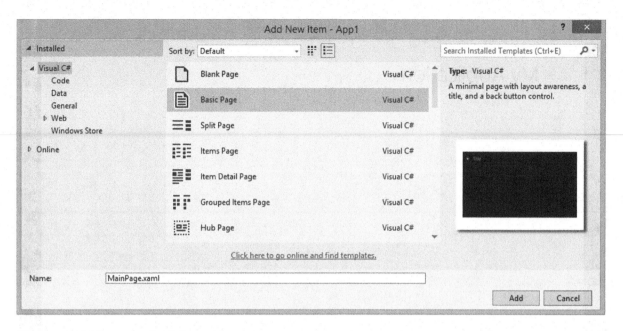

Figure 1-5. *Adding a new Basic Page*

■ **Note**   We call it `MainPage.xaml` so we don't have to change `App.xaml.cs`. If you want to call the files something else (or change the page that gets loaded when an app first starts, open `App.xaml.cs`, navigate to the end of the OnLaunched event handler, and change the following line to the name of the page you added:

```
rootFrame.Navigate(typeof(MainPage), e.Arguments);
```

When you add a new Basic Page, Visual Studio prompts you that it will add several files into your project. Say Yes! These are extremely helpful files and will be used extensively though the course of this book. However, for now, we just want to have some text to display. Change the option on the debug location toolbar to run in the simulator, and then press F5 (or click the green arrow to start debugging). You'll now see a title for the app (running in a window that resembles a tablet) and a series of controls on the right rail of the simulator, as shown in Figure 1-6.

Figure 1-6. *The Simulator*

The Simulator Controls

Most of the simulator controls are very self-explanatory, but I struggled in my early days of Windows 8 apps to remember what each icon stood for, so I've listed the explanations here to help you out.

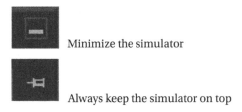 Minimize the simulator

Always keep the simulator on top

The touch modes in the simulator are important to be able to test your app's responsiveness to touch if you don't own (or develop on) a touch device. The mouse mode button takes you back out of touch mode to keyboard and mouse mode.

 Mouse mode

 Basic touch mode, pinch/zoom touch mode, rotation touch mode

The rotation and resolution controls help testing by responding to different orientations and form factors.

 Rotate clockwise (90 degrees)/rotate counterclockwise (90 degrees)

 Change the resolution

If you are building a location-aware application, you can test that by setting the location that is sent to the app from the hardware.

 Set location

The screenshot commands are invaluable for the submission process, as you will see in Chapter 12. They are also useful to create screenshots for building documentation, advertising your app on your website, and so on.

 Copy screenshot/screenshot settings

The network control allows for testing occasionally connected scenarios, bandwidth usage, and making other networks variables.

 Change network properties

 Help

Blend for Visual Studio 2013

Expression Blend has long been a staple of the WPF developer. Long sold as a separate product from Visual Studio, it was part of the Expression suite. Starting with Visual Studio 2012, Blend for Visual Studio was released as a free companion application for Visual Studio. Unfortunately, the first iteration left the XAML developer behind in the dust and completely focused on the HTML/JavaScript developers for Windows 8 apps.

That has been fixed, and Blend for Visual Studio 2013 is now back with a vengeance to help XAML developers. To open your project in Blend, you can right-click on any XAML file in Visual Studio 2013 and select Open in Blend. This will open not just the file that you selected but also the entire project/solution.

Many of the features of Blend are covered in subsequent chapters, but some of the biggest benefits of using Blend are:

- Full control of your UI in a compact layout—the Visual Studio XAML designer pales in comparison to what can be accomplished in Blend. While I am not a designer (and don't make any claims to having design skills), Blend has enabled me to make much-better-looking UIs as well as to make changes much faster than in Visual Studio (regardless of being in design or XAML mode in Visual Studio).

- The ability to easily add animations, gradients, and styles to your app/page

- The ability to quickly add states to your page (for layout updates) and state recording

- The ability to view your page in many layouts and form factors (much like the Simulator, but without the benefit of the page running—WinJS/HTML developers still have the advantage here)

Additionally, Visual Studio and Blend for Visual Studio keep your files in sync. If you have your project open in both, when you make changes (and save them) to your app/pages in one program, switching to the other program will prompt you to reload. Make sure that you actually save the changes, as making changes in both without saving will result in concurrency problems.

Opening Your Project in Blend for Visual Studio

Visual Studio and Blend work extremely well together. To open your project in Blend, right-click on the MainPage.xaml in your project and select Open in Blend (see Figure 1-7).

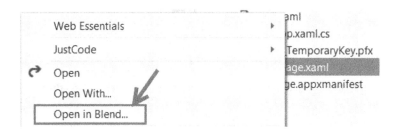

Figure 1-7. *Opening a file in Blend*

Visual Studio invokes Blend, opening your entire project (not just the file you clicked on). Once the file is opened, you will see a screen similar to Figure 1-8. Blend will open the file you right-clicked on in Visual Studio.

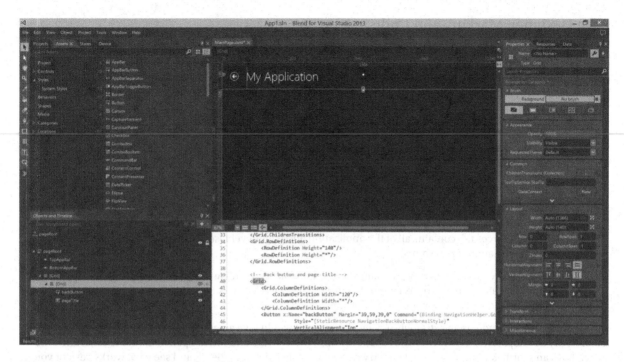

Figure 1-8. *MainPage.xaml opened in Blend*

That's a lot of windows, but at least in the default layout (much like Visual Studio, you can change the layout to suit your needs). Let's look at them in a little more detail.

Projects, Assets, States, and Device Tabs

The top-left corner of the window contains the Projects, Assets, States, and Device tabs, which allow you to do the following processes:

- The Projects tab shows all of the files in your solution (much like Solution Explorer in Visual Studio). Nothing too exciting to report here.

- The Assets tab lists all of the assets available to add to your page. Think of this as a turbo-charged Visual Studio Toolbox. In addition to controls and panels that you can add to your page, you can also add (and modify) styles, behaviors, and media.

- The States tab allows you to add the Visual State Manager XAML as well as Visual State groups to your page. It also allows for easy addition of transitions for your visual states.

- The Device tab allows you to change the resolution and orientation as well as connected edges (more on this in subsequent chapters). You can also change the theme (between light and dark) as well as the minimum width.

Objects and Timeline

The Objects and Timeline panel (lower left) provides the document outline as well as the ability to add and modify storyboards (to be used in conjunction with the Visual State Manager).

Page Designer, Markup, and Code

The center of the workspace is the designer and code editor. Just like in Visual Studio, you can have a split view, all design, or all markup. You can also load code files into the center pane. While you get features like Intellisense, the development experience doesn't contain all of the great features of Visual Studio like navigation and refactoring. Plus, you lose any productivity plug-ins like Telerik's JustCode that you might have installed in Visual Studio.

Properties, Resources, and Data Tabs

The right rail of the workspace contains the Properties, Resources, and Data tabs, which can be described as follows:

- The Properties tab is where I spend a significant portion of my time in Blend. In addition to the simple items like Name and Layout and properties like Width and Height, there are a host of properties that are difficult to set by hand in markup. Brushes, Transforms, and Interactions can all be set using the Properties panel.

- The Resources tab contains all of the application and page-level resources as well the option to edit and add more resources.

- The Data tab allows you to set the data context for your page, create sample data, and create different data sources. This is helpful to see what the page will look like with data at design time instead of always having to run the app.

Blend for Visual Studio is an extremely powerful tool and it would take an entire book to discuss all of the features. My development workflow involves keeping both Visual Studio and Blend open at the same time, and I switch back and forth depending on what I am trying to accomplish. Explore Blend, and see what works best for you.

Git

Software version control has been around for a long time. If you have been in the Microsoft space for a significant length of time, you might remember Visual Source Safe. In the .NET world, the MS developer was left with Team Foundation Server (TFS) as the only integrated source-code-management (SCM) system.

TFS is a powerful application lifecycle management (ALM) tool (including project management, bug tracking, SCM, and other components). That is a lot of tooling when you are only looking for SCM. The SCM portion of TFS is Team Foundation Version Control (TFVC) and is a centralized SCM system. This means that a single repository is the source of record, and all developers check their code in and out of this single repository. Later versions of TFVC have included the capability to shelve work and create branches, providing some isolation for work in progress.

Git, developed by Linus Torvalds in 2005 for the Linux kernel, is a distributed version control system (DVCS). This means that every developer using Git has a full-fledged repository on his local machine with complete history and tracking capabilities. Many Git users (especially in a team environment) have a central repository in addition to their local repository. This frees the developer to spike different ideas, work on features independent of the rest of the team, and check in rapidly as often as they like without worrying about network latency or affecting other team members.

Which SCM system you choose to use is completely up to you. They both have their merits (and there are many other SCM systems available to you as well that are very effective in what they do). It's more how you work and whom you work with that usually determines which system to use. So why do I bring up Git specifically in this book? Because if you are a single developer creating a Windows 8 app, Git is custom tailored to you, and with Visual Studio 2013 (and updated to Visual Studio 2012), Git support is now included.

There are entire books written about effectively using Git, so this is just a quick look into the Visual Studio integration, and not a treatise on DVCS.

Using Git in Visual Studio

One of the advantages of using Git is its simplicity. A Git repository can be created anywhere—on a local disk, network share, or web site (like GitHub).

GitHub for Windows

The easiest way to start working with Git if you are new to the system is to install GitHub for Windows, which is available from `https://windows.github.com/`. Creating a new repository is as easy as clicking on the Create button in GitHub for Windows. Once Visual Studio is configured to use Git, any projects created inside an existing repo will automatically tie into the Git repo.

Enabling Git in Visual Studio 2013

The first step to using Git with your project is to enable the Microsoft Git Provider. Do this by selecting Tools ➤ Options ➤ Source Control ➤ Plug-in Selection, and then select the Microsoft Git Provider for the Current source control plug-in, as in Figure 1-9.

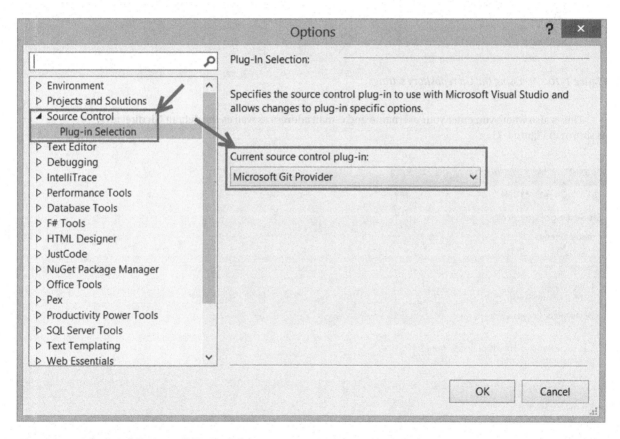

Figure 1-9. *Selecting the Microsoft Git Provider*

Selecting Team Explorer (View ➤ Team Explorer) in the right rail of Visual Studio (the default location) allows you to manage your local Git repository. By default, VS 2013 creates the appropriate Git ignore files so local files such as /bin and /obj files, temp files, user files, and so forth don't appear in the repository. There are also attributes on how Git should handle conflicts in project files. To view both of these files, select Git Settings, as shown in Figure 1-10.

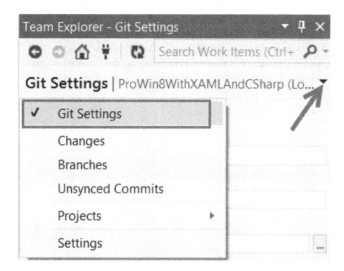

Figure 1-10. *Accessing the Git repository settings*

This is also where you enter your username and e-mail address as well as the default Git directory, as shown in Figure 1-11.

Figure 1-11. *Git Settings*

Checking in Changes

To check in changes, select Changes from the same menu, as shown in Figure 1-10. You will see changes that will be included in this check-in and excluded changes as well as untracked files. To commit the changes, enter a comment in the text box with the watermark "Enter a commit message <Required>" and click on Commit. You can also Commit and Push to a remote repository to share your changes, or Commit and Sync with a remote repository to share your changes and get the latest version from the remote repository as shown in Figure 1-12.

Figure 1-12. *Committing changes to the local repository*

Remote Repositories

There are many places where you can host remote Git repositories, with the most popular being GitHub (https://github.com). Once you set up a remote repository, you can point your project to it by entering its URL, as in Figure 1-13.

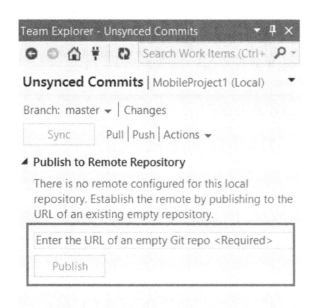

Figure 1-13. *Publishing to a remote repository*

Reverting Changes

If you totally mess up while developing, Git makes it very easy to restore from the repository. Right-click on your file in Solution Explorer and you will see the Git features exposed: Undo, View History, Compare with Unmodified, and Commit (see Figure 1-14). Undo does just what it says—it throws away your changes and restores the file from the repository. It's like your own personal security blanket!

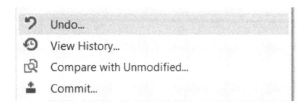

Figure 1-14. *Git functions exposed through Solution Explorer*

Again, this isn't a full explanation of how Git works but a quick overview of the Visual Studio features that support Git. If you've never used source code control systems, Git is an easy first one to use. You'll thank yourself in the end.

NuGet

From the official NuGet site (`www.nuget.org`): "NuGet is the package manager for the Microsoft development platform including .NET. The NuGet client tools provide the ability to produce and consume packages. The NuGet Gallery is the central package repository used by all package authors and consumers."

Instead of scouring the web for tools to add into Visual Studio, you can use NuGet as a single source to get a wide variety of add-ins for your solution. Rather than installing the tools on your development machine, the packages are installed at the *solution* level. This permits different versions to coexist on the same developer machine.

Another very large advantage to NuGet is that each package lists its dependencies within its package manifest. When a package is installed through NuGet, all of its dependencies get installed as well.

Yet another benefit of NuGet is the ability to create private NuGet package sources. To change the source, select Tools ➤ Options ➤ NuGet Package Manager ➤ Package Sources, as in Figure 1-15.

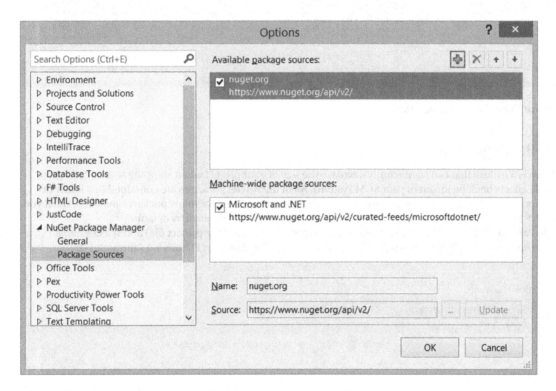

Figure 1-15. *NuGet Package Source dialog*

Installing NuGet

In the off chance that NuGet wasn't preinstalled with Visual Studio, installation is easy. It's available in the Visual Studio Extension Gallery (accessible from Tools ➤ Extensions and Updates).

Once the Extensions and Updates window is open, select Online ➤ Visual Studio Gallery in the left rail. In the search box, enter NuGet, and look for the NuGet Package Manager for Visual Studio 2013. In Figure 1-16, there is a green check mark by the extension since I already have NuGet installed.

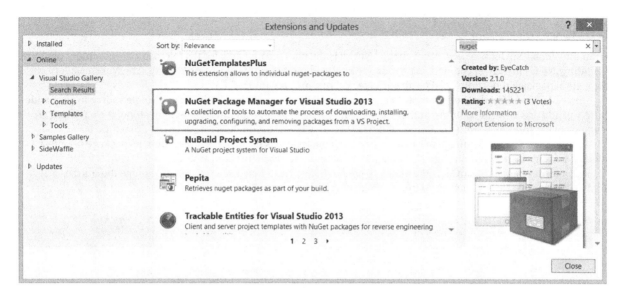

Figure 1-16. *Installing NuGet Package Manager*

Enabling Package Restore

Package Restore is a feature that can significantly decrease the size of your project when shipping source code (note that this doesn't affect checking in/out of your SCM system). All of the NuGet packages are contained in a folder in your solution aptly named "Packages." By default, Windows 8.1 projects don't have many packages installed, but if you create an ASP.NET project, you will see a lot of packages, only some of which are used by default.

To enable Package Restore, right-click on your solution (note that it is not the project file) and select Enable NuGet Package Restore. You will be prompted with a series of dialogs. as shown in Figures 1-17 through 1-19.

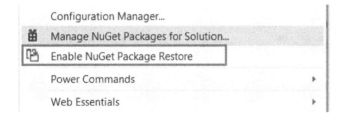

Figure 1-17. *Enabling Package Restore*

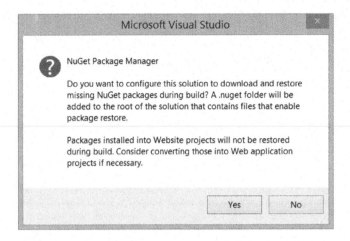

Figure 1-18. *Confirmation dialog for Package Restore*

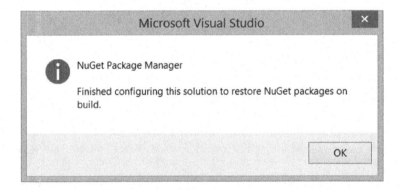

Figure 1-19. *Confirmation dialog*

Once you have enabled Package Restore, you will see the changes to your project as shown in Figure 1-20.

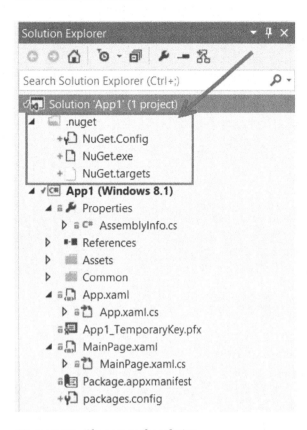

Figure 1-20. *Changes to the solution*

Installing Your First Package

One of the "Can't live without" packages for developing Windows 8.1 apps is Newtonsoft's Json.NET. We'll use Json. NET later in this book, but for now, let's just get it installed. There are two ways to install packages—by using the Package Manager Console command line or by using the Package Manager GUI.

Installing from the Command Line

Access the Package Manager Console by selecting View Ȩ Other Windows Ȩ Package Manager Console if it isn't currently visible in the bottom rail of Visual Studio.

Type "install-package newtonsoft.json" and you'll see the dialog shown in Figure 1-21. At the time of this writing, 6.0.1 is the current version. NuGet will install the current version unless you specify a version. Another benefit of using NuGet.

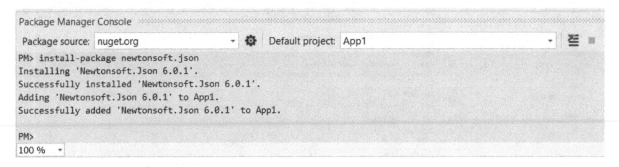

Figure 1-21. *Command line installation of Json.NET*

Installing from the Graphical User Interface

Installing from the graphical user interface (GUI) is very simple, and provides a search mechanism if you don't know the exact name of the package that you are looking for. For example, everyone refers to the package as "Json.NET." The actual package name in NuGet is "newtonsoft.json." This is a great example of where the search in the NuGet GUI is very helpful.

To access the GUI, right-click on your solution and select Manage NuGet Packages for Solution, as in Figure 1-22.

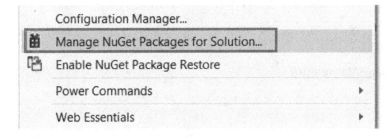

Figure 1-22. *Launching the NuGet GUI*

Select Online in the left rail and enter Json.NET in the search dialog. You will see results similar to Figure 1-23. Merely click install to install Json.NET.

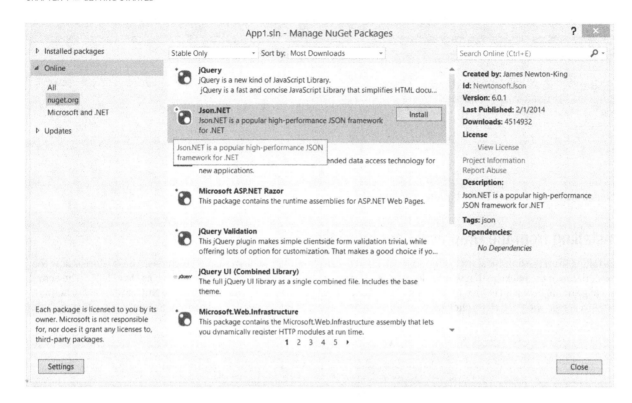

Figure 1-23. *Installing Json.NET with the Package Manager GUI*

Summary

Windows 8 apps represent a very large paradigm shift from traditional Windows desktop applications (such as WPF or WinForm) or web apps (such as ASP.NET Webforms or MVC). Whereas traditional applications were developed with a wide range of tools but no real design guidelines and no expectations of performance, Windows 8.1 apps must meet a series of expectations, both in terms of UI design and app performance. They are distributed through the Microsoft Store after a stringent certification process.

Developing Windows 8 apps involves a lot more than just Visual Studio. Blend for Visual Studio helps build compelling UIs, Git provides security for your source code, and NuGet enables easy addition of packages and add-ons to Visual Studio.

Now that you know the tools to use, let's build that first app!

■ ■ ■

CHAPTER 2

Building Your First Windows 8 App

Chapter 1 covered the design guidelines as well as the tooling commonly used to build Windows 8.1 apps. In this chapter, we will cover some of the core principles of Windows 8.1, including its architecture, all of the many parts of its apps in Visual Studio, the Model-View-ViewModel pattern, and navigation. All in the context of building your first Windows 8.1 app.

Windows Architecture (For Developers)

There are many options when choosing how to develop apps that can run on Windows 8.1 machines as you can see in Figure 2-1, and even more options when those Windows 8.1 machines are based on the x86 or x64 chipset.

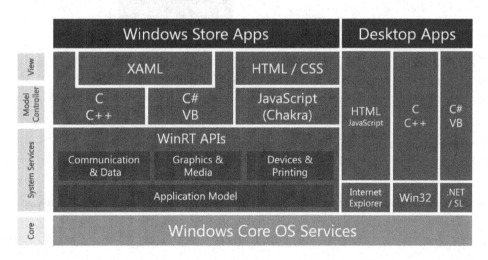

Figure 2-1. *Windows architecture*

Windows 8.1 apps that run in the modern interface (formerly called Metro; sometimes also called the Windows Store interface) can be developed with an XAML- or HTML-based UI. XAML-based apps can be written with C++, C#, or VB.NET. HTML-based apps are developed using JavaScript, leveraging the WinJS library. This book is about writing Windows 8.1 apps using XAML and C#. If you are interested in C++, VB.NET, or WinJS/HTML, Apress has an extensive library of books on those topics. Throughout this book, we'll dig deeper into the system services and the Windows 8.1 Core.

You can also develop applications for the desktop mode of Windows 8 on non-ARM-based devices (such as the Surface Pro). In desktop mode, you can still develop "traditional" applications such as smart client and browser-based ones, using all of the tools that you are familiar with such as Windows Presentation Foundation, ASP.NET, and even Silverlight and Winforms. For all of these topics, Apress has many books that can help you become even better with many great books on these subjects. (See www.apress.com for the full Apress catalog.)

Creating Your First App

To create our first app, let's start Visual Studio and select File ➤ New ➤ New Project, and then select Templates ➤ Visual C# ➤ Windows Store. We'll talk about the different templates in later chapters, but for now just select the Blank App and leave the default name as App1, as in Figure 2-2.

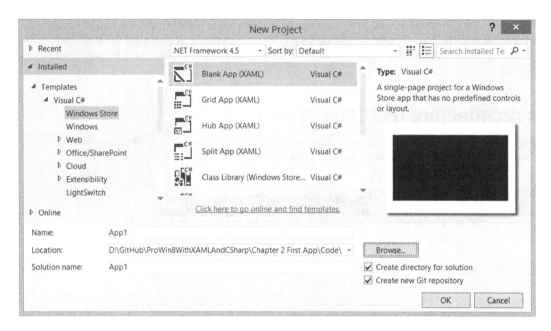

Figure 2-2. *Creating a new Windows 8.1 app*

Let's look at the nodes and files that are created as part of the template. Much of the project should be familiar to you.

App Project Overview

The New Project template introduces a significant number of folders and files, as shown in Figure 2-3.

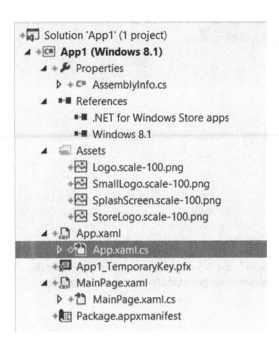

Figure 2-3. Folders and files in the Blank App template

Properties

Under the Properties node in the New Project template is the AssemblyInfo.cs file, the standard metainformation container for C# projects. Feel free to update the information such as description, copyright, and so on. Most of this information isn't necessary for modern apps, but I tend to update the information anyway out of habit.

References

The template also includes the standard References node, which is prepopulated with two references: .NET for Windows Store apps and Windows. These references provide that vast majority of functionality, as diagrammed in Figure 2-1, and must be included. Throughout this book, we will add additional references to supplement the default features available to us.

Assets

There is also the Assets folder, which contains all of the images that are part of your application. The tile images and splash screen graphics go in this folder as well as any other images or assets that need to be packaged with your app when it gets deployed. Click on one of the images in Solution Explorer (such as Logo.scale-100.png) and press F4 to view the properties. The Build Action for the images is set to Content and set not to copy to the Output directory, as in Figure 2-4. Alternatively, you can have the content copied to the Output directory or run a custom tool, although you will not want to do that for the images.

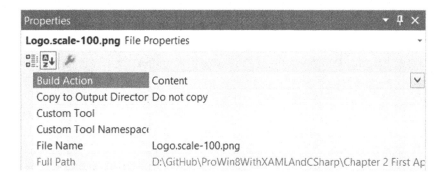

Figure 2-4. *Image Asset properties*

App1_TemporaryKey.pfx

App1_TemporaryKey.pfx (named after the app name—App1 in our case) is the developer license information for the app. We'll update this when we work with push notifications as well as when we get ready to submit our app to the Microsoft Store later in this book.

Package.appxmanifest

Package.appxmanifest contains six tabs that describe your application that we will go on to look at. The actual manifest file is an XML file, but Visual Studio provides a nice GUI to work with the elements in the file, saving us from having to memorize the format or definitions. Double-click on the Package.appxmanifest file to open it up in the Visual Studio editor.

The Application Tab

The Application tab largely replaces the AssemblyInfo.cs, but also provides many more options, as shown in Figure 2-5. The top section includes the Display Name, Entry Point, Default Language, and Description.

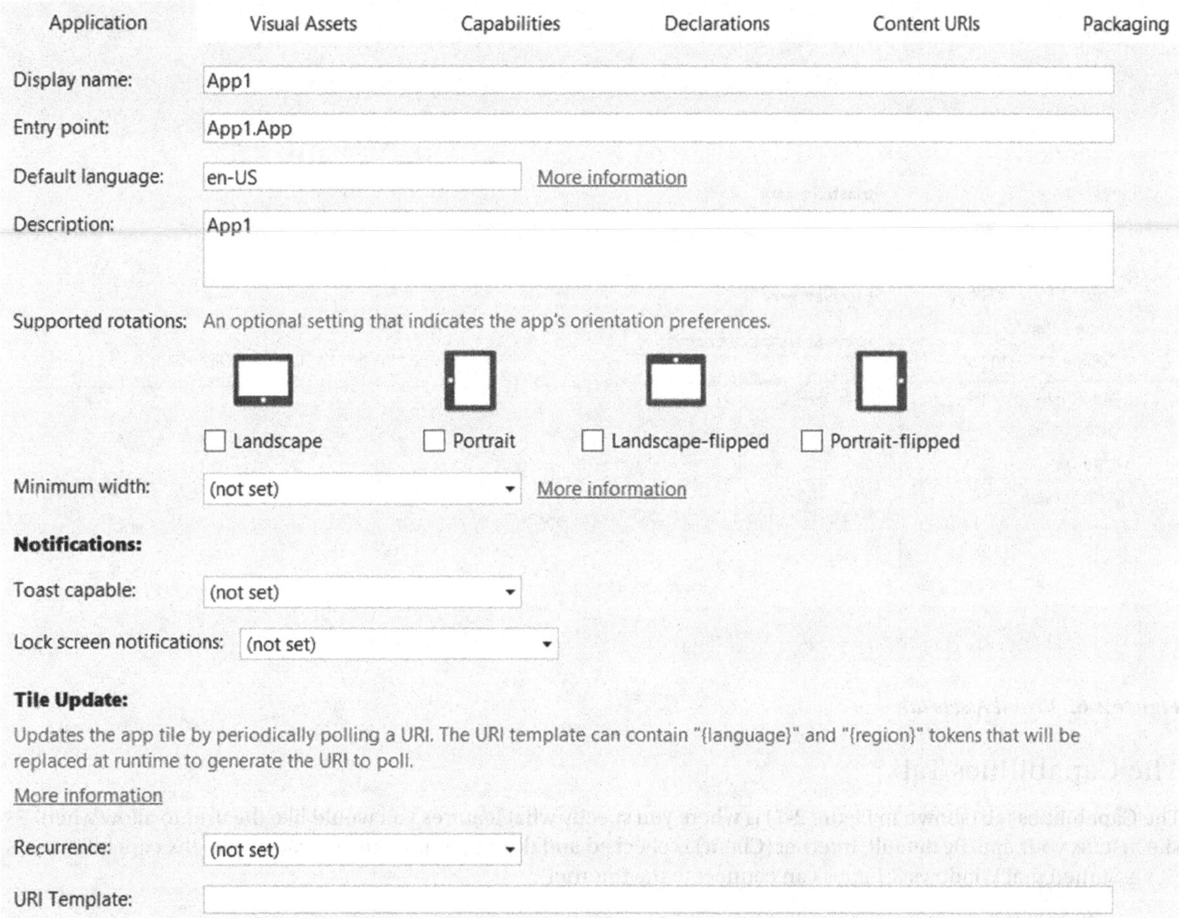

Application	Visual Assets	Capabilities	Declarations	Content URIs	Packaging

Display name: `App1`

Entry point: `App1.App`

Default language: `en-US`   More information

Description: `App1`

Supported rotations: An optional setting that indicates the app's orientation preferences.

☐ Landscape   ☐ Portrait   ☐ Landscape-flipped   ☐ Portrait-flipped

Minimum width: `(not set)` ▾   More information

Notifications:

Toast capable: `(not set)` ▾

Lock screen notifications: `(not set)` ▾

Tile Update:

Updates the app tile by periodically polling a URI. The URI template can contain "{language}" and "{region}" tokens that will be replaced at runtime to generate the URI to poll.

More information

Recurrence: `(not set)` ▾

URI Template:

Figure 2-5. *Application tab*

The next section under the tab is for the supported rotations, or the layout. You can select the rotations as well as the minimum width. For the layout preferences, if all of the options are checked (or none of them checked, as in the default), then all rotations are supported. If only some of the layouts are checked, such as Portrait and Portrait-Flipped, the app will not rotate when a tablet is changed from Portrait to Landscape. If the hardware does not support rotation (such as a traditional laptop), then the setting is essentially meaningless. The following section, Minimum Width, will be covered in detail in Chapter 5.

The first category, Notifications, has two sections, Toast Capable and Lock Screen notifications, which are covered in Chapter 9. The next category, Tile Update, provides a mechanism to enter Uri details for the source for notifications using a polling mechanism (instead of push notifications).

The Visual Assets Tab

The Visual Assets tab (shown in Figure 2-6) is where you set the Tile Images and Logo, Splash Screen, and Badge Logo, as well as text that can appear on the different tiles. The splash screen is what is shown as your app is activated. The default image is the white box on a dark screen. Select Splash Screen in the left rail to set a new splash screen for your app. By default, any images specified here should be stored in the Assets folder previously discussed. The other features of this screen are covered in detail in Chapter 9.

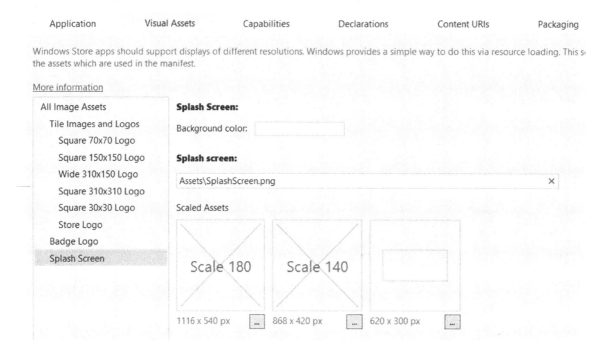

Figure 2-6. *Visual Assets tab*

The Capabilities Tab

The Capabilities tab (shown in Figure 2-7) is where you specify what features you would like the user to allow when she installs your app. By default, Internet (Client) is checked and doesn't require the user to accept the capability (it's assumed that Windows 8.1 apps can connect to the Internet).

| Application | Visual Assets | Capabilities | Declarations | Content URIs | Packaging |

Use this page to specify system features or devices that your app can use.

Capabilities:

☐ Enterprise Authentication
☑ Internet (Client)
☐ Internet (Client & Server)
☐ Location
☐ Microphone
☐ Music Library
☐ Pictures Library
☐ Private Networks (Client & Server)
☐ Proximity
☐ Removable Storage
☐ Shared User Certificates
☐ Videos Library
☐ Webcam

Description:

Provides outbound access to the Internet and networks in public places like airports and coffee shops. For example, Intranet networks where the user has designated the network as public. Most apps that require Internet access should use this capability.

More information

Figure 2-7. *Capabilities tab*

When users install your app, they will be prompted to allow or deny all of the Capabilities (such as the webcam, the libraries, and so forth). Those Capabilities will also get placed into the settings charm under permissions so that users can change their mind after installation.

The Declarations Tab

The Declarations tab (shown in Figure 2-8) adds additional capabilities to your app, such as Background Tasks and File Open and Save pickers, as well as Search and Share Target. Note that Share Target is just below Search, but due to scrolling doesn't appear in the image. Many of these features are also covered in later chapters.

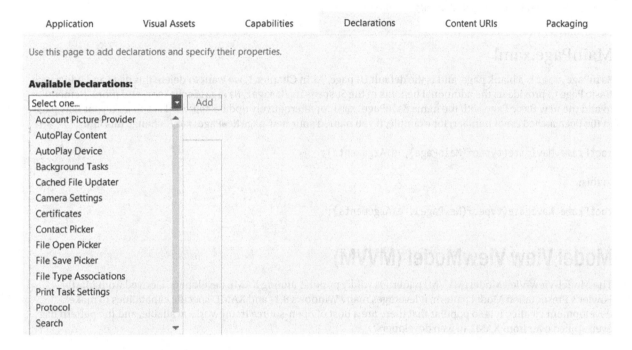

Figure 2-8. *Declarations tab*

The Content URIs Tab

The Content URIs tab is where you can specify an external web page that is permitted to fire the `ScriptNotify` event. Although we cover push notifications in Chapter 9, we use Azure Mobile Services instead of the mechanisms provided here, so this tab isn't covered in this book.

The Packaging Tab

The final tab, the Packaging tab, is for setting the packaging information. We will cover this in depth in Chapter 11.

App.xaml

The App.xaml file (and the related App.xaml.cs code behind file) is the entry point for your application. We will spend a lot of time in the code behind file throughout this book. For this example, we will simply comment out the following line of code in the OnLaunched event handler to turn off the frame rate counter.

```
this.DebugSettings.EnableFrameRateCounter = true;
```

Open up App.xaml.cs, navigate to the OnLaunched event handler, and add two slashes to the beginning of the line as such:

```
//this.DebugSettings.EnableFrameRateCounter = true;
```

MainPage.xaml

MainPage.xaml is a blank page, and is the default UI page. As in Chapter 1, we want to delete this page and add a new Basic Page to provide us the additional benefits of the SuspensionManager, NavigationHelper, and more. Remember to add the new Basic Page with the name MainPage.xaml, or alternatively update App.xaml.cs to load your new page in the OnLaunched event handler; for example, if you named your new page NewPage.xaml, change this line

```
rootFrame.Navigate(typeof(MainPage), e.Arguments);
```

to this:

```
rootFrame.Navigate(typeof(NewPage), e.Arguments);
```

Model View ViewModel (MVVM)

The Model-View-ViewModel (MVVM) pattern is wildly popular among XAML developers. Derived from Martin Fowler's Presentation Model pattern, it leverages many Windows 8.1- and XAML-specific capabilities to make development cleaner. It is so popular that there are a host of open-source frameworks available, and the pattern has even spilled over from XAML to web developers.

The Pattern

The goal of MVVM is to increase the separation of concerns between the layers of your app, increase testability, and promote code reuse. In this chapter, we will just scratch the surface of the pattern, starting with a brief explanation of the parts.

Model

The model is the data for your app. It is not the persistence layer (such as database or web service) but the object representation of your data. The structure of this data is typically in the form of entities or data transport objects (DTOs). They are commonly referred to as POCOs (Plain Old CLR Objects).

View

The view is the window (such as `MainPage.xaml`). The view shows data to the user and also takes input from the user. Beyond that, there shouldn't be any other intelligence behind the view. Often, MVVM proponents strive for zero code behind. My opinion (and this is not meant to start an architectural debate) is that removing code from the code behind is a pleasant side effect of implementing MVVM properly, but not the goal. But, either way, the view becomes very lightweight.

ViewModel

The ViewModel performs two functions in the MVVM pattern in an XAML world (it's a bit different in the web world):

- The first function is to be a transport mechanism for the model required for the window. There is typically a one-to-one correlation between windows and ViewModels in my code, but architectural differences exist, and your mileage may vary.

- The second job is to act as the controller for the view and the model, receiving the user actions from the view and brokering them accordingly.

ViewModels should also be very lightweight and leverage other classes such as commands and repositories to handle the heavy lifting.

Creating a Model

Let's start with the model. Add a new folder to your app named Models by right-clicking your project and selecting Add ➤ New Folder. Next, add a new Class file named `Customer` by right-clicking on the new project and selecting Add ➤ New Item, as in Figure 2-9.

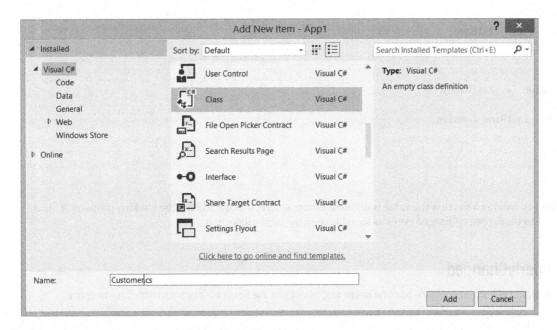

Figure 2-9. Adding the Customer model

Adding Customer Properties

For this simple example, we are only going to have two properties, a first name and a last name. We need to have backing properties to handle INotifyPropertyChanged events (as we will see in the next section). To create these properties, open up Customer.cs and add the following code:

```
public class Customer
{
  private string _firstName;
  private string _lastName;
  public string FirstName
  {
    get
    {
      return this._firstName;
    }
    set
    {
      if (value != _firstName)
      {
        this._firstName = value;
      }
    }
  }
  public string LastName
  {
    get
    {
      return this._lastName;
    }
    set
    {
      if (value != _lastName)
      {
        this._lastName = value;
      }
    }
  }
}
```

In the setters, we check to see w the value is different before setting it and updating the backing property. This is to save on calls to the PropertyChanged event as we will see in the next subsection.

INotifyPropertyChanged

The INotifyPropertyChanged interface has one event and resides in the System.ComponentModel namespace.

```
namespace System.ComponentModel
{
  public interface INotifyPropertyChanged
  {
    event PropertyChangedEventHandler PropertyChanged;
  }
}
```

To implement this interface, add a using for System.ComponentModel to the Customer class, and then add the interface and the event. The resulting code is shown next with the property setters and getters omitted for brevity:

```
using System.ComponentModel;
public class Customer : INotifyPropertyChanged
{
  // omitted for brevity
  public event PropertyChangedEventHandler PropertyChanged;
}
```

Next, we need to implement the event, and we want to make sure something is listening before firing the event off. Add a using for System.Runtime.CompilerServices as follows:

```
using System.Runtime.CompilerServices;
```

Then, add the code for the OnPropertyChanged method:

```
internal void OnPropertyChanged([CallerMemberName] string member = "")
{
  if (PropertyChanged != null)
  {
    PropertyChanged(this, new PropertyChangedEventArgs(member));
  }
}
```

The PropertyChanged event informs the binding engine to reinspect the data source for the property sent in the event arguments. You can also include the empty string, which will ask the binding engine to refresh all bindings on the Custom object. The attribute CallerMemberName will pass in the method name that executed the OnPropertyChanged method. For our purposes, we want the setters for each of the properties to call OnPropertyChanged when a value on the model is updated (but not when it is set to the same value; hence the added check that we did in the previous step). The full code is listed here:

```
public class Customer : INotifyPropertyChanged
{
  private string _firstName;
  private string _lastName;
  public string FirstName
  {
    get
    {
      return this._firstName;
    }
```

```
    set
    {
      if (value != _firstName)
      {
        this._firstName = value;
        OnPropertyChanged();
      }
    }
  }
  public string LastName
  {
    get
    {
      return this._lastName;
    }
    set
    {
      if (value != _lastName)
      {
        this._lastName = value;
        OnPropertyChanged();
      }
    }
  }

  internal void OnPropertyChanged([CallerMemberName]
    string member = "")
  {
    if (PropertyChanged != null)
    {
      PropertyChanged(this, new PropertyChangedEventArgs(member));
    }
  }

  public event PropertyChangedEventHandler PropertyChanged;
}
```

Creating the ViewModel

We are going to create a very simple ViewModel that starts by wrapping a Customer instance. In real-world examples, you would have ObservableCollections (discussed later in the book) and probably more than one model type in your window. As we are just showing the pattern here, we are going to keep things very simple.

Create a new folder called ViewModels (just like before) and then add a new class called MainPageViewModel. Note that there aren't firm rules around naming your ViewModels, but a popular convention is to add ViewModel to the end of the view that will be using it.

For starters, we want the ViewModel to instantiate an instance of the Customer class (again, in a real app, this would come from a repository in the Data Access Layer). First, add a using for the models.

```
using App1.Models;
```

And then create the ViewModel:

```
public class MainPageViewModel
{
  public Customer MyCustomer { get; set; }
  public MainPageViewModel()
  {
    MyCustomer = new Customer()
      { FirstName = "Bob", LastName = "Smith" };
  }
}
```

Next, we will create the RelayCommand. The RelayCommand class was added to our project when we added the Basic Page, and it takes care of a lot of plumbing that we would have to do ourselves if we created an instance of ICommand manually. The command (as you will soon see) gets tied to an actionable UI element, such as a button or a menu option. We will bind the command in the next section.

When you create a RelayCommand, it takes two parameters: The first is the delegate that gets executed when the action is taken. The second is optional and determines if the command is allowed to execute. We are only going to use the first parameter in this example. Add the namespace for the RelayCommand, App1.Common:

```
using App1.Common;
```

And then add the following code into the MainPageViewModel class:

```
private RelayCommand _updateNameCommand;
private void UpdateName()
{
  MyCustomer.FirstName = "Sue";
}
public RelayCommand UpdateNameCommand
{
  get
  {
    if (_updateNameCommand == null)
    {
      _updateNameCommand = new RelayCommand(UpdateName);
    }
    return this._updateNameCommand;
  }
  set
  {
    this._updateNameCommand = value;
  }
}
```

We want to make sure the RelayCommand is not null. We could easily do that in the constructor for the ViewModel, but I like to do that in the getter so that the related code is grouped together. The action will change the FirstName of the Customer to "Sue" from "Bob." That's it. We are done with the ViewModel.

Updating the Code Behind

Open up `MainPage.xaml.cs` and add the following using statements:

```
using App1.Models;
using App1.ViewModels;
```

Then add the following line of code to the constructor:

```
this.DataContext = new MainPageViewModel();
```

This creates a new instance of our ViewModel and sets the `DataContext` for the entire view to the ViewModel. Data binding needs two things—the object that is the source of the data and the path to the property that is being bound to. If a binding statement doesn't include a `DataContext`, the element will look up the element tree (to all of its parents, in order) to find a `DataContext`. Once it finds one, it stops and then attempts to bind the element based on the `Path` and the found `DataContext`. When we assign the `DataContext` to the entire view, everything will then use that specified source object.

That's it. No more code is necessary in the code behind!

Creating the View

For the view, we are going to create a very simple form that displays the first and last name and has a button to execute the name change. The finished view is shown in Figure 2-10. One thing you'll notice is the button right in the middle of the view, after all of that talk about content over chrome in Chapter 1. Yes, I broke the rules, but we are going to talk about command bars and app bars later in the book, and I didn't want to throw too much new content at you.

Figure 2-10. *View for the MVVM example*

Open up `MainPage.xaml` and add in the following XAML just before the final closing `</Grid>` tag:

```
<Grid Grid.Column="0" Grid.Row="1" Margin="120,0,0,0" Width="Auto">
  <Grid.ColumnDefinitions>
    <ColumnDefinition Width="Auto"/>
    <ColumnDefinition Width="Auto"/>
  </Grid.ColumnDefinitions>
```

```
<Grid.RowDefinitions>
  <RowDefinition Height="Auto"/>
  <RowDefinition Height="Auto"/>
  <RowDefinition Height="Auto"/>
</Grid.RowDefinitions>
<TextBlock Grid.Row="0" Grid.Column="0">First Name</TextBlock>
<TextBlock Grid.Row="1" Grid.Column="0">Last Name</TextBlock>
<TextBox Grid.Row="0" Grid.Column="1"
  Text="{Binding Path=MyCustomer.FirstName}"></TextBox>
<TextBox Grid.Row="1" Grid.Column="1"
  Text="{Binding Path=MyCustomer.LastName}"></TextBox>
<Button Grid.Row="2" Grid.Column="1"
  Content="Update Name" Command="{Binding Path=UpdateNameCommand}"/>
</Grid>
```

We will cover the controls and layouts in depth later in this book, so I just want to focus on the binding for the TextBox elements as well as the Command property of the Button element. The TextBox controls have a binding statement of Path=MyCustomer.FirstName and Path=MyCustomer.LastName. Each of these controls will look at the MainPageViewModel for the property MyCustomer and then look to the correct property on that object. This then binds these controls to the first and last name of the Customer.

Buttons also can leverage the command pattern. Instead of double-clicking on a button to create an event handler in the code behind, we bind the button's click action to a command. In this case, it's the UpdateNameCommand we created in the ViewModel. This gives a very clean implementation of the view and allows for separation of concerns all the way down.

Testing the App

Press F5 to run the app (either in the Simulator or on your local machine), and click the button. The First Name is changed to Sue (as in Figure 2-11), and the view is automatically updated! That is because TextBox bindings, by default, are TwoWay. If the source changes, the view is updated; if the view changes, the source is updated.

Figure 2-11. The First Name changed to Sue

Guidance

The MVVM pattern is very popular and extremely powerful, but it isn't for every app (or every developer). The rest of the code in this book does **not** use the pattern to keep the examples simple and clean, but I recommend that you spend some time learning the pattern so you can make an educated decision for yourself as to when it will help your architecture.

Navigation

The next topic that we will explore is Navigation. All Windows 8.1 apps are single-page apps. In XAML, this is implemented by creating a `Frame` that all subsequent pages get loaded into. This code was written for us when we created the new project from the Blank App template.

Open up `App.xaml.cs` and examine the following code (much of it I omitted to just show the relevant parts):

```
protected override void OnLaunched(LaunchActivatedEventArgs e)
{
  Frame rootFrame = Window.Current.Content as Frame;
  if (rootFrame == null)
  {
    rootFrame = new Frame();
    rootFrame.NavigationFailed += OnNavigationFailed;
    Window.Current.Content = rootFrame;
  }
  if (rootFrame.Content == null)
  {
    rootFrame.Navigate(typeof(MainPage), e.Arguments);
  }
  Window.Current.Activate();
}
```

After creating a Frame when the app is launched, the method determines if there is anything in the frame. If it is null, then the app was started fresh (and not resumed or restored from termination, as we discuss in Chapter 10, and a new frame is created. The current window's content is then assigned this frame. If the content is still null, the app navigates to the Main Page (the default start page for the app).

Navigation is a bit of a misnomer here. This is not like going from one web page to another. It is really swapping out the contents of the frame with the contents of the new page.

To see how this works, we are going to add a new Basic Page to the sample app we started to show the MVVM pattern.

Creating a New Page

Right-click on the project and select Add ➤ New Item ➤ Basic Page, and name it `PageTwo.xaml` like in Figure 2-12.

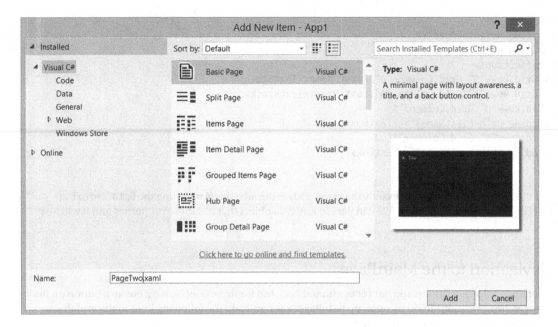

Figure 2-12. *Adding PageTwo.xaml*

Creating the UI

The UI for the second page will just be a copy of the MainPage without the buttons, as shown in Figure 2-13. Notice the back button? That comes along for free as part of the Basic Page template. More on that shortly.

Figure 2-13. *PageTwo UI*

To create this page, open `PageTwo.xaml` and enter the following XAML just before the final closing `</Grid>` tag:

```
<Grid Grid.Column="0" Grid.Row="1" Margin="120,0,0,0" Width="Auto">
  <Grid.ColumnDefinitions>
    <ColumnDefinition Width="Auto"/>
    <ColumnDefinition Width="Auto"/>
  </Grid.ColumnDefinitions>
```

```
<Grid.RowDefinitions>
  <RowDefinition Height="Auto"/>
  <RowDefinition Height="Auto"/>
</Grid.RowDefinitions>
<TextBlock Grid.Row="0" Grid.Column="0">First Name</TextBlock>
<TextBlock Grid.Row="1" Grid.Column="0">Last Name</TextBlock>
<TextBox Grid.Row="0" Grid.Column="1"
  Text="{Binding Path=FirstName}"></TextBox>
<TextBox Grid.Row="1" Grid.Column="1"
  Text="{Binding Path=LastName}"></TextBox>
</Grid>
```

Notice that the binding statements are exactly the same. This is the advantage of setting the DataContext at the window level instead of for each control. We can pass in any data object that has those properties and it will just simply work.

Adding Navigation to the MainPage

Navigation commands belong in the top app bar (or command bar), but for this example, we'll create a button on the Main Page to trigger the navigation. To do so, open up MainPage.xaml and add the following lines to the grid that we added for the previous example (the last grid in the XAML).

In the RowDefinitions block, add:

```
<RowDefinition Height="Auto"/>
```

At the end of the XAML (before the closing </Grid> tag for the same grid we've been working with), add:

```
<Button Name="NavigateBtn" Grid.Row="3" Grid.Column="1" Content="Navigate"
Click="NavigateBtn_Click"/>
```

The full XAML looks like this:

```
<Grid Grid.Column="0" Grid.Row="1" Margin="120,0,0,0" Width="Auto">
  <Grid.ColumnDefinitions>
    <ColumnDefinition Width="Auto"/>
    <ColumnDefinition Width="Auto"/>
  </Grid.ColumnDefinitions>
  <Grid.RowDefinitions>
    <RowDefinition Height="Auto"/>
    <RowDefinition Height="Auto"/>
    <RowDefinition Height="Auto"/>
    <RowDefinition Height="Auto"/>
  </Grid.RowDefinitions>
  <TextBlock Grid.Row="0" Grid.Column="0">First Name</TextBlock>
  <TextBlock Grid.Row="1" Grid.Column="0">Last Name</TextBlock>
  <TextBox Grid.Row="0" Grid.Column="1"
    Text="{Binding Path=MyCustomer.FirstName}"></TextBox>
  <TextBox Grid.Row="1" Grid.Column="1"
    Text="{Binding Path=MyCustomer.LastName}"></TextBox>
```

```
<Button Grid.Row="2" Grid.Column="1"
  Content="Update Name" Command="{Binding Path=UpdateNameCommand}"/>
<Button Name="NavigateBtn" Grid.Row="3" Grid.Column="1"
  Content="Navigate" Click="NavigateBtn_Click"/>
</Grid>
```

We now need to add the event handler for the button click event. Note that if we were sticking with MVVM, we would add a command for this, but to keep things simple (and to match the rest of the examples in this book), we are just going to add an event handler in the code behind.

To do this, open up MainPage.xaml.cs and add this code:

```
private void NavigateBtn_Click(object sender, RoutedEventArgs e)
{
  this.Frame.Navigate(typeof(PageTwo),
    ((this.DataContext as MainPageViewModel)!=null) ?
    (this.DataContext as MainPageViewModel).MyCustomer:
    (new Customer() {FirstName="Jane", LastName="Doe"}));
}
```

First and foremost, the code calls the Navigate method on the frame. This is the same frame that was created in App.xaml.cs (and previously explained in the text). The first parameter is required, and it requires the type of page that is to be loaded into the frame. In our case, it is typeof(PageTwo). The navigation framework will take this type, use reflection to create an instance of the page, and load it into the frame.

The second parameter is optional, and will be passed into the page that is being navigated to as the Parameter property of the NavigationEventArgs. In our case, we want to grab the Customer out of the ViewModel, and the easiest way to do that is to use the window's DataContext. If all went well, the DataContext is an instance of the MainPageViewModel, and we can call the MyCustomer property once we convert it back to the MainPageViewModel type. We added some defensive programming to pass in a new Customer instance in case there would be an error along the way.

Handling the NavigatedTo Event

Open up PageTwo.xaml.cs and navigate to the OnNavigatedTo event handler. You will have to expand the NavigationHelper registration region to find it. This and the other handlers in this region are provided for us when we load a Basic Page instead of using a Blank Page in our app.

Add the following code to the OnNavigatedTo event handler:

```
this.DataContext = e.Parameter as Customer;
```

This sets the data context for the window as the Customer that was passed in from the page that navigated to PageTwo, which in this simple case is the Main Page. Now the binding statements in the XAML will use the Customer passed in to show the values on the model, as in Figure 2-13. If the type conversion doesn't work, the DataContext will be set to null, and the bindings will fail silently, resulting in a blank form.

The Back Button

Now to the back button. Open up PageTwo.xaml and examine the XAML that created the back button, as shown here:

```
<Button x:Name="backButton" Margin="39,59,39,0"
  Command="{Binding NavigationHelper.GoBackCommand,
  ElementName=pageRoot}"
  Style="{StaticResource NavigationBackButtonNormalStyle}"
  VerticalAlignment="Top" AutomationProperties.Name="Back"
  AutomationProperties.AutomationId="BackButton"
  AutomationProperties.ItemType="Navigation Button"/>
```

The command is bound to the NavigationHelper class (added to our project when we added the first Basic Page). It handles everything for us. If the navigation back stack is empty, the button is hidden. If the back stack is not empty, clicking on the button will then reload the previous page. All of the styling is done for us, and the default layout of the Basic Page makes sure the back button is in the correct location on the screen.

As you can see, the navigation framework supplied for us by Microsoft and the Basic Page makes it super simple to load new pages into the mainframe, pass values from page to page, and ensure that users can navigate back through your app.

Summary

In this chapter, we looked at the anatomy of a Windows 8 app project in the myriad of options available to you. We touched on the MVVM pattern and data binding. Finally, we covered the single-page nature of Windows 8 apps and using navigation framework to load different pages into your app.

In the next chapter, we will take a deep look into all of the controls available for Windows 8 app development.

CHAPTER 3

■ ■ ■

Themes, Panels, and Controls

WHAT'S NEW IN WINDOWS 8.1

Windows 8.1 brings several new controls as well as updates existing controls. The new controls that we will be discussing in this chapter are the `DatePicker`, `TimePicker`, `Flyout`, and `MenuFlyout` controls.

Updates include the ability to add a `Header` to the `DatePicker`, `TimePicker`, `TextBox`, `PasswordBox`, `RichEditBox`, `ComboBox`, and `Slider`, and also add `PlaceholderText` (watermarks) to the `TextBox`, `PasswordBox`, `RichEditBox`, and `ComboBox`.

Themes provide a consistent display for all of the pages within your app. Controls provide a way for users to interact with your app. Panels hold the controls. Together, they help you define your UI. This chapter takes a quick look at the theme options and then dives deep into the panels and controls offered out of the box for the Windows 8.1 app.

Choosing a Theme

Windows 8 and Windows 8.1 applications use a Dark theme by default. Using a Dark theme is typically more user- and battery-friendly for tablet-based applications. However, based on your application, the Light theme might create a better user experience.

The best way to understand the themes is see them in action. To do so, open Visual Studio, select New Project ➤ Windows Store Application ➤ Blank App (XAML). Name the project Controls1, as shown in Figure 3-1.

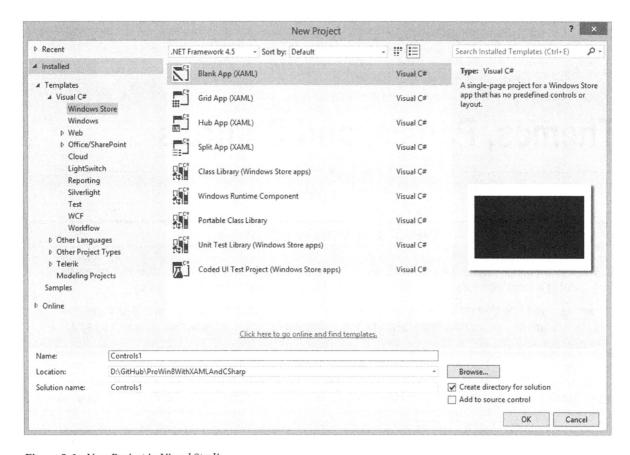

Figure 3-1. *New Project in Visual Studio*

In Windows 8, the application theme can be changed in App.xaml by specifying RequestedTheme="Light || Dark" as in the following code:

```
<Application
  x:Class="Controls1.App"
  xmlns="http://schemas.microsoft.com/winfx/2006/xaml/presentation"
  xmlns:x="http://schemas.microsoft.com/winfx/2006/xaml"
  xmlns:local="using:Controls1"
  RequestedTheme="Light">
```

In Windows 8.1 applications, setting the RequestedTheme in App.xaml changes the foreground theme but not the background theme for panels.

To see the Dark and Light themes in action, add a TextBlock to the Grid in MainPage.xaml, add a style for HeaderTextBlockStyle, and set the Text to "Hello, World". The resulting code is shown here:

```
<Grid>
  <TextBlock Text="Hello, World"
    Style="{StaticResource HeaderTextBlockStyle}"
/>
</Grid>
```

When you run the program, "Hello, World" is shown in light text on a dark background, as shown in Figure 3-2.

Figure 3-2. *A text block with the default Dark theme*

In App.xaml, add RequestedTheme="Light" to the <Application /> tag to switch to the Light theme:

```
<Application
  x:Class="Controls1.App"
  xmlns="http://schemas.microsoft.com/winfx/2006/xaml/presentation"
  xmlns:x="http://schemas.microsoft.com/winfx/2006/xaml"
  xmlns:local="using:Controls1"
  RequestedTheme="Light">
  <!-- Omitted for brevity -->
</Application>
```

When you run the program again, all that shows is a dark screen. This is because the control is set to use the Light theme. In the Light theme, controls are expecting a light background, so they are configured to use dark fonts. Panels (covered in the next section) must have their background set to use the ApplicationPageBackgroundThemeBrush in order for the RequestedTheme to take effect.

To do so, change the Grid it uses the ApplicationPageBackgroundThemeBrush as in the following code:

```
<Grid Background="{ThemeResource ApplicationPageBackgroundThemeBrush}">
  <TextBlock Text="Hello, World"/>
</Grid>
```

Run the application again, and you will see dark text on a light background, as in Figure 3-3.

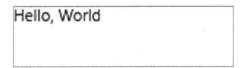

Figure 3-3. *A text block with a Light theme and the Grid configured to use the requested theme*

Using Panels

You can't discuss controls without first discussing panels. Panels are a special kind of UI control that "hold" other controls, supply a place to put your controls, and help with managing the layout of them. Panels are not new to Windows 8.1; they have been in XAML since the beginning, with WPF and Silverlight. The type of panel determines the behavior of the contained controls (as will be described). Conceptually, they are very similar to ASP.NET placeholder controls in that they contain other controls and they can both have controls added through code during runtime.

However, while ASP.NET placeholder controls are just another option for creating UIs, the XAML containers are the key components of creating UIs. There are a number of types of panels available out of the box with Windows 8.1, the most important of which are:

- Canvas

- Grid

- StackPanel

The Canvas

The Canvas is used primarily in games and other applications where you need precise (to the pixel) control over the placement of every object in your application. We'll show how to use the Canvas, but then we won't return to it for the rest of the book, as our focus is not on games.

To start, open MainPage.xaml and remove the Grid and the TextBlock. Next, add a Canvas. Again, to add a Canvas (or any other control), you can drag it from the toolbox onto the design surface or the XAML, or you can enter it by hand by typing the following where the Grid used to be:

```
<Canvas>

</Canvas>
```

METHODS FOR ADDING CONTROLS

Depending on how you add controls to your page, the resulting XAML can be very different. If you do so by dragging a control from the toolbox directly into the XAML editor, the resulting XAML will be very clean:

```
<Canvas/>
```

If you do so by dragging a control from the toolbox onto the design surface in Visual Studio, there will be a lot-more attributes set on the control, as the design surface interprets where on the design surface the control is dropped. For example, in my test app, dragging a control onto the design surface resulted in the following XAML:

```
<Canvas HorizontalAlignment="Left" Height="100" Margin="221,399,0,0"
   Grid.Row="1" VerticalAlignment="Top" Width="100"/>
```

There are advantages and disadvantages to the different methods of adding controls. The best option is to try them all and determine what works best for you.

You'll place controls within the Canvas (that is, between the opening and closing tags). If you drag an Ellipse onto the design surface, Visual Studio will fill in a number of properties for you so that the Ellipse is visible:

```
<Ellipse Fill="#FFF4F4F5"
  Height="100"
  Canvas.Left="205"
  Stroke="Black"
  Canvas.Top="111"
  Width="100" />
```

Setting the Height and Width to the same value (in this case, 100) makes the Ellipse into a circle. The properties Canvas.Left and Canvas.Top set the location of the Ellipse with respect to the left and top boundaries of the Canvas. In this case, the Ellipse is 205 pixels to the right of the left margin and 111 pixels down from the top boundary.

Change the Fill property to "Red" to see the circle more clearly.

You can place as many objects as you like onto the Canvas. Try the following XAML:

```
<Canvas>
  <Ellipse Fill="Red"
     Height="100"
     Canvas.Left="205"
     Stroke="Black"
     Canvas.Top="111"
     Width="100"
     Canvas.ZIndex="1"/>
  <Rectangle Fill="Blue"
     Height="188"
     Canvas.Left="82"
     Stroke="Black"
     Canvas.Top="40"
     Width="118" />
  <Rectangle Fill="Blue"
     Height="137"
     Canvas.Left="278"
     Stroke="Black"
     Canvas.Top="91"
     Width="140"
     Canvas.ZIndex="0"/>
</Canvas>
```

The result is shown in Figure 3-4.

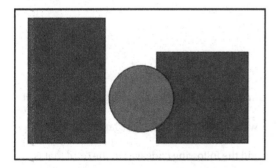

Figure 3-4. *Two Rectangles and an Ellipse*

Normally, this would create two rectangles and an ellipse (appearing as a circle since the height and the width are set to the same value). The second rectangle would partially cover the ellipse since it was declared after the Ellipse in the XAML. In this case, however, the ellipse occludes the rectangle because the ZIndex was set higher for the Ellipse (placing the ellipse "on top of" the rectangle). The ZIndex determines the layering as if the shapes were on a three-dimensional surface as shown in Figure 3-5.

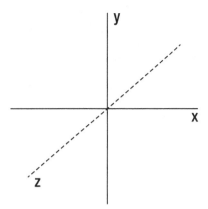

Figure 3-5. *ZIndex*

The Canvas really comes into its own when you work with animation, a topic beyond the scope of this book.

The Grid

The Grid is the workhorse panel of Windows 8.1. It is so commonly used that Microsoft made it the default panel for a new window.

Defining Rows and Columns

As one might expect, Grids are composed of rows and/or columns. You can define them using various measurements. The most common way is to define the actual size,

```
<RowDefinition Height="50" />
```

or to define the relative size of two or more rows,

```
<RowDefinition Height="*" />
<RowDefinition Height="2*" />
```

This code indicates that the second row will be twice as big as the first (and will take up two-thirds of the available space). An asterisk alone indicates 1*.

The last way to define them is by declaring a size to be "Auto," in which case it will size to the largest object in that row or column.

To see this all at work, create a new project named Controls2 and add the following code within the Grid that is provided:

```
<Grid Background="{StaticResource ApplicationPageBackgroundThemeBrush}">
  <Grid.RowDefinitions>
    <RowDefinition Height="100" />
    <RowDefinition Height="Auto" />
    <RowDefinition Height="*" />
    <RowDefinition Height="2*" />
  </Grid.RowDefinitions>
```

```
<Grid.ColumnDefinitions>
  <ColumnDefinition />
  <ColumnDefinition />
</Grid.ColumnDefinitions>
<Rectangle Fill="Red"
  Height="40"
  Width="20"
  Grid.Row="0"
  Grid.Column="0" />
<Rectangle Fill="Blue"
  Height="40"
  Width="20"
  Grid.Row="1"
  Grid.Column="0" />
<Rectangle Fill="Green"
  Height="40"
  Width="20"
  Grid.Row="2"
  Grid.Column="0" />
<Rectangle Fill="Yellow"
  Height="40"
  Width="20"
  Grid.Row="3"
  Grid.Column="0" />
</Grid>
```

Notice that all the rectangles are the same size (Height="40") but the rows are of differing sizes. The result is shown in Figure 3-6.

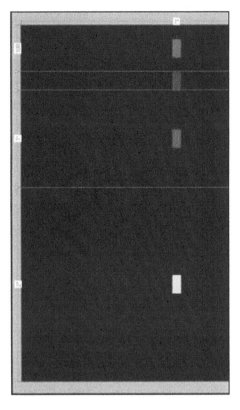

Figure 3-6. *Grid with varying heights*

The things to notice in this figure are: The first rectangle is centered in a row that is 100 pixels high. The second row is fit to the size of the rectangle. The next two rows divide the remaining space in the proportion 1:2 and the rectangles are centered in each. The image was cropped to make all of this more obvious.

Notice that the relative sizes are shown (e.g., 100, 1*, 2*, etc.) around the borders of the design surface to make it easier to see (and adjust) the sizes.

In this example, we placed everything in the first column to save space in the figure.

Alignment, Margins, and Padding

In setting objects into rows and columns of the Grid, you often want finer control over their placement. The first properties you might set are the horizontalAlignment and the VerticalAlignment. These are enumerated constants as shown in Figure 3-7.

```
<Rectangle Fill="Red"
           Height="40"
           Width="20"
           Grid.Row="0"
           Grid.Column="0"
           VerticalAlignment=""/>
                                    Bottom
                                    Center
                                    Stretch
                                    Top
```

Figure 3-7. *Setting the VerticalAlignment*

Margins are set to further fine-tune the placement of the object within the grid's cell. You can set margins as any of the following three types of values:

- *A single value*: If you set the margin as a single value in XAML, all four margins (top, left, bottom, right) will be set to the entered value.

- *A pair of values*: If you set the margin as a pair of values, the left and right margins will be assigned the value of the first number, and the top and bottom margins will be set to the second value.

- *Four values*: Finally, if you set the margins as four numbers, they will be assigned left, top, right, and bottom. This is different from cascading style sheets (CSS) in web development where the numbers are in top-right-bottom-left order.

Thus, if you set

```
Margin="5"
```

you create a margin of five pixels all around the object. But if you set

```
Margin = "10, 20"
```

you create a margin of 10 on the left and right and 20 on the top and bottom. And, finally, if you set

```
Margin = "5, 10, 0, 20"
```

you create a margin of 5 on the left, 10 on the top, 0 on the right, and 20 on the bottom.

Padding refers to the space *within* a control between its border and its contents. You can see padding at work when you create a button and set the padding—the contents are spaced further from the edges. In Controls2A, you see that we create three buttons, setting the padding to be quite small in the second and quite large in the third:

```
<Grid Background="{StaticResource ApplicationPageBackgroundThemeBrush}">
    <StackPanel Margin="50">
        <Button Content="Hello" />
        <Button Content="Hello"
                Padding="5" />
        <Button Content="Hello"
                Padding="25" />
    </StackPanel>
</Grid>
```

The result is shown in Figure 3-8.

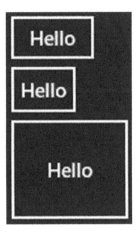

Figure 3-8. *Padding*

You can see in the figure that the padding affects the spacing around the content but only within the button, not the spacing between buttons (which is controlled by the margin).

The StackPanel

The StackPanel is both simple and useful. It allows you to "stack" one object on top of another, or one object to the right of another (horizontal stacking). No room is created between the objects, but you can easily add space by setting a margin. You can add any control inside a stack, including another stack.

For example, create a new application (Controls3) and add the following code:

```
<Grid Background="{StaticResource ApplicationPageBackgroundThemeBrush}">
  <StackPanel HorizontalAlignment="Left" Margin="50">
    <Rectangle Fill="Red"
      Height="50"
      Width="50" />
    <Ellipse Fill="Blue"
      Height="50"
      Width="50" />
    <StackPanel Orientation="Horizontal">
      <Ellipse Fill="Green"
        Height="20"
        Width="20" />
      <Ellipse Fill="Yellow"
        Height="20"
        Width="20" />
    </StackPanel>
  </StackPanel>
</Grid>
```

Here you have two instances of StackPanel, an outer StackPanel, and an inner StackPanel. The outer StackPanel consists of a Rectangle and an Ellipse stacked one on top of another. The inner StackPanel has its orientation set to Horizontal (the default is Vertical), and within the inner StackPanel are two somewhat smaller ellipses.

The result is shown in Figure 3-9.

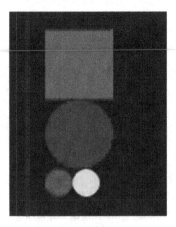

Figure 3-9. *StackPanel objects*

Border Control

The Border control is a container that can draw a border, background, or both around one or more other objects. Technically, the Border control, like many other controls, can only have a single object as its contents, but that object can be something like a StackPanel that can in turn have many objects within it, greatly increasing the utility of the Border. Create another project called Controls4 and add the following XAML to the main page:

```
<Border BorderBrush="Red"
  BorderThickness="5"
  Height="150"
  Width="150"
  Background="Wheat">
  <StackPanel VerticalAlignment="Center" >
    <Rectangle Height="50"
    Width="50"
    Fill="Blue"
    Margin="5"/>
    <Rectangle Height="50"
      Width="50"
      Fill="Black"
      Margin="5"/>
  </StackPanel>
</Border>
```

In Figure 3-10 the two squares have 10 pixels between them. That is because each declared a margin of 5, and the bottom margin of the upper rectangle was added to the top margin of the lower rectangle (5 + 5).

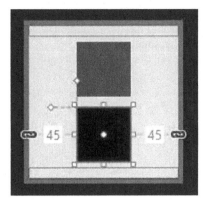

Figure 3-10. *Border control*

Working with Controls

In addition to the various panels, the Windows 8.1 toolbox is chock-full of additional controls for gathering or displaying information and/or for interacting with the end user. You can add controls to your page in a number of ways:

- Open Blend and drag a control onto the design surface.

- Open Blend and create the control by hand in the XAML.

- Open Visual Studio and drag a control onto the design surface.

- Open Visual Studio and drag a control into the XAML.

- Open Visual Studio and create the control by hand in the XAML.

Almost too many choices. For simplicity, we'll assume that readers of this book are working in Visual Studio. Blend is a powerful tool for XAML design work (for laying out controls, etc.), and we highly recommend you take a look at it, but the design work can often best be done in Blend.

Dragging a control from the toolbox onto either the design surface or directly into the XAML source itself is a great way to add controls to your page. If your control needs a special namespace, Visual Studio will add it for you automatically if you drag the control into place. If you add the control manually by typing the XAML, you'll have to add the namespace by hand.

This chapter will cover some of the more important controls and panels but does not endeavor to be exhaustive. A few controls, such as GridView won't be covered in detail until later in the book.

TextBlock and TextBox

There are a number of simple controls for displaying or retrieving data from the user. For example, text is typically displayed using a TextBlock control, and is retrieved from the user with a TextBox control. In Controls5, we create a very simple data entry form as follows:

```
<Grid Background="{StaticResource ApplicationPageBackgroundThemeBrush}">
  <Grid.RowDefinitions>
    <RowDefinition Height="50" />
    <RowDefinition Height="50" />
    <RowDefinition Height="50" />
  </Grid.RowDefinitions>
```

```xml
      <Grid.ColumnDefinitions>
        <ColumnDefinition />
        <ColumnDefinition />
      </Grid.ColumnDefinitions>
      <TextBlock Text="First Name"
        FontSize="20"
        Margin="5"
        HorizontalAlignment="Right"
        VerticalAlignment="Center" />
      <TextBox x:Name="FirstName"
        Width="200"
        Height="40"
        Grid.Row="0"
        Grid.Column="1"
        HorizontalAlignment="Left"
        Margin="5"
        VerticalAlignment="Center" />
      <TextBlock Text="Last Name"
        Grid.Row="1"
        FontSize="20"
        Margin="5"
        HorizontalAlignment="Right"
        VerticalAlignment="Center" />
      <TextBox x:Name="LastName"
        Width="200"
        Height="40"
        Grid.Row="1"
        Grid.Column="1"
        HorizontalAlignment="Left"
        Margin="5"
        VerticalAlignment="Center" />
      <TextBlock Text="Job Title"
        Grid.Row="2"
        FontSize="20"
        Margin="5"
        HorizontalAlignment="Right"
        VerticalAlignment="Center" />
      <TextBox x:Name="JobTitle"
        IsSpellCheckEnabled="True"
        IsTextPredictionEnabled="True"
        Width="200"
        Height="40"
        Grid.Row="2"
        Grid.Column="1"
        HorizontalAlignment="Left"
        Margin="5"
        VerticalAlignment="Center" />
    </Grid>
```

We start by giving the Grid three rows and two columns, and then populating the resulting cells with TextBlock and TextBox controls. Notice that the default position for a control is in Grid.Row="0" and Grid.Cell="0", and so we only need to specify when we want a different row or cell. While it is best programming practice to specify the default as well, it is so common to assume 0 for cell or row if not specified, that we show it that way here.

The result of this code is shown in Figure 3-11.

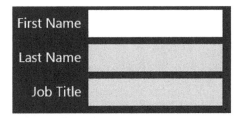

Figure 3-11. *Simple data entry form*

The text boxes in the data entry form have an X that shows up on the right-hand side once the user starts typing, allowing her to delete the text and start over, as shown in Figure 3-12.

Figure 3-12. *X in text box for deleting*

Also, notice in the XAML that the two TextBox controls are assigned names with the x:Name attribute:

```
<TextBox x:Name="FirstName"
```

This is so that we can refer to them programmatically. That is, we can refer to them in code, such as in an event handler, which we'll see in the next section.

Spell Check

Windows 8.1 XAML supports system-driven spell checking and auto-complete. Built in and right out of the box. Figure 3-13 shows spell checking at work. Notice the squiggly underlining of the misspelled word and the options to correct or add to the dictionary or ignore.

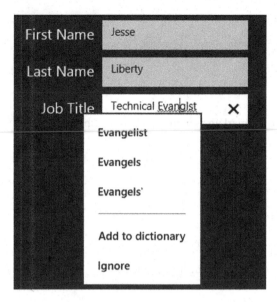

Figure 3-13. *SpellCheck*

You get both spell checking and auto-completion by setting just two properties on the TextBox:

```
IsSpellCheckEnabled="True"
IsTextPredictionEnabled="True"
```

The complete XAML for the Job Title text box is shown here:

```
<TextBox x:Name="JobTitle"
  IsSpellCheckEnabled="True"
  IsTextPredictionEnabled="True"
  Width="200"
  Height="40"
  Grid.Row="2"
  Grid.Column="1"
  HorizontalAlignment="Left"
  Margin="5"
  VerticalAlignment="Center" />
```

Headers and Watermarks

In the previous examples, we used a two-column Grid and created text blocks next to the text boxes in order to create a data entry form. New in Windows 8.1 is the ability to create headers in place with many input controls, including the TextBox, the PasswordBox, and the ComboBox (all shown later in this chapter).

To demonstrate this, create a project Controls5a and add the following row definitions into the Grid. The main difference between this Grid and the one we created in Controls5 is setting the height to "Auto" and not including column definitions.

```
<Grid.RowDefinitions>
  <RowDefinition Height="Auto" />
  <RowDefinition Height="Auto" />
  <RowDefinition Height="Auto" />
  <RowDefinition />
</Grid.RowDefinitions>
```

To create headers for the controls, add the Header attribute into the markup as in the sample code shown here:

```
<TextBox x:Name="FirstName"
  Header="First Name"
  Width="200"
  Grid.Row="0"
  HorizontalAlignment="Left"
  Margin="5"
  VerticalAlignment="Center" />
```

To add a watermark, use the PlaceHolderTextAttribute as shown in the following sample code:

```
<TextBox x:Name="FirstName"
  Header="First Name"
  PlaceholderText="[Enter First Name]"
  Width="200"
  Grid.Row="0"
  HorizontalAlignment="Left"
  Margin="5"
  VerticalAlignment="Center" />
```

The full code for the page is listed here:

```
<Grid
  Background="{StaticResource ApplicationPageBackgroundThemeBrush}">
  <Grid.RowDefinitions>
    <RowDefinition Height="Auto" />
    <RowDefinition Height="Auto" />
    <RowDefinition Height="Auto" />
    <RowDefinition />
  </Grid.RowDefinitions>
  <TextBox x:Name="FirstName"
    Header="First Name"
    PlaceholderText="[Enter First Name]"
    Width="200"
    Grid.Row="0"
    HorizontalAlignment="Left"
    Margin="5"
    VerticalAlignment="Center" />
  <TextBox x:Name="LastName"
    Header="Last Name"
    PlaceholderText="[Enter Last Name]"
    Width="200"
    Grid.Row="1"
```

```
      HorizontalAlignment="Left"
      Margin="5"
      VerticalAlignment="Center" />
    <TextBox x:Name="JobTitle"
      Header="Job Title"
      PlaceholderText="[Enter Job Title]"
      IsSpellCheckEnabled="True"
      IsTextPredictionEnabled="True"
      Width="200"
      Grid.Row="2"
      HorizontalAlignment="Left"
      Margin="5"
      VerticalAlignment="Center" />
  </Grid>
```

When you run the project, you get the result shown in Figure 3-14:

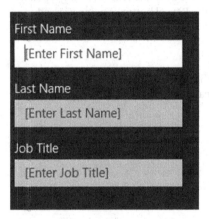

Figure 3-14. *Password box*

PasswordBox

A variation on the TextBox is the PasswordBox, which allows you to collect information from the user that is masked by a "password character"—which is by default a bullet (●). To demonstrate this, create a new project called Controls5b. Add a PasswordBox into MainPage.xaml and substitute a question mark as the password character. Also, we turn on the Reveal button. which allows the user to temporarily see the password in clear text. The XAML is as follows:

```
<Grid Background="{StaticResource
  ApplicationPageBackgroundThemeBrush}">
  <PasswordBox Margin="5"
    Width="200"
    Header="Password"
    PlaceholderText="Please Enter Your Password"
    IsPasswordRevealButtonEnabled="True"
    PasswordChar="?"
    VerticalAlignment="Top"/>
</Grid>
```

The before-and-after results of typing an entry are shown in Figure 3-15.

Figure 3-15. *Password boxes waiting for input (top) and with input (bottom)*

The "eye" on the right side of the password box is the Reveal button. It allows the actual characters being typed to be shown to the user. It is not a toggle, as the characters are only revealed while the Reveal button is being pressed.

Buttons and Event Handlers

Create a new project named Controls6. The main page is a form with two TextBox instances, a Button, and an event handler that will respond to the button being clicked. In that event handler, we can get the values in the two TextBox instances. The result will be displayed in a text block.

```
<Grid Background="{StaticResource
  ApplicationPageBackgroundThemeBrush}">
  <Grid.RowDefinitions>
    <RowDefinition Height="50" />
    <RowDefinition Height="50" />
    <RowDefinition Height="50" />
    <RowDefinition />
  </Grid.RowDefinitions>
  <Grid.ColumnDefinitions>
    <ColumnDefinition />
    <ColumnDefinition />
  </Grid.ColumnDefinitions>
  <TextBlock Text="First Name"
    FontSize="20"
    Margin="5"
    HorizontalAlignment="Right"
    VerticalAlignment="Center" />
  <TextBox x:Name="FirstName"
    Width="200"
    Height="40"
    Grid.Row="0"
    Grid.Column="1"
    HorizontalAlignment="Left"
    Margin="5"
    VerticalAlignment="Center" />
```

```xml
<TextBlock Text="Last Name"
  Grid.Row="1"
  FontSize="20"
  Margin="5"
  HorizontalAlignment="Right"
  VerticalAlignment="Center" />
<TextBox x:Name="LastName"
  Width="200"
  Height="40"
  Grid.Row="1"
  Grid.Column="1"
  HorizontalAlignment="Left"
  Margin="5"
  VerticalAlignment="Center" />
<TextBlock x:Name="Output"
  HorizontalAlignment="Right"
  VerticalAlignment="Center"
  Text=""
  Margin="5"
  FontSize="20"
  Grid.Column="0"
  Grid.Row="2" />
<Button Name="ShowName"
  Content="Show Name"
  HorizontalAlignment="Left"
  VerticalAlignment="Center"
  Margin="5"
  Grid.Row="2"
  Grid.Column="1" />
</Grid>
```

There are numerous ways to add an event handler for the click event. The simplest is to type Click=, and when you hit space Visual Studio will offer to create (and name) an event handler for you, as shown in Figure 3-16.

```xml
<Button Name="ShowName"
        Content="Show Name"
        HorizontalAlignment="Left"
        VerticalAlignment="Center"
        Margin="5"
        Grid.Row="2"
        Grid.Column="1"
        Click=""
              ⊡ <New Event Handler>
```

Figure 3-16. *Event handler*

The name created for you by Visual Studio is <objectName>_Click, so if your button is named ShowName then the event handler will be ShowName_Click, though you are free to override this name with anything you like.

Not only does Visual Studio set up the name for your event handler but it stubs out the event handler in the code behind (e.g., `MainPage.xaml.cs`).

```
private void ShowName_Click( object sender, RoutedEventArgs e )
{
}
```

All you need do is fill in the logic. In this case, we'll obtain the string values from the Text properties of the FirstName and LastName TextBoxes, concatenate them, and then place them into the Text property of the TextBlock Output as follows:

```
private void ShowName_Click( object sender, RoutedEventArgs e )
{
  string fn = FirstName.Text;
  string ln = LastName.Text;
  Output.Text = fn + " " + ln;
}
```

You can of course shorten this by leaving out the intermediate string variables:

```
private void ShowName_Click( object sender, RoutedEventArgs e )
{
  Output.Text = FirstName.Text + " " + LastName.Text;
}
```

We will typically show the longer version, as it makes it easier to see what is happening and it makes it easier to debug if anything goes wrong.

HyperLinkButton

The HyperLinkButton looks like a HyperLink but acts like a button. That is, you can assign a click event handler to the HyperLinkButton that will be handled before the user is navigated to the URL represented by the HyperLinkButton. HyperLinkButtons are often used inline with text blocks.

Create a new project names Controls6a, and add the following XAML to show a simple HyperLinkButton at work:

```
<Grid Background="{StaticResource
  ApplicationPageBackgroundThemeBrush}">
  <StackPanel Margin="50">
    <TextBlock Name="Message" />
    <HyperlinkButton Content="Phil Japikse"
      NavigateUri="http://skimedic.com"
      Click="HyperlinkButton_Click" />
  </StackPanel>
</Grid>
```

Notice that the HyperLinkButton has an event handler. This method is implemented in the code behind, like any event handler.

```
private void HyperlinkButton_Click( object sender, RoutedEventArgs e )
{
  Message.Text = "Hello Hyperlink!";
}
```

The code will be called before the hyperlink is navigated to, and so in this case the message "Hello Hyperlink!" will flash just before we navigate to the URL. While you can write code that requires user interaction to take place before the URL is navigated to, it is more common use the HyperLinkButton just to navigate to the URL. This gives you the appearance of a normal (HTML) hyperlink within an XAML application.

CheckBoxes, ToggleSwitches, and RadioButtons

There are a number of controls to help the user to make selections. Two of the most popular that allow the user to select from a number of options are the CheckBox and RadioButton. The ToggleSwitch is the Windows 8.1 control of choice for when the user is selecting one of two mutually exclusive choices. Controls7 shows a small form with all three of these controls added:

```
<Grid Background="{StaticResource
  ApplicationPageBackgroundThemeBrush}">
  <StackPanel Name="OuterPanel" Margin="50">
    <StackPanel Orientation="Horizontal" Name="RadioButtonsPanel">
      <RadioButton Name="Soft"
        Content="Soft"
        GroupName="Loudness"
        Margin="5" />
      <RadioButton Name="Medium"
        Content="Medium"
        GroupName="Loudness"
        Margin="5" />
      <RadioButton Name="Loud"
        Content="Loud"
        IsChecked="True"
        GroupName="Loudness"
        Margin="5" />
    </StackPanel>
    <StackPanel Orientation="Horizontal"
      Name="CheckBoxPanel">
      <CheckBox Name="ClassicRock"
        Content="Classic Rock"
        Margin="5" />
      <CheckBox Name="ProgRock"
        Content="Progressive Rock"
        Margin="5" />
      <CheckBox Name="IndieRock"
        Content="Indie Rock"
        Margin="5" />
    </StackPanel>
    <ToggleSwitch Header="Power" OnContent="On"
      OffContent="Off" />
    <ToggleButton Content="Toggle me!"
      Checked="ToggleButton_Checked"
      Unchecked="ToggleButton_Unchecked"/>
    <TextBlock Name="Message"
      Text="Ready…"
      FontSize="40" />
  </StackPanel>
</Grid>
```

The first thing to notice about this form is that rather than creating the layout with cells in a Grid, we laid out the controls in a StackPanel. Either way is valid.

The first StackPanel consists of three RadioButton controls. RadioButton controls are grouped using a GroupName (every RadioButton in a group is mutually exclusive). We set the IsChecked property to true for the third button—the default is false, and in a RadioButton group only one button will have the IsChecked value set to true at a time.

The second StackPanel has three CheckBox controls and they are not mutually exclusive; the user is free to pick any or all of the music choices.

Next, we have a ToggleSwitch. You can see that it has a header and text for when it is in the on and in the off position.

Finally, we have a ToggleButton, which looks like a button but toggles between a checked and unchecked state and has events that correspond to being checked or unchecked.

Run the program and click on the buttons and check boxes to see how they behave, and toggle the switch to see the text and the switch change, as shown in Figure 3-17.

Figure 3-17. *Radio buttons, check boxes, a toggle switch, and a toggle button*

The only code for all of the previous controls are the event handlers for clicking the Toggle button,

```
private void ToggleButton_Checked( object sender, RoutedEventArgs e )
{
  Message.Text = "Button was toggled on!";
}

private void ToggleButton_Unchecked( object sender, RoutedEventArgs e )
{
  Message.Text = "Button was toggled off!";
}
```

ListBox, ListView, and ComboBox

Windows 8.1 continues to support the ListBox control though it has, in many ways, been replaced by the ListView. They work very similarly, and they both provide a scrolling list of data, though the ListView is more powerful and more suited to Windows 8.1 Store applications. In their simplest form, the use and appearance is identical, as shown in Controls8:

```
<Grid Background="{StaticResource
  ApplicationPageBackgroundThemeBrush}">
  <StackPanel Orientation="Horizontal" Margin="50">
    <ListBox Name="myListBox"
      Background="White"
      Foreground="Black"
      Width="150"
      Height="250"
      Margin="5">
      <x:String>ListBox Item 1</x:String>
      <x:String>ListBox Item 2</x:String>
      <x:String>ListBox Item 3</x:String>
      <x:String>ListBox Item 4</x:String>
    </ListBox>
    <ListView Name="myListView"
      Background="White"
      Foreground="Black"
      Width="150"
      Height="250"
      Margin="5">
      <x:String>ListView Item 1</x:String>
      <x:String>ListView Item 2</x:String>
      <x:String>ListView Item 3</x:String>
      <x:String>ListView Item 4</x:String>
    </ListView>
  </StackPanel>
</Grid>
```

The output is nearly identical in this case, as shown in Figure 3-18.

Figure 3-18. *ListBox and ListView*

The ComboBox is very similar to the ListBox. It provides a drop-down list, but you can also provide watermark text and a header (through the PlaceHolderText and Header attributes, respectively), as shown in Controls8a:

```
<ComboBox Name="myComboBox"
  Background="White"
  Foreground="Black"
  Width="Auto"
  Height="60"
  Margin="5"
  PlaceholderText="Please Select and Item"
  Header="ComboBox Example">
  <x:String>ComboxBox Item 1</x:String>
  <x:String>ComboxBox Item 2</x:String>
  <x:String>ComboxBox Item 3</x:String>
  <x:String>ComboxBox Item 4</x:String>
</ComboBox>
```

The result, with all three controls, is shown in Figure 3-19.

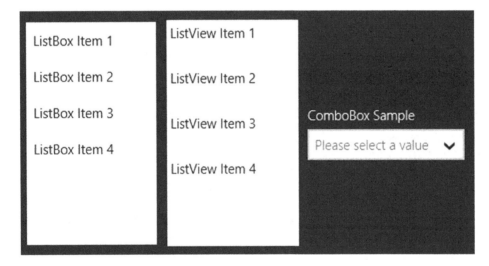

Figure 3-19. *ListBox and ListView with ComboBox*

Typically, you'll use the ComboBox when space is tight and when users select just one choice at a time. You'll use the ListBox (if you use it at all) when you want to display all the choices at once and when you want to allow multiple selections.

Image

The Image control is used to display (surprise!) an image, typically a jpg or png file. Its most important property is Source, which is the URI of the image itself. Controls9 shows how to add two Image controls to the page:

```
<Grid Background="{StaticResource
  ApplicationPageBackgroundThemeBrush}">
  <StackPanel Margin="50">
```

```
    <Image Height="240"
      Width="360"
      Source="Assets/Sheep.jpg"
      Margin="5" />
    <Image Height="240"
      Width="360"
      Source="Assets/PaintedDesert.jpg"
      Margin="5" />
  </StackPanel>
</Grid>
```

The result is shown in Figure 3-20.

Figure 3-20. *Images presented with Image controls*

To add the images to your page, copy two images into your Assets folder, click on Add Existing Item to add them to the project and then update the name in the Source property of the Image. You can use any images that you have on your local system or use the images from the sample code provided along with the book.

If your image does not fit the rectangle described for it by the Image control, you can set the Stretch property, which is an enumerated constant, as shown in Figure 3-21.

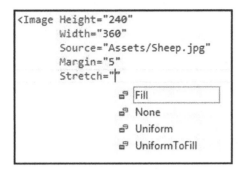

Figure 3-21. *Stretch property*

The effect of each of these constants can be seen in Figure 3-22.

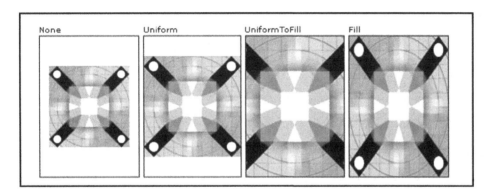

Figure 3-22. *Stretch settings in action*

Slider

The `Slider` control allows the user to select from a range of values by sliding a thumb control along a track. While the thumb is being moved, the actual value is automatically displayed above the slider, as shown in Figure 3-23.

Figure 3-23. *Slider control*

The code for creating the slider is shown in Controls10:

```
<StackPanel Margin="50">
  <Slider
    Header="Select a Value"
    Minimum="0"
    Maximum="100"
    Value="50"
    Width="100"/>
</StackPanel>
```

Progress Bar

The ProgressBar control is used to indicate progress, typically while waiting for an asynchronous operation to complete. If you know the percentage of progress achieved at any moment, you can use a standard progress bar, setting its value as you progress toward completion. Otherwise, you will want to use the indeterminate progress bar.

A ProgressRing works just like the indeterminate ProgressBar but is typically used to indicate waiting for the system rather than for program progress.

The code for creating progress bars is shown in Controls11:

```
<StackPanel Margin="50">
  <ProgressBar Value="50" Width="150" Margin="20"/>
  <ProgressBar IsIndeterminate="True"
    Width="150" Margin="20" />
  <ProgressRing IsActive="True" Margin="20" />
</StackPanel>
```

The result is shown in Figure 3-24.

Figure 3-24. *A progress bar*

ToolTip

Tooltips pop up and display information associated with an element. A tooltip will appear if the user hovers over the element with a mouse or by tapping and holding the element with their finger. Controls12 shows the code for adding a ToolTip control to a button:

```
<Grid Background="{StaticResource
  ApplicationPageBackgroundThemeBrush}">
  <StackPanel Margin="50">
```

```
    <Button Content="Button"
      ToolTipService.ToolTip="Click to perform action" />
  </StackPanel>
</Grid>
```

The tooltip is shown in Figure 3-25.

Figure 3-25. *Tooltip*

DatePickers and TimePickers

Windows 8.1 allows you to add date and time pickers for XAML-based applications. To do so, create a new project
Controls13 and add the following XAML to demonstrate the core functionality of the controls:

```
<Grid.ColumnDefinitions>
  <ColumnDefinition Width="120"/>
  <ColumnDefinition Width="Auto"/>
  <ColumnDefinition Width="40"/>
  <ColumnDefinition Width="Auto"/>
  <ColumnDefinition Width="*"/>
</Grid.ColumnDefinitions>
<TimePicker Grid.Column="1" Header="Select a Time" />
<DatePicker Grid.Column="3" Header="Select a Date"/>
```

The controls are shown in Figure 3-26:

Figure 3-26. *TimePicker and DatePicker*

Flyouts

Flyouts have been available for HTML/JavaScript developers since Windows 8. Windows 8.1 adds flyouts for XAML
developers. A flyout is an UI element that overlays the current UI to provide additional information to the user or
provide a mechanism to get confirmation of an action.

Flyouts are attached to other controls and are shown in response to an action. For example, a flyout attached to
a button will show when the button is clicked. Flyouts are container controls themselves and can hold and number of
additional controls by using a panel.

To show the different types of flyouts, create another project called Controls14. Add the following column definitions in preparation for the different examples:

```
<Grid.ColumnDefinitions>
  <ColumnDefinition Width="120"/>
  <ColumnDefinition Width="Auto"/>
  <ColumnDefinition Width="Auto"/>
</Grid.ColumnDefinitions>
```

Basic Flyouts

To show how to add a flyout, add the following XAML to the Grid, run the program, and you will see the result shown in Figure 3-27 (after clicking the button).

```
<Button Grid.Column="0" Content="This is a button to launch a flyout">
  <Button.Flyout>
    <Flyout>
      <StackPanel>
        <TextBlock>This is a flyout message</TextBlock>
        <Button>This is a flyout button</Button>
      </StackPanel>
    </Flyout>
  </Button.Flyout>
</Button>
```

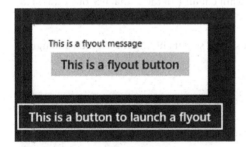

Figure 3-27. *Flyout attached to a button*

Menu Flyouts

Menu flyouts allow for building menus that remain hidden until needed. Add the following XAML into Controls14 and run the program to get the result shown in Figure 3-28.

```
<Button Grid.Column="1"
  Content="This is a button to launch Menu Flyout">
  <Button.Flyout>
    <MenuFlyout>
      <MenuFlyoutItem Text="First Item"/>
      <MenuFlyoutSeparator/>
      <ToggleMenuFlyoutItem Text="Toggle Item"/>
    </MenuFlyout>
  </Button.Flyout>
</Button>
```

Figure 3-28. *Menu flyout with a regular menu item and a toggle menu item*

Understanding Dependency Properties

Dependency properties are like the electric wires and pipes running under the streets of a big city. You can ignore them, you can even be oblivious to their existence, but they make all the magic happen and when something breaks you suddenly discover that you need to understand how they work.

Before we begin exploring dependency properties, let's review properties themselves. To do that, we go back into the dark early days of C++ when what we had available in a class were methods and member variables (fields).

Data Hiding

Back in these dark days, we wanted to store values in fields but we didn't want clients (methods that use our values) to have direct access to those fields (if nothing else, we thought we might later change how we store the data). Thus, we used accessor methods.

The accessor methods had method semantics (you used parentheses), and so data hiding was explicit and ugly. You ended up with code that looked like this:

```
int theAge = myObject.GetAge();
```

which just seems all wrong when what you wanted was

```
int theAge = myObject.age;
```

Enter properties. Properties have the wonderful characteristic of looking like a field to the consumer but looking like a method to the implementer. Now you can change the way the property is "backed" without breaking the any code that uses the property.

```
private int _age;
public int Age { get { return _age; } set { _age = value; } }
```

Age is the property; _age is the backing variable. The consumer can now write

```
int theAge = myObject.Age;
```

Age is a property and so you can put anything you like in the getter, including accessing a database or computing the age.

If your property getters and setters only return and set the value (in other words, no additional logic), you can use automatic properties to save typing. The private field and public property we looked at could have been written with this single line:

```
public int Age { get; set; }
```

The compiler turns this single statement into a declaration of a private backing variable and a `public` property whose get returns that backing variable, and whose set, sets that variable.

Dependency Properties

Dependency properties are an extension to the CLR and to C# and were created because normal properties just don't provide what we need: *declarative syntax that supports data binding as well as storyboards and animations.*

Most of the properties exposed by Windows 8.1 elements are dependency properties, and you've been using these properties without realizing it. That is possible because dependency properties are designed to look and feel like traditional C# properties.

In short, what was needed was a system that could establish the value of a property at runtime based on input from a number of sources. The value of a dependency property is computed based on inputs such as

- User preferences

- Data binding

- Animation and storyboards

- Templates and styles

- Inheritance

A key value of the dependency properties system is the ability to build properties that automatically notify any interested party that is registered each time the value of the property changes. This free, painless, and automatic implementation of the observer pattern[1] is tremendously powerful and greatly reduces the burden on the client programmer (in fact, the data-binding system depends on it!).

You normally will not have to create dependency properties unless you are creating a custom control (a topic beyond the scope of this book).

The first thing to know is that in order to support a dependency property, the object that defines the property (your custom control) must inherit from the DependencyObject. Virtually all of the types you use for a Windows Store app with XAML and C# will be a DependencyObject subclass.

You might then declare your property like this:

```
public bool Valuable
{
    get { return (bool) GetValue( ValuableProperty ); }
    set { SetValue( ValuableProperty, value ); }
}
```

It's a pretty standard get and set except that you access your backing variable using GetValue and SetValue to get and set the value of a dependency property named ValuableProperty (and that is the idiom, the CLR property name plus the word *property* equals the name of the dependency property, thus Valuable plus Property equals ValuableProperty).

---

[1]See "Exploring the Observer Design Pattern" on the Microsoft Developer Network for more information: http://msdn.microsoft.com/en-us/library/Ee817669(pandp.10).aspx.

The declaration of the dependency property itself is a bit weirder:

```
public static readonly DependencyProperty ValuableProperty =
  DependencyProperty.Register(
  "Valuable",
  typeof( bool ),
  typeof( MyCustomControl ),
  new PropertyMetadata( new PropertyChangedCallback(
    MyCustomControl.OnValuablePropertyChanged ) ) );
```

Let's break this down. The first line declares my object (which is really a reference to a dependency property) as public; it must be static and read only, and its type is DependencyProperty and its name (identifier) is ValuableProperty.

We set that reference to what we'll get back by calling the static Register method on the DependencyProperty class. Register takes four arguments:

- The name of the dependency property wrapper

- The type of the dependency property being registered

- The type of the object registering it

- The Callback

The Callback is of type PropertyMetaData. You can imagine a world in which there are various pieces of metadata for the DependencyProperty. At the moment, however, in Windows 8.1, there is only one: the Callback.

The constructor for the PropertyMetaData takes an object of type PropertyChangedCallback that will be called any time the effective property value of the dependency property changes. We pass it a reference to the method to call (which equates to a Callback).

The net of all of this is that we present to the world a CLR property (Valuable) that is in fact backed by a DependencyProperty that will call back to the method OnValuablePropertyChanged any time the effective value of the property changes.

The Callback method will take two arguments:

- A DependencyObject (the control)

- An object of type DependencyPropertyChangedEventArgs

Typically you'll cast the first argument to be the type of the control that contains the property, and you'll cast the NewValue property of the DependencyPropertyChangedEventArgs object to the DependencyProperty that changed. You can then take whatever action you need to based on the change in the dependency property's value

```
public class MyCustomControl : Control
{
  public static  readonly DependencyProperty
    ValuableProperty = DependencyProperty.Register(
      "Valuable",
      typeof( bool ),
      typeof( MyCustomControl ),
      new PropertyMetadata( new PropertyChangedCallback(
      MyCustomControl.OnValuablePropertyChanged ) ) );
  public bool Valuable
  {
    get { return (bool) GetValue( ValuableProperty );}
    set { setValue( ValuableProperty, value );}
  }
```

```
  private static void OnValuablePropertyChanged(
    DependencyObject d,
    DependencyPropertyChangedEventArgs e )
  {
    MyCustomControl control = d as MyCustomControl;
    bool b = (bool) e.NewValue;
  }
}
```

The key thing is that when you bind to a property (either through data binding or element binding), it must be a dependency property. Similarly, if you are going to use animations (for example, to change the opacity of a control or the style based on values), the animation storyboard only works on dependency properties. This is normally not a problem, as the properties you will be inclined to animate or bind to (almost always) are dependency properties anyway. You can see that quickly by looking at the documentation for the properties for any of the UI elements. These will all be UI elements (or the FrameworkElement, which derives from UIElement) and UIElement derives from the DependencyObject, which provides the support for dependency properties.

Summary

There are a wide variety of controls available for use in your Windows 8.1 apps that ship with Visual Studio, plus many more available through the rich third-party ecosystem. Every page starts with a Panel control (the most common being the Grid), and then additional controls are added to make the desired UI.

Using controls and handling events for those controls is very similar to what you find in other XAML environments such as WPF and Silverlight. This chapter did not cover every type of control available but provides information about the core controls, and the remaining controls are all conceptual extensions of the ones described.

The next step in your journey into using Windows 8.1 controls is data binding, which is covered in the next chapter.

CHAPTER 4

■ ■ ■

Binding

The essential glue in any meaningful Windows 8.1 application is showing data in your user UI. This is referred to as binding. At its simplest, binding allows you to connect the value of one object to a property on another object. This connection is referred to as a binding. The most common use is binding the properties of a data object (a .NET class) to the controls in the UI. For example, a customer's information might be bound to a series of text boxes. This use case is so prevalent that binding is commonly referred to as data binding.

The *target* of the binding must be a dependencyproperty on a UI element; the source can be any property of any object. That is a very powerful statement; it means that you don't have to create anything special in the source. A simple class such as a POCO (Plain Old CLR Object) will do. The classes that represent the data are typically referred to as models.

It is important to note that *any* dependencyproperty on the control can be bound to any accessible property on the data source. We'll see an example of this later in this chapter.

■ **Note** Please see Chapter 3 for more information on dependency properties.

DataContext

As stated earlier, data binding needs a model to supply the data and a dependencyproperty to receive the value of one of the model's properties. If the binding statement specifies the information directly, the binding engine sends the data value(s) from the model to the control. However, when multiple controls are bound to the model, *a lot* of typing is required, as each binding statement must provide the model's information. In addition to the additional work required upfront to bind the UI, if anything changes about the model (or if the model must be exchanged for another one), you must update each control with the new information.

If the binding statement does not contain information that specifies how to find the model, the binding engine will use the DataContext. If the control does not have a DataContext specified, the binding engine will walk up the control tree until it finds a DataContext. Once the binding engine finds a control in the UIElement tree that has a DataContext specified, the binding engine will use that definition in the binding statements for all of the controls contained by that element.

Using a DataContext instead of explicitly referencing a model in each of the binding statements leads to a much more supportable UI. It also greatly enhances the ability to change the data source during runtime with a single statement.

Creating a Simple Binding

The best way to move from theory to practice is to write some simple code as follows: Create a new Windows 8.1 project by selecting the Blank App (XAML) Windows Store template and naming it Binding1. Add a new class to the project named Person. This class will become the model to hold the data and will be bound to the UI. The Person class is shown in the following:

```
public class Person
{
    public string FirstName { get; set; }
    public string LastName { get; set; }
}
public Person person = new Person { FirstName = "Jesse", LastName = "Liberty" };
```

Figure 4-1 shows a prompt with the output we want to display and the value of the first and last name.

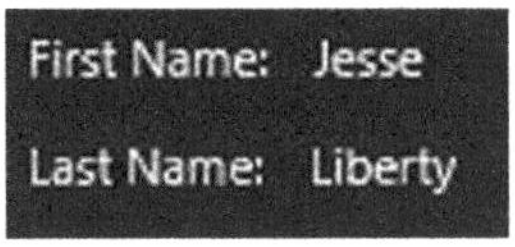

Figure 4-1. *First Name and Last Name*

We certainly could create this by adding four TextBlocks like this:

```
<StackPanel>
    <StackPanel Orientation="Horizontal">
        <TextBlock Text="First Name: " Margin="5"/>
        <TextBlock Name="txtFirstName" Margin="5"/>
    </StackPanel>
    <StackPanel Orientation="Horizontal">
        <TextBlock Text="Last Name: "  Margin="5"/>
        <TextBlock Name="txtLastName" Margin="5"/>
    </StackPanel>
</StackPanel>
```

We would then populate the text blocks by writing the value from the Person instance into the Text property of the TextBlock:

```
protected override void OnNavigatedTo(NavigationEventArgs e)
{
    txtFirstName.Text = person.FirstName;
    txtLastName.Text = person.LastName;
}
```

The OnNavigated event is raised when a XAML pages loads into view. It will be covered later in the book when we talk about navigation. It is used to set up the state for each page.

While this works, and it is perfectly valid code, it is inflexible and incredibly tedious when working with collections. Data binding is much more powerful, flexible, easier to maintain, and generally more desirable.

To change the controls to data bind to the model start by changing the XAML as follows:

```
<StackPanel>
    <StackPanel Orientation="Horizontal">
        <TextBlock Text="First Name: " Margin="5"/>
        <TextBlock Text="{Binding FirstName}" Margin="5"/>
    </StackPanel>
    <StackPanel Orientation="Horizontal">
        <TextBlock Text="Last Name: " Margin="5"/>
        <TextBlock Text="{Binding LastName}" Margin="5"/>
    </StackPanel>
</StackPanel>
```

The data binding statements are contained as strings enclosed with curly braces and start with the word *binding*. In these examples, the Text properties of TextBlocks are bound to the FirstName and LastName properties, respectively. This is much better; if nothing else, we've moved from procedural to declarative code, which is more easily manipulated in tools such as Blend or Visual Studio. We'll look deeper into the binding syntax in the next section, but for now, this amount of description is adequate.

Only the properties on the model are specified, not the model. This causes the data binding engine to next check the TextBlock for a DataContext. Not finding one, it would then check the two StackPanels (starting with the inner StackPanel), finally moving on to the window itself.

The DataContext can be set programmatically (in code) or declaratively (in XAML). In this example, I'll set the DataContext at the page level, and I'll do so programmatically by setting the DataContext of the class (which is the page itself). The page is the highest-level container, so all of the elements on the page will inherit the Person class as the DataContext. To do this, replace the assignments to the TextBlocks in the OnNavigatedTo event to the following code:

```
protected override void OnNavigatedTo(NavigationEventArgs e)
{
    DataContext = person;
}
```

When the application runs, the DataContext is set to the Person instance, and the values are filled into the TextBlocks. Very gratifying.

Data Binding Statements

As mentioned earlier, a declarative binding statement in its simplest form is as follows:

```
<dependencyobject dependencyproperty="{Binding bindingArgs}" />
```

The `bindingArgs` are a set of name-value pairs that further refine the binding. There are a lot more options to explore, but here are some of the most commonly used binding arguments:

Path. The path defines the property from the model that will be data bound to the dependencyproperty. It can be a simple property or a complex property chain in dot notation, walking down the properties of the model, such as `Address.StreetName`. If there is only one argument, and that argument is not a `binding` property, the binding engine will use that as the path. For example, these two statements are equivalent:

```
{Binding Path=Address.Streetname}
{Binding Address.Streetname}
```

Source. The `Source` property specifies the model that the binding statement will use to get the data. This is unnecessary when the `DataContext` is set.

FallbackValue (New in 8.1). The `Binding.FallbackValue` provides a value to display in the control when the binding fails.

TargetNullValue (New in 8.1). The `TargetNullValue` provides a value to display in the control when the bound value is null.

ElementName. XAML allows a control to bind one of its properties to the property of another control. This is commonly called element binding. Instead of using a data context, the binding is set to the name of the element.

Mode. The binding mode specifies whether the binding is `OneWay`, `TwoWay`, or `OneTime`. If `Mode` is not specified it will be set to `OneWay`.

UpdateSourceTrigger. The `UpdateSourceTrigger` determines when an update will be triggered in two-way binding situations. The possible values are `Default`, `Explicit`, and `PropertyChanged`.

Converter. Value converters enable binding of disparate types, such as changing the color of an element based on the numeric value of a property on the model.

Binding Errors

If you haven't worked in XAML before, there is a very important fact about data binding that you should know: When a binding statement fails, nothing happens. That's right, the user doesn't get any notification, there aren't any error dialogs, just a silent failure.

On one hand, this is very good. In the days of Windows Forms, when there was a binding error, the user would get a modal dialog box. This dialog came from the framework, and could be very disruptive. Especially if the binding problem was in a grid, the user would get a steady stream of modal dialog boxes.

Data-binding errors in the XAML world are very different. Nothing is presented to the user (unless you purposely add that interaction), and the default behavior is that the error will *only* be displayed in one place—in the output window of Visual Studio. To illustrate this, update the binding statement for the `LastName` property to this:

```
<TextBlock Text="{Binding LastName1}" Margin="5"/>
```

When you run the app, look in the Output window in Visual Studio. There will be a statement similar to the one that follows (it is actually a lot longer and might differ slightly on your machine):

```
Error: BindingExpression path error: 'LastName1' property not found on 'Binding1.Person,
Binding1,...
```

■ **Note** If you don't have the Output window open, you can find it on the Debug menu under Windows ➤ Output.

Windows 8.1 provides two new features in data binding specifically for problem situations: The `FallbackValue` provides a safety valve if the binding is in error, and the `TargetNullValue` provides a value to display if the source is null.

FallbackValue

New in Windows 8.1 is the ability to specify a value to be shown if the binding fails. To specify a fallback value, update the binding statement to the following:

```
<TextBlock Text="{Binding LastName1, FallbackValue='Doe'}" Margin="5"/>
```

Now, when you run the app, the result will be like Figure 4-2.

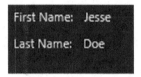

Figure 4-2. *Window using FallbackValue*

It is important to note that the control is not data bound. It is essentially showing a watermark.

TargetNullValue

Another new binding option allows you to specify what to show when the bound property is null. To illustrate this, correct the binding statement to once again bind to `LastName` and add the `TargetNullValue`:

```
"{Binding LastName, FallbackValue='Doe', TargetNullValue='Unknown'}"
```

The next change is to alter the creation of the `Person` class so that it does not provide a last name.

```
public Person person = new Person { FirstName = "Jesse"};
```

When you run the project, you get the result as shown in Figure 4-3.

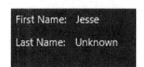

Figure 4-3. *TargetNullValue*

Just like the `FallbackValue`, the value shown in the UI is window dressing. It does not affect the value of the model.

Binding to Elements

In addition to binding to objects such as the Person object, you are also free to bind to the value of other controls. For example, you might add a slider to your page and a TextBlock and bind the Text property of the TextBlock to the Value property of the Slider.

To see this, create a new project and name it Binding2. Add the following XAML:

```
<StackPanel Orientation="Horizontal" Margin="100">
    <Slider Name="MySlider"
            Minimum="0"
            Maximum="100"
            Value="50"
            Width="300"
            Margin="10" />
    <TextBlock Margin="10"
            Text="{Binding ElementName=MySlider, Path=Value}"
            FontSize="42" />
</StackPanel>
```

That's all you need; no code required. You've bound the text block to the slider. As the slider changes value, the value in the TextBlock will be updated, as shown in Figure 4-4.

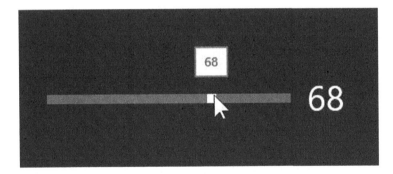

Figure 4-4. *Element binding*

You might be thinking at this point: "That's interesting. Why would I use that?" Element binding is a very powerful technique that can make your applications UI much more interactive.

A common example is enabling or disabling controls based on the state of other controls. Figure 4-5 is an example where users must check a box to accept the conditions (perhaps an End User License Agreement) before they continue. Selecting the check box should enable the button so the user can continue.

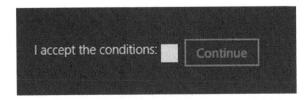

Figure 4-5. *Accept/Continue button appearing after controls have been disabled*

This can certainly be done with code, but it can also be done entirely in markup by leveraging element binding. Simply binding the IsEnabled property of the button to the IsChecked property of the check box links them together. The binding statement is writtent like this:

```
IsEnabled="{Binding ElementName=MyCheckBox,Path=IsChecked}"
```

When the check box is checked, the button becomes enabled, as shown in Figure 4-6.

Figure 4-6. *Button that is enabled after check box is checked*

The entire XAML of this example is shown in the following:

```
<TextBlock Text="I accept the conditions:" Style="{StaticResource BodyTextStyle}"/>
<CheckBox Name="MyCheckBox" HorizontalAlignment="Left"/>
<Button Content="Continue" IsEnabled="{Binding ElementName=MyCheckBox,Path=IsChecked}"/>
```

Binding Modes

The binding mode sets the direction(s) in which binding takes place. Binding comes in three "modes":

- OneWay
- TwoWay
- OneTime

Specifying the mode in a binding statement is optional. If it's not specified, the mode gets set to the default value of OneWay. The OneTime mode sets the value of the target when the window first loads and then severs the binding. Any changes to the source will not update the target. To see this, update the binding statement on the TextBlock by adding Mode=OneTime like this:

```
Text="{Binding ElementName=MySlider, Path=Value, Mode=OneTime}"
```

Run the project and the value in the text block will be set to 50 (the initial value of the slider). Changing the slider will not change the value in the text block.

OneWay binding mode sets the initial value just like OneTime but then keeps the connection alive so that changes to the source can be reflected in the target. Changing the mode to OneWay (or removing the Mode property completely) returns the example back to one direction, and changing the slider will change the value in the text block.

It is important to note that this example works because the target is binding to a dependencyproperty on the Slider. If you were to bind to the Person class we built for the first binding example and then to update the source, the target value would not change. This is due to the class (as we have written it) missing some needed infrastructure. Fortunately, the fix is to leverage INotifyPropertyChanged. This is very simple and is covered in the next section.

TwoWay binding allows for binding back to the source so that user input can update the data source. This is what you should expect when your application is binding to application data. To see TwoWay binding at work, change the TextBlock to a TextBox and set the binding mode to TwoWay as shown:

```
<StackPanel Orientation="Horizontal"
            Margin="100">
    <Slider Name="xSlider"
            Minimum="0"
            Maximum="100"
            Value="50"
            Width="300"
            Margin="10" />
    <TextBox Margin="10"
             Text="{Binding ElementName=xSlider, Path=Value, Mode=TwoWay}"
             FontSize="42"
             Height="75"
             VerticalAlignment="Top" />
</StackPanel>
```

Run the application and move the slider; the value in the TextBox updates. Now type a new value between 0 and 100 into the TextBox and hit tab. The value of the slider changes to reflect the value you entered. That is two-way binding at work.

UpdateSourceTrigger

In the previous example, the Slider value didn't change until the TextBox lost focus, but the TextBox updated immediately when the Slider's value changed. Why the different behavior? It is actually very clever how the framework determines when to send the update. By default, the update gets sent when the value changes on a non-text-based control and when a text based control loses focus. If the screen were to jump around at every keystroke (or send a lot of error messages while the user is still typing), users would not be kept around for long.

There are three options for the UpdateSourceTrigger binding property:

- Default
- Explicit
- PropertyChanged

Default leaves the behavior the same as previously explained. Explicit prevents the binding framework from updating the target, requiring it to programmatically update values with the call to UpdateSource method. PropertyChanged will fire every time a property changes (except on lost focus).

Change the binding statement from the previous example by adding UpdateSourceTrigger=PropertyChanged as follows:

```
Text="{Binding ElementName=MySlider, Path=Value, Mode=TwoWay, UpdateSourceTrigger=PropertyChanged}"
```

Run the program and start typing into the text box. As you type, the slider will update.

INotifyPropertyChanged

It is possible for the value of a property in your data to change after it is displayed to the user. You would like for that value to be updated in the view. For example, you might be retrieving the data from a database and the data gets changed by another instance of the program. It can be imperative that the UI keep up with these changes.

Imagine that a customer calls a certain store asking for *A History of the English Speaking Peoples* by Winston Churchill. The employee looks on our application to find out how many books are in stock and sees that there is one copy left. While he's negotiating the price with the potential buyer, another employee sells the last copy of the book. If the first employee's screen does not update to show that the store is now sold out of the book, he's in real danger of selling a product he doesn't have.

To prevent this type of situation from occurring, we typically have the classes that will serve as models in the view implement the INotifyPropertyChanged interface. This interface consists of exactly one event: PropertyChanged. You raise this event each time your property changes, passing in an EventArg that contains the name of your property. The XAML framework listens for this event and will then update any control bound to the property on the model that matches the name in the event arg. If the EventArg is blank, all properties will be updated.

To illustrate this, create a copy of the Binding1 project and name it Binding3. Add a helper method to the Person class called NotifyPropertyChanged that wraps the event to cut down on repetitive code.

```
public event PropertyChangedEventHandler PropertyChanged;
private void NotifyPropertyChanged(string caller = "" )
{
    if ( PropertyChanged != null )
    {
        PropertyChanged( this, new PropertyChangedEventArgs( caller ) );
    }
}
```

To fire this event, change the getters and setters for the Person class so that they call the NotifyPropertyChanged method from each setter, passing in the name of the property that is changed. That way, each time you set the value of the property for any reason, the UI will be notified.

```
private string firstName;
 public string FirstName
 {
     get { return firstName; }
     set
     {
         firstName = value;
         NotifyPropertyChanged("FirstName");
     }
 }
 private string lastName;
 public string LastName
 {
     get { return lastName; }
     set
     {
         lastName = value;
         NotifyPropertyChanged("LastName");
     }
 }
```

One problem with this implementation is the prevalence of magic strings. Every time a property is added, you have to remember to add the string name. And if the property name changes and you forget to update the string passed into the NotifyPropertyChanged method, you won't get a compiler error. The data-bound control just won't get updated.

To solve this problem, we can use the `CallerMemberName` attribute. This will set the value of the caller parameter to the name of the property that called the method, greatly simplifying the process.

```
public event PropertyChangedEventHandler PropertyChanged;
private void NotifyPropertyChanged( [CallerMemberName] string caller = "" )
{
    if ( PropertyChanged != null )
    {
        PropertyChanged( this, new PropertyChangedEventArgs( caller ) );
    }
}
```

The updated properties are listed here:

```
private string firstName;
 public string FirstName
 {
     get { return firstName; }
     set
     {
         firstName = value;
         NotifyPropertyChanged("FirstName");
     }
 }
 private string lastName;
 public string LastName
 {
     get { return lastName; }
     set
     {
         lastName = value;
         NotifyPropertyChanged("LastName");
     }
}
```

To test this, add a button to `MainPage.xaml` below the TextBlocks as follows:

```
<Button Name="cmdChange"
        Content="Change"
        Click="cmdChange_Click" />
```

When the button is pressed, modify the `FirstName` of the person object as shown:

```
private void cmdChange_Click( object sender, RoutedEventArgs e )
{
    person.FirstName = "Stacey";
}
```

Because of INotifyPropertyChanged, the UI will be updated when the value is changed, as shown in Figure 4-7.

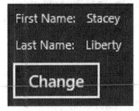

Figure 4-7. *Person changed*

Binding to Collections

One of the key processes of data binding is showing lists of items. The two main controls to show lists are the ListView and the GridView. To show binding to collections, we will create an app that takes a list of People and displays it in two ways: first in a ListView (shown in Figure 4-8) and then in a GridView (shown in Figure 4-9).

Figure 4-8. *A data-bound ListView*

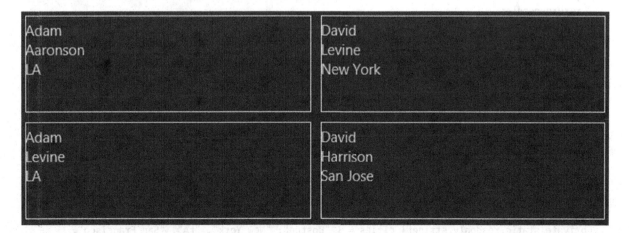

Figure 4-9. *A data-bound GridView*

Creating the Collection

Before we see this at work, we need to create a list. Start by creating a new application named Binding4. Instead of manually creating a list of Person objects, we are going to create a helper function that will generate names for each of the Person objects. In the Person class, create arrays to hold some first and last names as well as an array of cities as follows:

```
private static readonly string[] firstNames = { "Adam", "Bob", "Carl", "David", "Edgar", "Frank",
"George", "Harry", "Isaac", "Jesse", "Ken", "Larry" };
 private static readonly string[] lastNames = { "Aaronson", "Bobson", "Carlson", "Davidson",
"Enstwhile", "Ferguson", "Harrison", "Isaacson", "Jackson", "Kennelworth", "Levine" };
 private static readonly string[] cities = { "Boston", "New York", "LA", "San Francisco", "Phoenix",
"San Jose", "Cincinnati", "Bellevue" };
```

We can then "assemble" new Person objects by randomly selecting from each of the arrays, creating as many people as we need. To keep things simple, we'll do this in a static method so that we can call it from our MainPage.xaml.cs without instantiating an object. Instances of ListViews and GridViews bind very well with IEnumerables, so we'll have it return an IEnumerable<Person> as shown:

```
public static IEnumerable<Person> CreatePeople( int count )
{
    var people = new List<Person>();

    var r = new Random();

    for ( int i = 0; i < count; i++ )
    {
        var p = new Person()
        {
            FirstName = firstNames[r.Next( firstNames.Length )],
            LastName = lastNames[r.Next( lastNames.Length )],
            City = cities[r.Next( cities.Length )]
        };
        people.Add( p );
    }
    return people;
}
```

The entire Person class now looks like this:

```
public class Person
{
    public string FirstName { get; set; }
    public string LastName { get; set; }
    public string City { get; set; }

    private static readonly string[] firstNames = { "Adam", "Bob", "Carl", "David", "Edgar",
"Frank", "George", "Harry", "Isaac", "Jesse", "Ken", "Larry" };
    private static readonly string[] lastNames = { "Aaronson", "Bobson", "Carlson", "Davidson",
"Enstwhile", "Ferguson", "Harrison", "Isaacson", "Jackson", "Kennelworth", "Levine" };
    private static readonly string[] cities = { "Boston", "New York", "LA", "San Francisco",
"Phoenix", "San Jose", "Cincinnati", "Bellevue" };
```

```
public static IEnumerable<Person> CreatePeople( int count )
{
    var people = new List<Person>();

    var r = new Random();

    for ( int i = 0; i < count; i++ )
    {
        var p = new Person()
        {
            FirstName = firstNames[r.Next( firstNames.Length )],
            LastName = lastNames[r.Next( lastNames.Length )],
            City = cities[r.Next( cities.Length )]
        };
        people.Add( p );
    }
    return people;
}
}
```

Creating a Data-Bound ListView

A ListView lays out the data vertically in a single column. A ListView is most often used when an application is in Portrait or Snapped mode due to the reduced width of the view screen when apps are in those two layouts. A ListView scrolls vertically, which is the preferred scrolling direction for Portrait and Snapped views.

To create a new ListView, open up MainPage.xaml and either drag a ListView from the ToolBox onto the page and name it MyListView or enter the following XAML:

```
<ListView Name="MyListView">
</ListView>
```

We need to set the ItemsSource property of the ListView to the result of calling the static CreatePeople function we added to the Person class. Add the following line of code in MainPage. We'll do this in MainPage.xaml.cs, in the constructor as follows:

```
public MainPage()
{
    this.InitializeComponent();
    MyListView.ItemsSource = Person.CreatePeople(25);
}
```

When you run this, you won't get quite what you were hoping for, as shown in the cropped Figure 4-10.

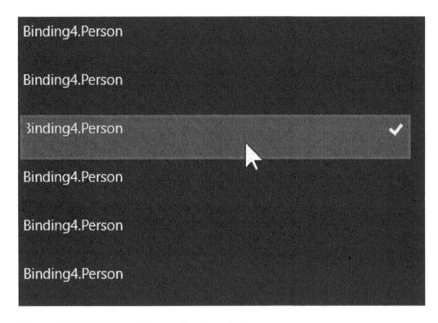

Figure 4-10. *Binding without a data template*

The binding is working perfectly; there is one entry for each of the 25 Person objects. The problem is that the ListView doesn't know how to display a Person object and so it falls back to just showing the name of the type. Data-bound list controls such as the ListView and the GridView require an ItemTemplate to define how each item in the list is displayed. The ItemTemplate needs to have a DataTemplate that contains the defining markup to display each item. Update the ListView XAML to match the following:

```
<ListView Name="MyListView">
    <ListView.ItemTemplate>
        <DataTemplate>
            <Border Width="300" Height="Auto" BorderBrush="Beige" BorderThickness="1">
            <StackPanel>
                <TextBlock>
                    <Run Text="{Binding FirstName}" />
                    <Run Text=" " />
                    <Run Text="{Binding LastName}" />
                    <Run Text=" " />
                    <Run Text="(" />
                    <Run Text="{Binding City}" />
                    <Run Text=")" />
                </TextBlock>
            </StackPanel>
            </Border>
        </DataTemplate>
    </ListView.ItemTemplate>
```

Let's break down the ItemTemplate. The main container is the DataTemplate whose DataContext is the current item in the collection. It's just a matter of formatting the data to your liking. Inside the TextBlock in the sample is a XAML trick that allows for more complex binding into a single TextBlock. By using the <Run/> markup, you can add multiple binding statements to build a single TextBlock. In our case, we are combining the FirstName, LastName, and City data elements with some punctuation. This pattern will be repeated for all 25 entries in the ListView as shown in Figure 4-11.

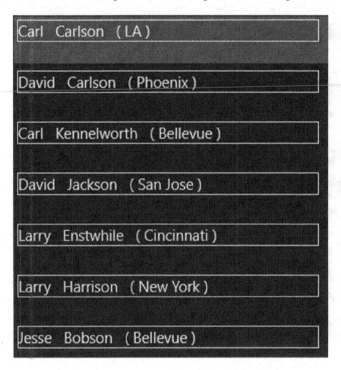

Figure 4-11. *ListView*

Creating a Data-Bound GridView

While the ListView scrolls vertically, the GridView layout fills in vertically until the container is filled and then starts in the next column and so on. If the entire screen is filled, the GridView will scroll horizontally. This layout container is used for apps while they are in Portrait or Filled mode and usually shows a bit more information than a ListView.

To show a GridView in action, comment out the ListView we just created in MainPage.XAML and add the following XAML into the page:

```
<GridView Name="MyGridView">
    <GridView.ItemTemplate>
        <DataTemplate>
            <Border Width="300" Height="100" BorderBrush="Beige" BorderThickness="1">
                <StackPanel Orientation="Vertical">
                    <TextBlock Text="{Binding FirstName}"
                        Style="{StaticResource ItemTextStyle}"/>
                    <TextBlock Text="{Binding LastName}"
                        Style="{StaticResource ItemTextStyle}"/>
                    <TextBlock Text="{Binding City}" Style="{StaticResource ItemTextStyle}"/>
                </StackPanel>
            </Border>
        </DataTemplate>
    </GridView.ItemTemplate>
</GridView>
```

93

You'll see that the techniques are the same, just with a little different styling. The resulting GridView is shown in Figure 4-12.

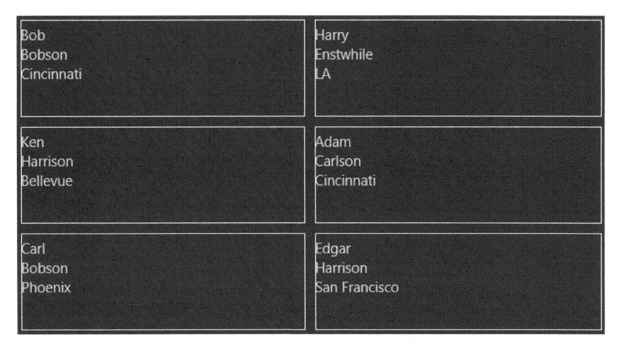

Bob	Harry
Bobson	Enstwhile
Cincinnati	LA

Ken	Adam
Harrison	Carlson
Bellevue	Cincinnati

Carl	Edgar
Bobson	Harrison
Phoenix	San Francisco

Figure 4-12. GridView

INotifyCollectionChanged

Just as you want the application to be updated when the value of a property changes, you want it to be notified if the contents of a collection changes (e.g., if an item is added, deleted, etc.). Similar to INotifyPropertyChanged, there is an interface made just for this scenario: INotifyCollectionChanged. This interface has just one event:

```
public event NotifyCollectionChangedEventHandler CollectionChanged;
```

This event needs to be called each time an item is added or removed from the collection. We could inherit from a specialized collection and code this ourselves (much like we did in the Person class for INotifyPropertyChanged), but Microsoft has already done the work for us and provided a custom class called ObservableCollection<T>. You can use the ObservableCollection<T> class in the same way you use other collection classes.

In fact, you can modify Person.cs to use an ObservableCollection<Person> and the program will continue to work just like it did before with the added feature that the ListView or GridView will be updated if an item is added or removed from the collection. All we need to do is simply change the return type of the CreatePeople method to return ObservableCollection<Person> and change the internal variable from List<Person> to ObservableCollection<Person>:

```
public static ObservableCollection<Person> CreatePeople( int count )
{
    var people = new ObservableCollection<Person>();
```

■ **Note** The ObservableCollection class only updates the client if an item is added or deleted but not if the item is changed (e.g., a property on an item in the collection is changed). If you want to receive a notification of the item being changed, you need to implement INotifyPropertyChanged on the items.

Data Converters

There are times that you will want to bind an object to a control but the types won't match up correctly. For example, you might want to bind a check box to a value, setting the check mark if the value is anything other than zero. To do this, you need to convert the integer value to a Boolean, and for that you need a DataConverter. A DataConverter is any class that implements IValueConverter, which takes two methods: Convert and ConvertBack.

To see this at work, create a new project and name it Binding5. In MainPage.xaml, we'll have a CheckBox that will be set if the Num property of the Person object is not zero. A TextBlock will display the Num property, and there will be a button which will generate a new Num property at random.

```
<StackPanel Margin="100"
            Orientation="Horizontal"
            Height="100">
    <CheckBox Name="xCheckBox"
              Content="Is Not Zero"
              Margin="10"
              IsChecked="{Binding Num, Converter={StaticResource numToBool}}"/>
    <TextBlock Name="xTextBlock"
               Margin="10"
               FontSize="42"
               VerticalAlignment="Center"
               Text="{Binding Num}"/>
    <Button Name="xButton"
            Content="Generate Number"
            Click="xButton_Click"
            Margin="10" />
</StackPanel>
```

Notice that the IsChecked binding for the CheckBox calls on the DataConverter that was identified in the Resources section:

```
<Page.Resources>
    <local:IntegerToBooleanConverter x:Key="numToBool" />
</Page.Resources>
```

We'll use the Person class we used in previous iterations, adding a Num property to the Person class so that we can bind to it (e.g., number of children, etc.):

```
public class Person : INotifyPropertyChanged
{
    private string firstName;
    public string FirstName
    {
        get { return firstName; }
        set
        {
            firstName = value;
            NotifyPropertyChanged();
        }
    }
    private string lastName;
    public string LastName
    {
        get { return lastName; }
        set
        {
            lastName = value;
            NotifyPropertyChanged();
        }
    }

    private int num;
    public int Num
    {
        get { return num; }
        set
        {
            num = value;
            NotifyPropertyChanged();
        }
    }

    public event PropertyChangedEventHandler PropertyChanged;
    private void NotifyPropertyChanged( [CallerMemberName] string caller = "" )
    {
        if ( PropertyChanged != null )
        {
            PropertyChanged( this, new PropertyChangedEventArgs( caller ) );
        }
    }

}
```

The key to making this work, of course, is the converter. Create a new class IntegerToBooleanConverter and have it implement IValueConverter as shown:

```
public class IntegerToBooleanConverter : IValueConverter
{
    public object Convert( object value, Type targetType, object parameter, string language )
    {
        int num = int.Parse( value.ToString() );
        if ( num != 0 )
            return true;
        else
            return false;

    }

    public object ConvertBack( object value, Type targetType, object parameter, string language )
    {
        throw new NotImplementedException();
    }
}
```

The binding mechanism will take care of passing in the value (in this case num), the targetType (in this case Boolean), a parameter if there is one, and the language. Our job is to convert the value to a Boolean, which we do in the body of the Convert method. The net effect is to convert any nonzero value to the Boolean value true, which sets the check box as shown in Figure 4-13.

Figure 4-13. *Boolean converter*

ConvertBack is used in TwoWay binding scenarios. For example, if you needed to format a number from the model to resemble the user's local currency, you could do that in the ConvertMethod. In order to save that number back into the model, it would need to be changed back into a number from the string representation that includes the currency symbol and the commas.

Summary

Binding is a key element of programming for Windows 8.1. With data binding, you can connect a data source, which can be virtually any object, to a property on a visual element (or you can bind two visual elements together). Along the way, you can convert data from one type to another to facilitate the binding. The INotifyPropertyChanged interface allows your view to be updated when your data changes. TwoWay binding allows your data object to be changed based on user input.

CHAPTER 5

Views

An application can be presented in landscape or portrait orientation as well as one of four visual states:

- Adjacent to the left edge
- Adjacent to the right edge
- Adjacent to both edges (full screen)
- Adjacent to neither edge (between two apps)

Before discussing the resize events, we will examine the two principal controls used to display data: the GridView for wide views (such as landscape) and the ListView for narrow views (such as minimum width or portrait).

The GridView and ListView Controls

As we covered in the previous chapter on binding, the GridView and ListView controls are nearly identical, both inheriting all their methods, properties, and events from the ListViewBase. The key difference is that GridView is designed to scroll horizontally and ListView vertically.

Building the Sample

You can get a GridView out of the box using the Grid App template, as will be covered later in this chapter, but things are a lot clearer and simpler if you start with a blank application, or Blank App, and then implement your own GridView.

GridView is one of the most powerful out-of-the-box controls in Windows 8, and fully understanding how to use it is not trivial. The complexity is a result of the fact that GridViews are often used to hold groups of collections rather than simple collections. The GridView template assumes that it will be displaying groups of collections of items, and this can add complexity to working with the GridView.

A basic GridView is shown in Figure 5-1, with people sorted into groups by city.

Bellevue		Boston			Cincinnati	
Harry Carlson (Bellevue) ✔	Larry Carlson (Bellevue)	Isaac Kennelworth (Boston)	Larry Aaronson (Boston)	Frank Kennelworth (Boston)	Larry Carlson (Cincinnati)	Jesse
Jesse Davidson (Bellevue)	Carl Davidson (Bellevue)	Edgar Kennelworth (Boston)	Ken Kennelworth (Boston)	Jesse Kennelworth (Boston)	Carl Carlson (Cincinnati)	Carl Ja
Carl Isaacson (Bellevue)	Edgar Ferguson (Bellevue)	Ken Davidson (Boston)	Harry Davidson (Boston)	Harry Bobson (Boston)	Carl Bobson (Cincinnati)	Carl E
Edgar Aaronson (Bellevue)	Adam Levine (Bellevue)	George Isaacson (Boston)	Carl Jackson (Boston)	Edgar Harrison (Boston)	Carl Bobson (Cincinnati)	Jesse
Edgar Ferguson (Bellevue)	David Bobson (Bellevue)	Harry Kennelworth (Boston)	Bob Enstwhile (Boston)	David Harrison (Boston)	Edgar Kennelworth (Cincinnati)	Isaac
Harry Harrison (Bellevue)	Isaac Aaronson (Bellevue)	Larry Aaronson (Boston)	Frank Kennelworth (Boston)		Bob Kennelworth (Cincinnati)	Ken A
George Harrison (Bellevue)	David Isaacson (Bellevue)	Adam Harrison (Boston)	Larry Harrison (Boston)		Larry Harrison (Cincinnati)	Ken D
George Bobson (Bellevue)	Adam Kennelworth (Bellevue)	Bob Aaronson (Boston)	Isaac Davidson (Boston)		George Harrison (Cincinnati)	
Carl Kennelworth (Bellevue)	David Harrison (Bellevue)	Bob Carlson (Boston)	Carl Davidson (Boston)		Carl Jackson (Cincinnati)	
Adam Levine (Bellevue)	Larry Bobson (Bellevue)	Harry Isaacson (Boston)	Isaac Bobson (Boston)		Adam Davidson (Cincinnati)	
Carl Jackson (Bellevue)	David Ferguson (Bellevue)	Bob Ferguson (Boston)	Frank Enstwhile (Boston)		Jesse Enstwhile (Cincinnati)	
Carl Enstwhile (Bellevue)	Carl Harrison (Bellevue)	Harry Jackson (Boston)	Frank Enstwhile (Boston)		Adam Enstwhile (Cincinnati)	
Edgar Isaacson (Bellevue)	Bob Kennelworth (Bellevue)	George Kennelworth (Boston)	Larry Jackson (Boston)		Frank Bobson (Cincinnati)	
Jesse Kennelworth (Bellevue)		David Aaronson (Boston)	Harry Levine (Boston)		Carl Enstwhile (Cincinnati)	

Figure 5-1. *GridView: people sorted into groups by city*

Getting Started

The basics of creating a list and binding it to a GridView have already been covered in the previous chapter. In this chapter, we are going to focus on the customization of the layout and features such as grouping and sorting.

Creating a program to illustrate GridView is nearly trivial. To do so, we will create a new Blank App and name it . We will divide our page's grid (not to be confused with GridView) into rows and columns. In the left column we'll add two buttons: Add and Insert. In the right hand column we'll add a very simple GridView. The procedure follows:

```
<Grid Background="{StaticResource ApplicationPageBackgroundThemeBrush}">
    <Grid.ColumnDefinitions>
        <ColumnDefinition Width="1*" />
        <ColumnDefinition Width="3*" />
    </Grid.ColumnDefinitions>
    <Grid.RowDefinitions>
        <RowDefinition Height="Auto"/>
        <RowDefinition Height="Auto"/>
        <RowDefinition Height="Auto"/>
        <RowDefinition Height="*" />
    </Grid.RowDefinitions>
</Grid.RowDefinitions>
```

```
<Button Name="Add"
        Content="Add"
        Grid.Row="0"
        Grid.Column="0"
        Click="Add_Click"/>
<Button Name="Insert"
        Content="Insert"
        Grid.Row="1"
        Grid.Column="0"
        Click="Insert_Click" />
<GridView Name="myGridView"
          Grid.RowSpan="4"
          Grid.Column="1"
          Grid.Row="0" />
```

```
</Grid>
```

The event handlers for both the Add button and the Insert button are nearly intuitive:

```
private int counter = 1;

rivate void Add_Click( object sender, RoutedEventArgs e )
 {
     myGridView.Items.Add( "Item " + counter++ );
 }

 private void Insert_Click( object sender, RoutedEventArgs e )
 {
     myGridView.Items.Insert( 0, "Item " + counter++ );
 }
```

Clicking Add and/or Insert a number of times will fill the first column of the grid, and then the second column will begin to fill. Unfortunately, the grid will size all the items based on the size of the first item, and things get crowded quickly, as shown in Figure 5-2.

Add

Insert

Item 1	Item 1	Item 3	Item 4	Item 6	Item 7	Item 9	Item 1	Item 1	Item 1
Item 2	Item 1	Item 3	Item 4	Item 6	Item 7	Item 9	Item 1	Item 1	Item 1
Item 3	Item 1	Item 3	Item 4	Item 6	Item 7	Item 9	Item 1	Item 1	Item 1
Item 4	Item 1	Item 3	Item 4	Item 6	Item 7	Item 9	Item 1	Item 1	Item 1
Item 5	Item 2	Item 3	Item 5	Item 6	Item 8	Item 9	Item 1	Item 1	Item 1
Item 6	Item 2	Item 3	Item 5	Item 6	Item 8	Item 9	Item 1	Item 1	Item 1
Item 7	Item 2	Item 3	Item 5	Item 6	Item 8	Item 9	Item 1	Item 1	Item 1
Item 8	Item 2	Item 3	Item 5	Item 6	Item 8	Item 9	Item 1	Item 1	Item 1
Item 9	Item 2	Item 3	Item 5	Item 6	Item 8	Item 9	Item 1	Item 1	
Item 1	Item 2	Item 4	Item 5	Item 7	Item 8	Item 1	Item 1	Item 1	
Item 1	Item 2	Item 4	Item 5	Item 7	Item 8	Item 1	Item 1	Item 1	

Figure 5-2. *Crowded grid*

We can fix this by adding a style:

```
<GridView Name="myGridView"
        Grid.RowSpan="4"
        Grid.Column="1"
        Grid.Row="0" >
    <GridView.ItemContainerStyle>
        <Style TargetType="GridViewItem">
            <Setter Property="Width"
                    Value="150" />
        </Style>
    </GridView.ItemContainerStyle>
</GridView>
```

Now when the grid is populated there is a bit more breathing room between the columns and nothing is truncated, as shown in Figure 5-3.

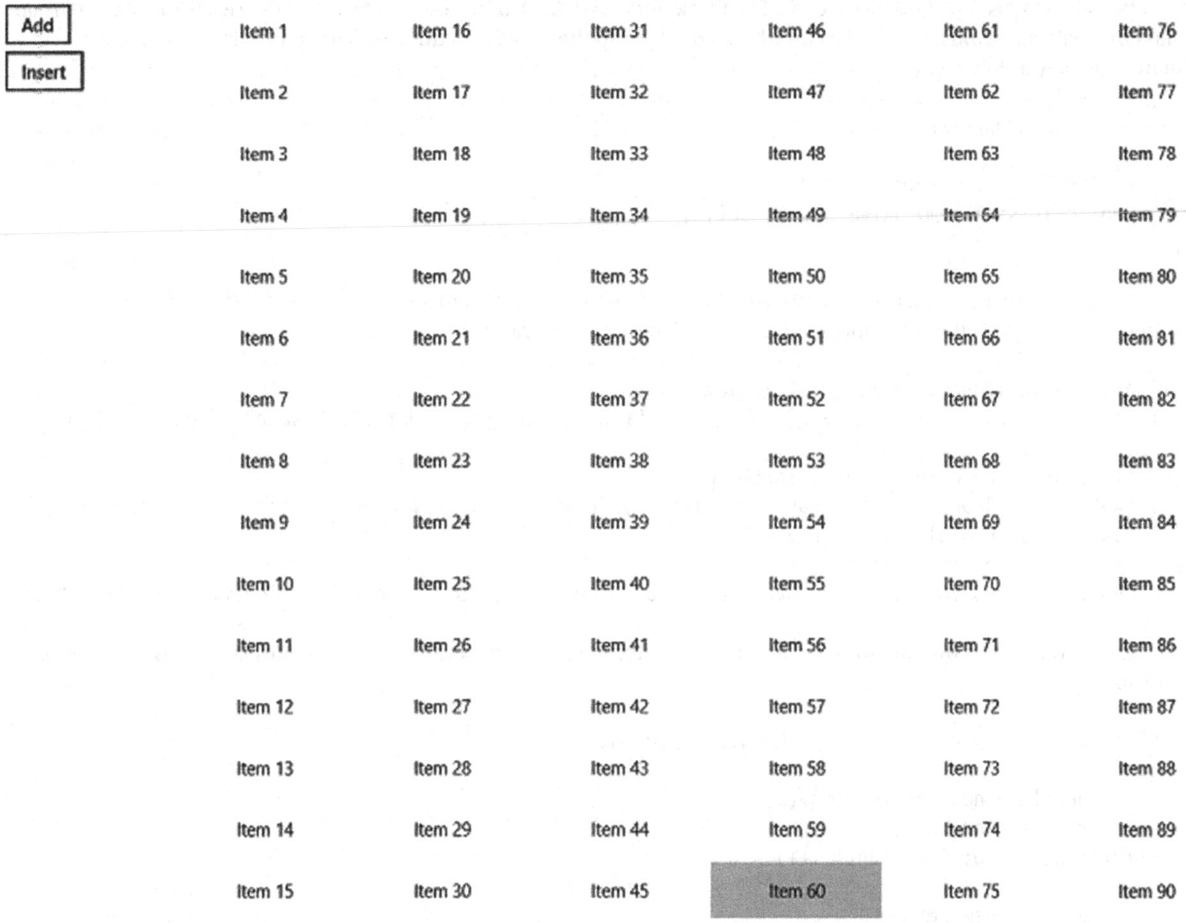

Add	Item 1	Item 16	Item 31	Item 46	Item 61	Item 76
Insert	Item 2	Item 17	Item 32	Item 47	Item 62	Item 77
	Item 3	Item 18	Item 33	Item 48	Item 63	Item 78
	Item 4	Item 19	Item 34	Item 49	Item 64	Item 79
	Item 5	Item 20	Item 35	Item 50	Item 65	Item 80
	Item 6	Item 21	Item 36	Item 51	Item 66	Item 81
	Item 7	Item 22	Item 37	Item 52	Item 67	Item 82
	Item 8	Item 23	Item 38	Item 53	Item 68	Item 83
	Item 9	Item 24	Item 39	Item 54	Item 69	Item 84
	Item 10	Item 25	Item 40	Item 55	Item 70	Item 85
	Item 11	Item 26	Item 41	Item 56	Item 71	Item 86
	Item 12	Item 27	Item 42	Item 57	Item 72	Item 87
	Item 13	Item 28	Item 43	Item 58	Item 73	Item 88
	Item 14	Item 29	Item 44	Item 59	Item 74	Item 89
	Item 15	Item 30	Item 45	Item 60	Item 75	Item 90

Figure 5-3. Grid with style

GridView with Collections of Collections

GridViews are typically used to display more complex data: specifically groups of collections, and, unlike creating a simple list and displaying it, implementing grouping is not trivial. To implement grouping, create a new Blank App(XAML) project and call it GridView2.

Let's assume that our data consists of people, with each person having a first name, a last name, and a city:

```
public class Person
{
    public string FirstName { get; set; }
    public string LastName { get; set; }
    public string City { get; set; }
```

We'd like to display these people in a GridView but organize (group) the data by city. The trick is to create a Group class that will allow you to have a key on which you'll group the people (in this case city) and a list of people who match that key as follows:

```
public class Group<TKey, TItem>
{
    public TKey Key { get; set; }
    public IList<TItem> Items { get; set; }
}
```

To generate your initial (ungrouped) list of people, you might go out to a service, read in XML, or in our case, generate names and cities at random. To do so, we'll have three arrays:

```
private static readonly string[] firstNames =
  { "Adam", "Bob", "Carl", "David", "Edgar", "Frank", "George", "Harry", "Isaac", "Jesse", "Ken",
    "Larry" };
private static readonly string[] lastNames =
  { "Aaronson", "Bobson", "Carlson", "Davidson", "Enstwhile", "Ferguson", "Harrison", "Isaacson",
    "Jackson", "Kennelworth", "Levine" };
private static readonly string[] cities =
  { "Boston", "New York", "LA", "San Francisco", "Phoenix", "San Jose", "Cincinnati", "Bellevue" };
```

And you'll need a method to generate a given number of people randomly mixing names and cities, which might look like

```
public static IEnumerable<Person> CreatePeople(int count)
{
    var people = new List<Person>();
    var r = new Random();
    for (int i = 0; i < count; i++)
    {
        var p = new Person()
        {
            FirstName = firstNames[r.Next(firstNames.Length)],
            LastName = lastNames[r.Next(lastNames.Length)],
            City = cities[r.Next(cities.Length)]
        };
        people.Add(p);
    }
    return people;
}
```

Creating the GridView

Let's turn now to the view. Before we create the GridView, we need to create a CollectionViewSource. The CollectionViewSource manages the collection of lists and is created in the Resources section of the page that will host the GridView. To do so, open up the MainPage.xaml file and add the following XAML after the page tag. Be sure to set the IsSourceGrouped property to True and set the ItemsPath to the list of objects (in our case, the Items property in the Group class).

```
<Page.Resources>
    <CollectionViewSource x:Name="cvs"
                          IsSourceGrouped="True"
                          ItemsPath="Items" />
</Page.Resources>
```

Next, add a GridView control that will bind its ItemsSource to a CollectionViewSource:

```
<Grid Background="{StaticResource ApplicationPageBackgroundThemeBrush}">
<GridView x:Name="myGridView"
          ItemsSource="{Binding Source={StaticResource cvs}}">
```

Within the GridView itself we want to determine how the groups will be organized, and for that we use the ItemsControl.ItemsPanel:

```
<ItemsControl.ItemsPanel>
    <ItemsPanelTemplate>
        <StackPanel Orientation="Horizontal" />
    </ItemsPanelTemplate>
</ItemsControl.ItemsPanel>
```

To ensure that there is sufficient room between each entry, we'll want to add some padding around each item. We do that with the ItemsControl.ItemContainerStyle that follows:

```
<ItemsControl.ItemContainerStyle>
    <Style TargetType="GridViewItem">
        <Setter Property="HorizontalContentAlignment"
                Value="Left" />
        <Setter Property="Padding"
                Value="5" />
    </Style>
</ItemsControl.ItemContainerStyle>
```

Next, we want to determine how each group will be laid out. This consists of two templates: one for the header and one for the items themselves. The HeaderTemplate will, in our case, display the city, which is, you'll remember, the Key property in the Group class:

```
<ItemsControl.GroupStyle>
    <GroupStyle>
        <GroupStyle.HeaderTemplate>
            <DataTemplate>
                <TextBlock Text="{Binding Key}"
                           FontSize="26.67" />
            </DataTemplate>
        </GroupStyle.HeaderTemplate>
```

We then add an ItemsPanelTemplate to ensure that the members of each group are listed vertically and have an appropriate width:

```
<GroupStyle.Panel>
    <ItemsPanelTemplate>
        <VariableSizedWrapGrid Orientation="Vertical" ItemWidth="220" />
    </ItemsPanelTemplate>
</GroupStyle.Panel>
```

Finally, we close out the XAML:

```
            </GroupStyle>
        </ItemsControl.GroupStyle>
    </GridView>
</Grid>
```

The Supporting Code

The GridView that we are creating and the ListView (that will be created in the next section) use same code to create the collection and the groups. In the code behind, we generate 200 people into a list and then use a LINQ statement to obtain a list of Group objects, which is set as the source for the CollectionViewSource. To do so, open MainPage.xaml.cs and create two lists as follows:

```
private IList<Person> people;
private IList<Group<object, Person>> groupedPeople;
```

Next, add the code to generate 200 people. Add this to the constructor after the call to InitializeComponent. This is because the code uses the CollectionViewSource, and the XAML on a page doesn't get instantiated until after the InitializeComponent is called.

```
people = Person.CreatePeople( 200 ).ToList();
groupedPeople = ( from person in people
                  group person by person.City into g
                  orderby g.Key
                  select new Group<object, Person>
                  {
                      Key = g.Key.ToString(),
                      Items = g.ToList()
                  } ).ToList();
cvs.Source = groupedPeople;
```

Notice that an Item template isn't needed, as the ToString method of Person has been overridden:

```
public override string ToString()
{
    return string.Format("{0} {1} ({2})", FirstName, LastName, City);
}
```

The result is a fully populated grid with people rather than random data, as shown in Figure 5-4.

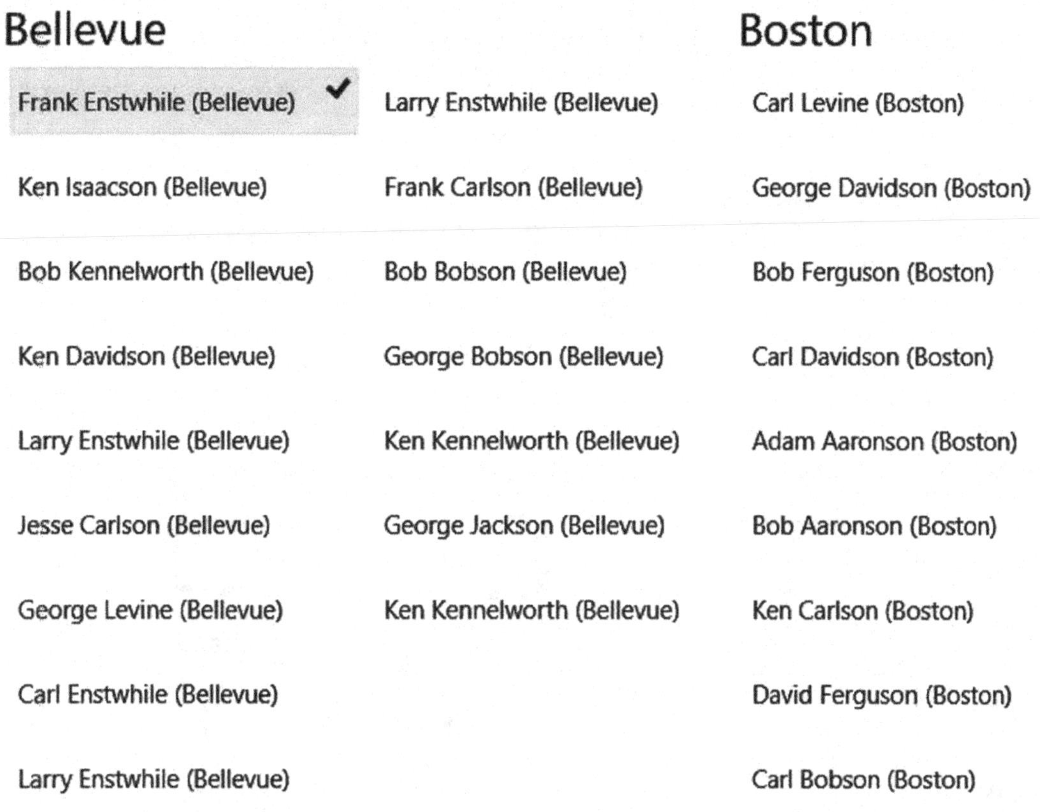

Bellevue

Frank Enstwhile (Bellevue) ✔	Larry Enstwhile (Bellevue)
Ken Isaacson (Bellevue)	Frank Carlson (Bellevue)
Bob Kennelworth (Bellevue)	Bob Bobson (Bellevue)
Ken Davidson (Bellevue)	George Bobson (Bellevue)
Larry Enstwhile (Bellevue)	Ken Kennelworth (Bellevue)
Jesse Carlson (Bellevue)	George Jackson (Bellevue)
George Levine (Bellevue)	Ken Kennelworth (Bellevue)
Carl Enstwhile (Bellevue)	
Larry Enstwhile (Bellevue)	

Boston

Carl Levine (Boston)

George Davidson (Boston)

Bob Ferguson (Boston)

Carl Davidson (Boston)

Adam Aaronson (Boston)

Bob Aaronson (Boston)

Ken Carlson (Boston)

David Ferguson (Boston)

Carl Bobson (Boston)

Figure 5-4. *GridView with people*

Resizing the Application

Unlike Windows 8.0, Windows 8.1 allows for a variety of sizes for an app (down to the minimum size specified in the App Manifest). Figure 5-5 shows the application tab in the Package App Manifest file.

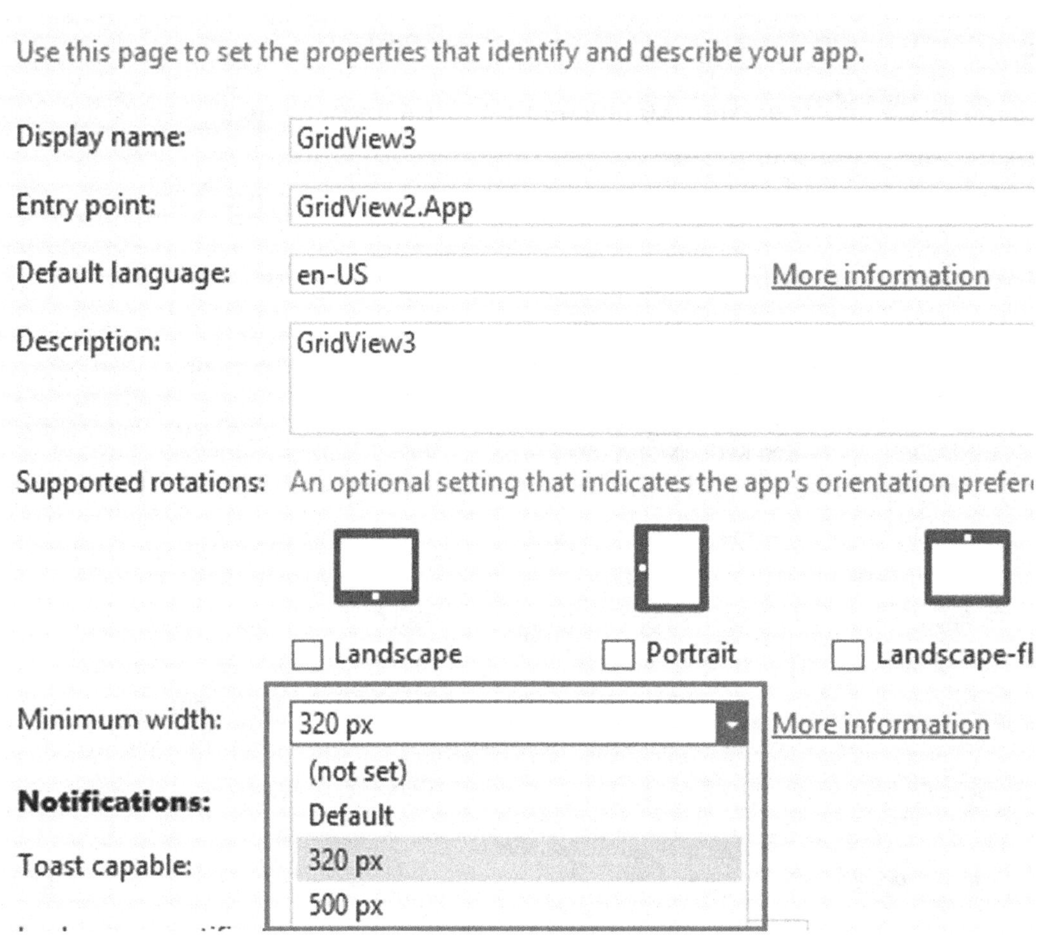

Use this page to set the properties that identify and describe your app.

Display name: GridView3

Entry point: GridView2.App

Default language: en-US   More information

Description: GridView3

Supported rotations: An optional setting that indicates the app's orientation prefer

☐ Landscape   ☐ Portrait   ☐ Landscape-fl

Minimum width: 320 px ▾   More information

(not set)

Notifications: Default

Toast capable: 320 px

500 px

Figure 5-5. Setting the minimum size

Run the app and resize it to the left or right edge. You can resize it and snap it to the left or right edge by holding the Windows key and pressing the left or right arrow. Alternatively, you can drag the app down from the top (not so far as to close the app) and then move it left or right.

When the sample app is pinned to the right side, the GridView leaves much to be desired when seen in SnapView, as seen in Figure 5-6.

Figure 5-6. *GridView pinned to the right edge*

The common solution for a GridView that looks poor in a vertical UI state is to hide the GridView and display the same data in a ListView. This works well in those dimensions as it scrolls vertically, as shown in Figure 5-7.

Figure 5-7. *Using the ListView*

Creating the ListView

The `ListView` and `GridView` controls share all of the same methods, events, and properties. For this example, create a new project GridView3 from the Blank App (XAML) template, delete the `MainPage`, and add the pages and code from the GridView2 example (`MainPage.XAML`, `Group.cs`, `Person.cs`). Set the application to a minimum size of 320 px.

To add the `ListView`, copy and paste the `GridView` in `MainPage.XAML` so that you have two, one above the other. Change the second `GridView` to a `ListView` and fix any place in that `ListView` that says `GridView` (e.g., change the `ItemContainerStyle TargetType` from `GridViewItem` to `ListViewItem`). Change the name of the `ListView` to `myListView`.

Here's the complete `ListView`:

```
<ListView x:Name="myListview"
        Grid.Row="1"
        ItemsSource="{Binding Source={StaticResource cvs}}"
        Visibility="Collapsed">
    <ItemsControl.ItemsPanel>
        <ItemsPanelTemplate>
            <StackPanel Orientation="Vertical" />
        </ItemsPanelTemplate>
    </ItemsControl.ItemsPanel>
    <ItemsControl.ItemContainerStyle>
        <Style TargetType="ListViewItem">
            <Setter Property="HorizontalContentAlignment"
                    Value="Left" />
            <Setter Property="Padding"
                    Value="5" />
        </Style>
    </ItemsControl.ItemContainerStyle>
    <ItemsControl.GroupStyle>
        <GroupStyle>
            <GroupStyle.HeaderTemplate>
                <DataTemplate>
                    <TextBlock Text="{Binding Key}"
                            FontSize="26.67" />
                </DataTemplate>
            </GroupStyle.HeaderTemplate>
            <GroupStyle.Panel>
                <ItemsPanelTemplate>
                    <VariableSizedWrapGrid Orientation="Vertical"
                                        ItemWidth="220" />
                </ItemsPanelTemplate>
            </GroupStyle.Panel>
        </GroupStyle>
    </ItemsControl.GroupStyle>
</ListView>
```

Notice that it is nearly identical to the `GridView` and that, most important, its ItemsSource is bound to the same `CollectionViewSource` as the `GridView`. This is very important, as it will enable both controls to point to the same data. In fact, by using the `CollectionViewSource`, if we select an item in the `GridView` and then switch to `SnapView`, the same item will be selected.

Switching Views

When you run the app now, it looks like a bit of a mess. That's because *both* the GridView and the ListView are shown, one on top of the other. To effectively handle resizing of the application, we need to show one control and hide the other.

Switching Views Manually

Switching views could be as simple as changing one view to Visible and the other one to Collapsed. Add two ColumnDefinitions to the grid (not the GridView) on MainPage.XAML and add a button to the first column. The partial XAML looks like this:

```
<Grid Background="{StaticResource ApplicationPageBackgroundThemeBrush}">
    <Grid.ColumnDefinitions>
        <ColumnDefinition Width="Auto" />
        <ColumnDefinition Width="*"/>
    </Grid.ColumnDefinitions>
    <Button Name="cmdSwitch" Content="Switch" VerticalAlignment="Top" Click="cmdSwitch_Click">
    </Button>
```

We need to change the GridView and ListView so they are rendered in the second column by adding the attribute Grid.Column="1". We also want to set the Visibility of the GridView to Visible and the ListView to Collapsed. The top lines of the GridView and the ListView are shown in the following:

```
<GridView x:Name="myGridView" Grid.Column="1" Visibility="Visible"
        ItemsSource="{Binding Source={StaticResource cvs}}">
<ListView x:Name="myListView" Grid.Column="1" Visibility="Collapsed"
        ItemsSource="{Binding Source={StaticResource cvs}}">
```

Finally, we need to add code to alternate the Visibility of the controls. In MainPage.XAML.cs, add the following code:

```
private void cmdSwitch_Click(object sender, RoutedEventArgs e)
{
    myGridView.Visibility = (myGridView.Visibility == Visibility.Collapsed) ?
            Visibility.Visible : Visibility.Collapsed;
    myListView.Visibility = (myListView.Visibility == Visibility.Collapsed) ?
            Visibility.Visible : Visibility.Collapsed;
}
```

When you run the app, you can switch between the GridView and the ListView by clicking on the button. Both views are shown in figures 5-8 and 5-9.

Switch	Bellevue		Boston
	Jesse Davidson (Bellevue) ✔	Jesse Davidson (Bellevue)	Larry Isaacson (Boston)
	Isaac Bobson (Bellevue)	Isaac Levine (Bellevue)	David Aaronson (Boston)
	Bob Carlson (Bellevue)	David Levine (Bellevue)	Edgar Isaacson (Boston)
	Harry Levine (Bellevue)		Jesse Aaronson (Boston)
	Frank Harrison (Bellevue)		Ken Kennelworth (Boston)
	Frank Aaronson (Bellevue)		Larry Bobson (Boston)
	David Harrison (Bellevue)		Bob Levine (Boston)
	Larry Aaronson (Bellevue)		Harry Davidson (Boston)

Figure 5-8. GridView

Switch	Bellevue	Boston	Cincinnati
	Jesse Davidson (Bellevue) ✔	Larry Isaacson (Boston)	Isaac Aaronson (Cincinnati)
	Isaac Bobson (Bellevue)	David Aaronson (Boston)	Larry Enstwhile (Cincinnati)
	Bob Carlson (Bellevue)	Edgar Isaacson (Boston)	Carl Davidson (Cincinnati)
	Harry Levine (Bellevue)	Jesse Aaronson (Boston)	Adam Isaacson (Cincinnati)
	Frank Harrison (Bellevue)	Ken Kennelworth (Boston)	Carl Carlson (Cincinnati)
	Frank Aaronson (Bellevue)	Larry Bobson (Boston)	Frank Ferguson (Cincinnati)
	David Harrison (Bellevue)	Bob Levine (Boston)	Edgar Isaacson (Cincinnati)
	Larry Aaronson (Bellevue)	Harry Davidson (Boston)	Bob Jackson (Cincinnati)

Figure 5-9. ListView

Using the VisualStateManager

Suddenly changing the view, such as by collapsing one and showing the other, can have a jarring effect on the user. It is much better to use an animation to transition from one view to the next. The previous example is also a very manual process for the developer to create and maintain.

It would be much better to leverage the capabilities of the framework to modify the layout based on size changes of the application and not to have to litter your code with something similar to that which we placed in the event handler for the button click.

The VisualStateManager provides solutions to both of these issues. Using the VisualStateManager combines creating VisualStateGroups in XAML and reacting to the SizeChanged event in code.

The VisualStateManager defines VisualStateGroups. Each VisualStateGroup contains one or more VisualState sections that define a StoryBoard. StoryBoards are used to define animations. The name comes from the practice of sketching out ideas for animations on large boards and flipping through them to show the concepts before spending the money on actual animation or filming. The term has grown to mean a container that defines animations and transitions. In XAML, the StoryBoard tags contain the information necessary for the framework to make the desired changes and animations.

Defining the StoryBoards

We will no longer need a button to change the layout, so we can delete the button that we created in the previous section. Since we will be making this process automatic, open MainPage.XAML and remove the button that switches the Visibility of the controls.

Add the following XAML after the ListView control:

```
<VisualStateManager.VisualStateGroups>
    <VisualStateGroup>
        <VisualState x:Name="DefaultLayout">
            <Storyboard>
            </Storyboard>
        </VisualState>
        <VisualState x:Name="MinimalLayout">
            <Storyboard>
            </Storyboard>
        </VisualState>
        <VisualState x:Name="PortraitLayout">
            <Storyboard>
            </Storyboard>
        </VisualState>
    </VisualStateGroup>
</VisualStateManager.VisualStateGroups>
```

Here, we define three VisualStates: a DefaultLayout, a MinimalLayout, and a PortraitLayout. Each VisualState contains a single StoryBoard. This is the animation that will execute when the state is activated.

■ **Note**   Unlike Windows 8, where the states were defined my Microsoft, Windows 8.1 leaves the number and name of the states completely up to you, the developer.

The animations that we will use are simple. XAML is capable of very powerful animations, but just because they exist doesn't mean we need to use them for simple tasks (think of the Blink and Marquee tags). For this example, we will be using KeyFrames. KeyFrames define the start- and endpoint of a transition. KeyFrame animation is a very common animation used in XAML development because of its gentle nature and ease of use.

Add the following to the MinimalLayout StoryBoard:

```
<ObjectAnimationUsingKeyFrames Storyboard.TargetName="myGridView"
        Storyboard.TargetProperty="Visibility">
    <DiscreteObjectKeyFrame KeyTime="0:0:1" Value="Collapsed"/>
</ObjectAnimationUsingKeyFrames>
<ObjectAnimationUsingKeyFrames Storyboard.TargetName="myListView"
        Storyboard.TargetProperty="Visibility">
    <DiscreteObjectKeyFrame KeyTime="0:0:1" Value="Visible"/>
</ObjectAnimationUsingKeyFrames>
```

The StoryBoard adds attached properties to the KeyFrame elements, and that is how the animation target is specified. We then use a DiscreteObjectKeyFrame (an animation that uses discreet interpolation) on the value of the target element. In this VisualState, the Visibility properties of the GridView and the ListView are set to "Collapsed" and "Visible", respectively, over one second.

■ **Note** I set the KeyTime to one second for demonstration purposes. It is perfectly acceptable to set the animation time to zero so that the transformation happens immediately. This is because the act of a user changing the visual aspects of an app by resizing it is explicit.

Next, we need to create the remaining StoryBoards using the same techniques. The complete XAML is listed here:

```
<VisualStateManager.VisualStateGroups>
    <VisualStateGroup>

        <VisualState x:Name="DefaultLayout">
            <Storyboard>
                <ObjectAnimationUsingKeyFrames Storyboard.TargetName="myGridView"
                        Storyboard.TargetProperty="Visibility">
                    <DiscreteObjectKeyFrame KeyTime="0:0:1" Value="Visible"/>
                </ObjectAnimationUsingKeyFrames>
                <ObjectAnimationUsingKeyFrames Storyboard.TargetName="myListView"
                        Storyboard.TargetProperty="Visibility">
                    <DiscreteObjectKeyFrame KeyTime="0:0:1" Value="Collapsed"/>
                </ObjectAnimationUsingKeyFrames>
            </Storyboard>
        </VisualState>
        <VisualState x:Name="MinimalLayout">
            <Storyboard>
                <ObjectAnimationUsingKeyFrames Storyboard.TargetName="myGridView"
                        Storyboard.TargetProperty="Visibility">
                    <DiscreteObjectKeyFrame KeyTime="0:0:1" Value="Collapsed"/>
                </ObjectAnimationUsingKeyFrames>
                <ObjectAnimationUsingKeyFrames Storyboard.TargetName="myListView"
                        Storyboard.TargetProperty="Visibility">
```

```
                <DiscreteObjectKeyFrame KeyTime="0:0:1" Value="Visible"/>
              </ObjectAnimationUsingKeyFrames>
          </Storyboard>
      </VisualState>
      <VisualState x:Name="PortraitLayout">
          <Storyboard>
              <ObjectAnimationUsingKeyFrames Storyboard.TargetName="myGridView"
                      Storyboard.TargetProperty="Visibility">
                  <DiscreteObjectKeyFrame KeyTime="0:0:1" Value="Collapsed"/>
              </ObjectAnimationUsingKeyFrames>
              <ObjectAnimationUsingKeyFrames Storyboard.TargetName="myListView"
                      Storyboard.TargetProperty="Visibility">
                  <DiscreteObjectKeyFrame KeyTime="0:0:1" Value="Visible"/>
              </ObjectAnimationUsingKeyFrames>
          </Storyboard>
      </VisualState>
    </VisualStateGroup>
</VisualStateManager.VisualStateGroups>
```

Handling the Resize Event

When a Windows 8.1 app is resized, the framework raises the size changed event. Open MainPage.XAML.cs and add the following code into the constructor to register the event handler:

```
this.SizeChanged += MainPage_SizeChanged;
```

And then add in the code for the event handler:

```
void MainPage_SizeChanged(object sender, SizeChangedEventArgs e)
{
}
```

The SizeChangedEventArgs contains three properties that we leverage in adjusting the layout of our app: NewSize, OriginalSize, and PreviousSize. For this scenario (and most for that matter), all that is important is the NewSize. When the NewSize is less than or equal to 500 px, we want to apply the MinimalLayout. If the height is greater than the width, we want to apply the PortraitLayout. Otherwise, we want to apply the DefaultLayout.

To apply the layout of your choice, use the static GoToState method of the VisualStateManager. The VisualStateManager class loads the XAML that we configured in the page and executes the specified StoryBoard.

Add the following code to the event handler:

```
if (e.NewSize.Width <= 500)
{
    VisualStateManager.GoToState(this, "MinimalLayout", true);
}
else if (e.NewSize.Width < e.NewSize.Height)
{
    VisualStateManager.GoToState(this, "PortraitLayout", true);
}
else
{
    VisualStateManager.GoToState(this, "DefaultLayout", true);
}
```

Run it again and pin the app to the right edge. You will see something similar to Figure 5-10. You should also see a short pause before the data appears due to the KeyTime value that we entered.

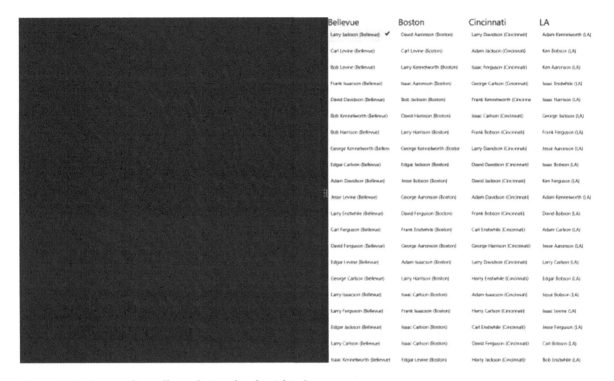

Figure 5-10. *App made smaller and pinned to the right edge*

You can now run the application and switch between snapped and unsnapped views and you should see the application "Do the right thing."

The Grid App Template

As mentioned earlier, the GridView control is perhaps the most complex control you'll work with in Windows Store XAML applications since it works with collections of collections. The Grid App template was designed to help you get started with a GridView-based application, but it's (necessarily) also a bit complex for the same reason.

Compounding things a bit, there's no owner's manual or even an obvious "Start here!" to tell you what's going on. It's worth figuring out though: once you understand the Grid App template, it can really help by providing a useful architecture for managing multidimensional data.

What's Included in the Template

To see the Grid App template in action, create a new Grid App project called Grid App and take a look at the generated files as shown in Figure 5-11.

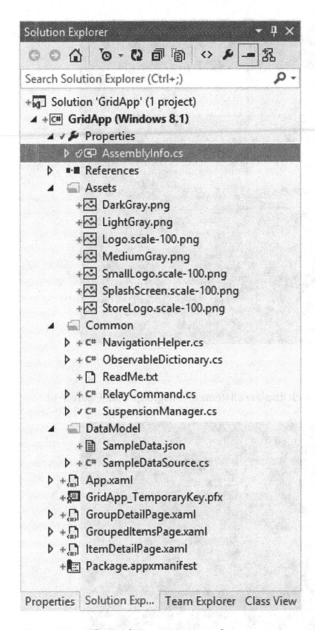

Figure 5-11. The GridView project template

The Pages

There are three pages in the template: the GroupedItemsPage, the GroupDetailPage, and the ItemDetailPage.

The GroupedItemsPage is the home page. It displays grouped collections of items. Running the app shows the page loaded, as in Figure 5-12.

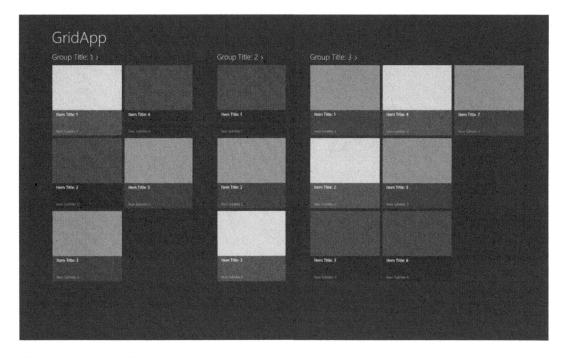

Figure 5-12. *The GridView template in action*

Clicking on a group title shows the `GroupDetailPage`, which displays all items in that group, as in Figure 5-13.

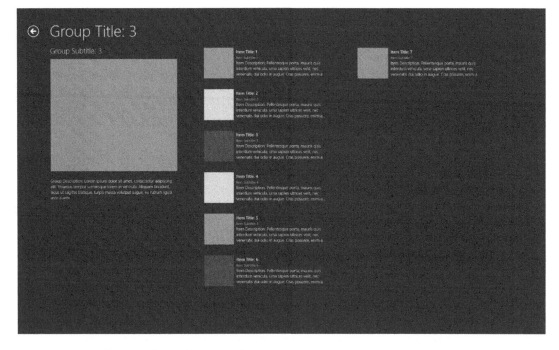

Figure 5-13. *Drilling into the GridView template*

Finally, clicking on an individual item displays the `ItemDetailPage`, which (as you probably guessed) shows details for that one item, as in Figure 5-14.

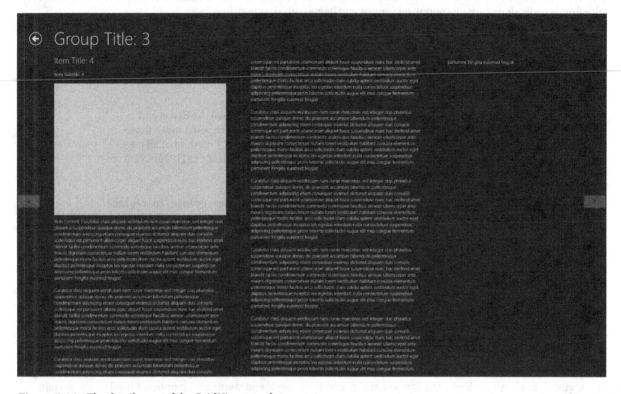

Figure 5-14. *The detail page of the GridView template*

The Common Folder

The `Common` folder contains several files, introduced via a `ReadMe.txt` file, which basically says "Hands off the XAML, be very careful with the class files."

The SampleDataSource

`SampleDataSource.cs` (found in `/DataModel`) actually contains three classes:

- *SampleDataItem*: This class represents a single item. It represents the core model of the app and has a set of properties already configured to define the item.

- *SampleDataGroup*: This class consists of a `Group` that includes an `Items` property that is an ObservableCollection of all items in the group as well as metadata that describes the group.

- *SampleDataSource*: This class populates the items and groups on start-up and maintains a catalog in a static collection. It's also got a few static utility methods to allow retrieving a group or item by unique ID.

Options for Integrating Your Data into a Grid App Project

The Grid App template works fine out of the box, but it's just displaying hard-coded data. The SampleDataConstructor initializer is really simple—it just populates groups and items with simple strings.

There are a few ways to integrate with the Grid App template:

1. You can just modify the way that SampleDataSource loads data. This is ideal if the properties in SampleDataCommon, SampleDataItem, and SampleDataGroup fit your data model. That's not all that far-fetched—these classes have very generic names that would work in quite a few cases.

2. You can throw out the SampleDataSource class completely and load the Group and Item collections using your own custom logic. To see exactly where you'd make these changes, search the application for //TODO: since the LoadState() method of all pages (GroupedItemsPage.xaml.cs, GroupDetailPage.xaml.cs, and ItemDetailPage.xaml.cs) all begin with the comment:

   ```
   //TODO: Create an appropriate data model for your problem domain to replace
   the sample data.
   ```

3. An important third option to keep in mind is that the Grid App may not be a good fit for your specific application. If your Item properties and display need to be substantially different, you're going to end up doing more work than if you just were to build custom views in a Blank App, as shown earlier in this chapter.

If you've settled on option 3, our work here is done!

If you're choosing whether to go with option 1 or 2, it's a little bit harder. While it may be tempting to think that your application is a unique snowflake, keep in mind that the SampleDataSource classes do handle a lot of helpful things for you, like raising property change notifications through BindableBase and keeping the TopItems collection for each group up-to-date. Unless you're fairly certain that you're in that narrow range that will profit from the Grid App template but can't work with the SampleDataSource, I'd recommend starting with option 1 until you're certain you've outgrown it.

For this example, we'll look at integrating with the SampleDataSource.

Integrating Your Own Data into SampleDataSource

While it may be tempting to delete all the sample data loaded in the SampleDataSource constructor, remember that this data is helpful when you're editing the application pages in design mode. A better solution is to include a check for design mode and, when you do, load the existing sample data.

The data in the SampleDataSource is loaded in the GetSampleDataAsync() method, so we need to add an if-else block that checks if you're in design mode; otherwise, we'll call out to a service that loads the data.

```
if (Windows.ApplicationModel.DesignMode.DesignModeEnabled)
{
    //Template generated code here
}
else
{
    //TODO: Load production data here
}
```

Now, when you run the app, there isn't any data displayed. However, if you look at one of the main pages in the Visual Studio designer, the sample data is loaded. Open `GroupDetailPage.XAML` in the Visual Studio designer, as shown in Figure 5-15.

Figure 5-15. *Sample data loaded in the Visual Studio designer*

Blend for Visual Studio 2013 fully supports Windows 8.1 XAML. To open it, right-click on `GroupDetailPage.xaml` in Solution Explorer, select Open in Blend, and the data again is loaded. This page is shown in Figure 5-16.

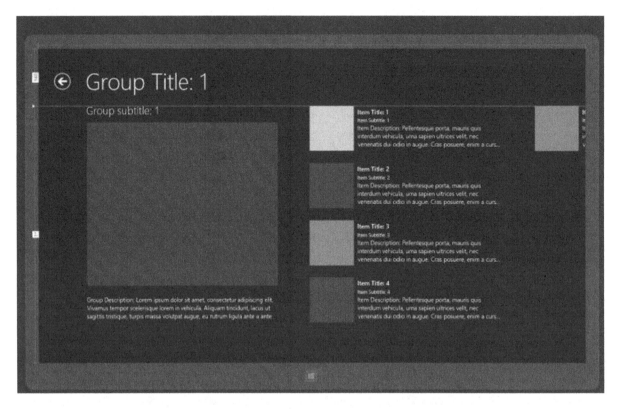

Figure 5-16. *Sample data loaded in Blend for Visual Studio 2013*

Adding the Person Class

Our first task is to create the classes and services needed to generate the "real" data for the application—that is, the data that is shown at run time (rather than at design time). We'll use a modified version of the Person class defined earlier in this chapter. Notice that we will create the names randomly, but we will assign the city from a parameter passed in to the CreatePeople method.

To do so, add the following Person class to the DataModels folder:

```
using System;
using System.Collections.Generic;
using System.Linq;
using System.Text;
using System.Threading.Tasks;

namespace Grid App.DataModel
{
  public class Person
  {
      public string FirstName { get; set; }
      public string LastName { get; set; }
      public string City { get; set; }
```

```
    private static readonly string[] firstNames =
      { "Adam", "Bob", "Carl", "David", "Edgar", "Frank", "George", "Harry", "Isaac", "Jesse",
        "Ken", "Larry" };
    private static readonly string[] lastNames =
      { "Aaronson", "Bobson", "Carlson", "Davidson", "Enstwhile", "Ferguson", "Harrison",
        "Isaacson", "Jackson", "Kennelworth", "Levine" };

    public override string ToString()
    {
       return string.Format( "{0} {1} ({2})", FirstName, LastName, City );
    }

    public static IEnumerable<Person> CreatePeople( int count, string city )
    {
        var people = new List<Person>();
        var r = new Random();
        for ( int i = 0; i < count; i++ )
        {
           var p = new Person()
           {
               FirstName = firstNames[r.Next( firstNames.Length )],
               LastName = lastNames[r.Next( lastNames.Length )],
               City = city
           };
           people.Add( p );
        }
        return people;
    }
  }
}
```

Creating the PeopleService

Normally, we will go out to a database or a web service to retrieve the collection of People to display. We will mimic that by creating a local class with a GetTimes method that will create all the People we need for the application.

To do so, add the following PeopleService class to the DataModels folder:

```
using System;
using System.Collections.Generic;
using System.Linq;
using System.Text;
using System.Threading.Tasks;
using Grid App.Data;
```

```csharp
namespace Grid App.DataModel
{
    public class PeopleService
    {
        public string[] GetGroups()
        {
            string[] cities =
                { "Boston", "New York", "LA", "San Francisco", "Phoenix",
                  "San Jose", "Cincinnati", "Bellevue" };
            return cities;
        }
        internal Data.SampleDataGroup GetItems(string group)
        {
            var r = new Random();
            int i = 0;
            var people = Person.CreatePeople(r.Next(50), group);
            SampleDataGroup dataGroup = new SampleDataGroup("Group-" + group,
                        group,
                        string.Empty,
                        "Assets/DarkGray.png",
                        "Group Description: Some description for " + group + " goes here.");
            foreach (var person in people)
            {
                dataGroup.Items.Add(new SampleDataItem("Group-" + group + "-Item-" + ++i,
                    person.FirstName + " " + person.LastName,
                    "(" + person.City + ")",
                    "Assets/LightGray.png",
                    "Person Description: (none)",
                    "Here's where the extended content for each person goes"));
            }
            return dataGroup;
        }
    }
}
```

Then, navigate back to the SampleDataSource.cs class and open the GetSampleDataAsync method and replace the following line:

```csharp
//TODO: Load production data here
```

with the following code:

```csharp
this.AllGroups.Clear();
var peopleService = new PeopleService();

string[] groups = peopleService.GetGroups();
foreach(string group in groups)
{
    this.AllGroups.Add(peopleService.GetItems(group));
}
```

This method will now do the following:

- Clear the `SampleDataSource` groups
- Retrieve the list of groups
- Populate each group

Run the app again, and you will see something similar to figures 5-17 and 5-18.

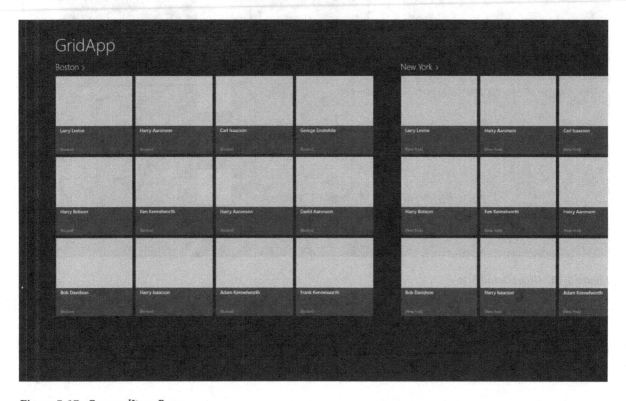

Figure 5-17. *GroupedItemsPage*

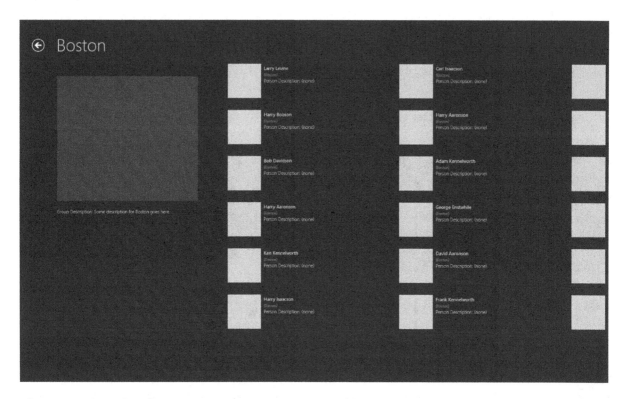

Figure 5-18. *GroupDetailPage*

The Split App Template

In addition to the Grid App template, Visual Studio offers the Split App template as shown in Figure 5-19.

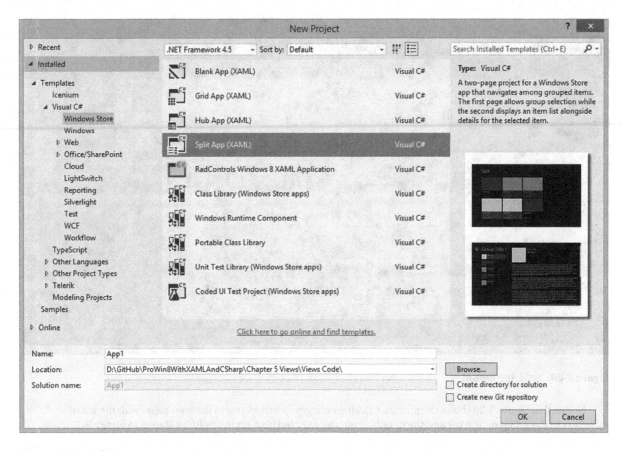

Figure 5-19. *Split App*

The Split App is in essence a simplified version of the Grid App, and you can use it in exactly the same way. In fact, to see how this works, create a new project of the type Split App called Split App and then follow the identical steps from above for the Grid App. The net effect is that your data is now shown in the Split App main page, as shown in Figure 5-20.

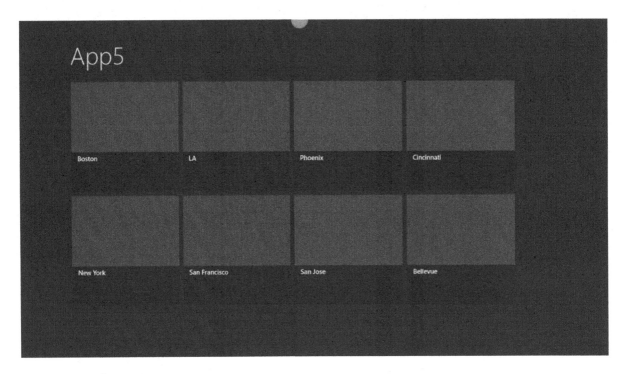

Figure 5-20. *Split App groups*

Notice that Figure 5-20 shows the groups. Clicking on a group brings you to the split page, with the list of members of the group on the left and the details about the selected item on the right, as shown in Figure 5-21.

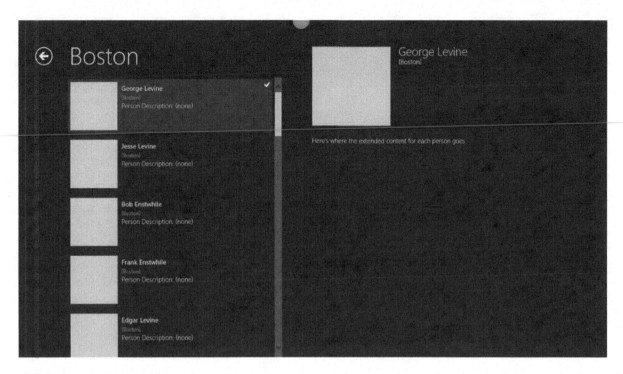

Figure 5-21. *Split App details*

Summary

An extremely important consideration as a developer is making sure that your app will scale gracefully not only to different devices but also to different layouts and sizes. The fluid nature of XAML provides a significant amount of support for different device sizes.

The `VisualStateManager` can contain one or more `VisualStates` that you use to define a layout for a specific view through animations. When the `SizeChanged` event is raised, you can specify which controls to show/hide as well as any other changes to improve the user experience.

We looked at two of the most complex app templates in the Grid App and the Split App. If your app requirements match one of these templates, there is a lot of power right at your fingertips.

CHAPTER 6

■ ■ ■

Local Data

All significant Windows 8 Store applications manage and store data of some sort. This data can be arbitrarily divided into application data and user data. The former, application data, refers to the state of the application at any given time, including:

- What page the user is on

- What form fields have been filled out

- What selections and other choices have been made

User data, on the other hand, is data entered by the user specifically to be processed and stored by the application. User data can be stored in a number of formats, and it can be stored in a number of places on your disk or in the cloud.

This chapter will start off by showing how to store application data and then will explore some of the most popular ways to store user data.

Application Data

While your Windows 8 Store application is running, you want to be saving data all the time. After all, you can switch to another application at any time, and you only have five seconds to store out your data at that point.

But, while that it's true that you want to be saving all the time for major data points, there are certain "status" values that you want to store only at the last minute. This might include which information is visible, what is selected, the currently filled-in fields, and so forth.

A great way to store that information is in with an `ApplicationDataContainer`. This can be stored with your local settings or your roaming settings, and it requires no special permission from the operating system; these files are considered safe.

Settings Containers

There are three settings containers that can be used for local storage: local, roaming, and temporary. Local is stored on the device and persists across app launches. Roaming is also stored locally but will sync across devices based on the currently logged-in user. Temporary is, well, temporary. It can be deleted by the system at any time.

Saving, Reading, and Deleting Local Data

Let's create an application that stores, reads, and deletes application data. Our UI is very simple: a text box to enter information into, a text block to display recalled information, and three buttons, as shown in Figure 6-1.

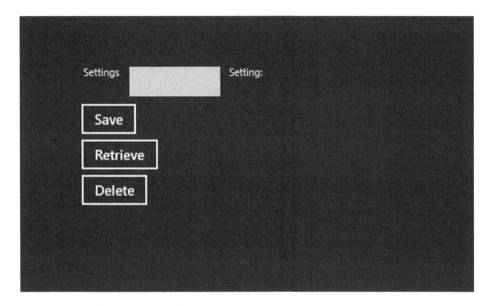

Figure 6-1. *View for saving, retrieve, and deleting data*

Start with a new project based on the Blank App template and name your app AppSettings. Open MainPage.xaml.cs and add the following using statement to the very top of the file:

```
using Windows.Storage;
```

Then, add the following declaration to the top of the class:

```
private ApplicationDataContainer settings =
    ApplicationData.Current.LocalSettings;
```

This creates a local variable that references the local data storage.
Next, open MainPage.xaml and replace the default Grid with the following XAML:

```
<Grid Background="{ThemeResource ApplicationPageBackgroundThemeBrush}">
    <Grid.ColumnDefinitions>
        <ColumnDefinition Width="120"/>
        <ColumnDefinition Width="*"/>
    </Grid.ColumnDefinitions>
```

```
<Grid.RowDefinitions>
    <RowDefinition Height="140"/>
    <RowDefinition Height="*"/>
</Grid.RowDefinitions>
<StackPanel Grid.Column="1" Grid.Row="1">
    <StackPanel Orientation="Horizontal">
        <TextBlock Text="Settings"
                    Margin="5" />
        <TextBox Width="100"
                    Height="30"
                    Name="txtSettings"
                    Margin="5"/>
        <TextBlock Text="Setting: " Margin="5"/>
        <TextBlock Name="txtSettingOutput"
                    Text=""
                    Margin="5"/>
    </StackPanel>
    <Button Name="SaveSettings"
            Content="Save"
            Click="SaveSettings_Click" />
    <Button Name="RetrieveSettings"
            Content="Retrieve"
            Click="RetrieveSettings_Click" />
    <Button Name="DeleteSettings"
            Content="Delete"
            Click="DeleteSettings_Click" />
</StackPanel>
</Grid>
```

Go on to open up the MainPage.xaml.cs file again and add another class-lever variable. This variable will be used to eliminate the use of "Magic Strings," which can lead to typos and runtime errors.

```
string settingName = "UserSetting";
```

When the user clicks the Save button, the content from the text box gets written to the settings collection, and then the text box is cleared. Create the event handler for the SaveSettings button in MainPage.xaml.cs, and enter in the following code:

```
private void SaveSettings_Click(object sender, RoutedEventArgs e)
{
    string userValue = txtSettings.Text;
    settings.Values[settingName] = userValue;
    txtSettings.Text = String.Empty;
}
```

If a UserSetting already exists in the dictionary, the current value will be overwritten. If it doesn't exist, it will be created.

Retrieving the text is equally simple. We pull the text out of the settings collection as an object, and if it is not null we turn it into a string. If the setting does not exist, it will come back as null. While still in `MainPage.xaml.cs`, create the event handler for the `RetrieveSettings` button, and add the following code:

```
private void RetrieveSettings_Click(object sender, RoutedEventArgs e)
{
    object val = settings.Values[settingName];
    if (val != null)
    {
        txtSettingOutput.Text = val.ToString();
    }
}
```

Finally, deleting a setting just requires a call to the `Remove` method. We also clear out the output text box. Create the event handler for the `DeleteSettings` button and add the following code:

```
private void DeleteSettings_Click(object sender, RoutedEventArgs e)
{
    settings.Values.Remove(settingName);
    txtSettingOutput.Text = String.Empty;
}
```

That's all it takes to manage your application state. Piece of cake. Easy as pie. The complete code is listed here:

```
public sealed partial class MainPage : Page
{
  private ApplicationDataContainer settings =
      ApplicationData.Current.LocalSettings;
  string settingName = "UserSetting";
  public MainPage()
  {
    this.InitializeComponent();
  }
  private void SaveSettings_Click(object sender, RoutedEventArgs e)
  {
    string userValue = txtSettings.Text;
    settings.Values[settingName] = userValue;
    txtSettings.Text = String.Empty;
  }
  private void RetrieveSettings_Click(
    object sender, RoutedEventArgs e)
  {
    object val = settings.Values[settingName];
    if (val != null)
    {
      txtSettingOutput.Text = val.ToString();
    }
  }
```

```
private void DeleteSettings_Click(object sender, RoutedEventArgs e)
{
    settings.Values.Remove(settingName);
    txtSettingOutput.Text = String.Empty;
}
}
```

Creating the Data Layer

Applications that rely on data are wise to separate data-related classes into a separate layer. Often, in large applications, this data-access layer is a separate project. To keep things simple in our examples, we will say that all classes are the same project for simplicity.

To begin, create a new Windows 8 Store application using the Blank Application template and call it LocalFolderSample. In the following sections, you will create the foundation for the rest of the examples in this chapter.

Creating the Repository Interface

Basic data operations include Create, Read, Update, and Delete, commonly referred to as CRUD operations. A very common pattern to use is the repository pattern. While this section does not attempt to fully execute the pattern, we will place these functions into repository classes. We start by creating a common interface for all repositories in the data-access layer. This is a good practice, even though we are only creating a single repository in this example.

To begin, create a new folder in your project named Data by right-clicking the project name and selecting Add ➤ New Folder. Next, add a new interface by right-clicking the folder you just created and selecting Add ➤ New Item and then Interface. Name the folder IDataRepository and enter the following code:

```
public interface IDataRepository<T>
{
    Task Add(T customer);
    Task<ObservableCollection<T>>Load();
    Task Remove(T customer);
    Task Update(T customer);
}
```

To use the ObservableCollection, you need to add a using to System.ComponentModel. At the top of the file, add this statement:

```
using System.Collections.ObjectModel;
```

There's a lot going on in this interface, and it merits some discussion before we move on. The interface is created using generics so that the implementing classes can be strongly typed. The ObservableCollection class has been around since Windows Presentation Foundation (WPF), and it is a class that implements INotifyCollectionChanged and INotifyPropertyChanged. These events are raised anytime items are added to or deleted from the collection, or when any other changes are made to the collection class. The data-binding engine in Windows 8.1 XAML apps listens for those events and will automatically update the bound elements to the new values. Additionally, all of the methods have been defined to return a Task<T> to enable asynchronous operations.

Creating the DataModel

Next, we need to create the class that will hold and transport the data. Sometimes referred to as Data Transfer Objects (DTOs) or Plain Old CLR Objects (POCOs), the term most commonly used is *model*. Add a new class by right-clicking the Data folder and selecting Add ➤ New Item ➤ Class. Name the class Customer.cs, and add the following code:

```
public class Customer
{
    public int Id { get; set; }
    public string Email { get; set; }
    public string FirstName { get; set; }
    public string LastName { get; set; }
    public string Title { get; set; }
}
```

Creating the ViewModel

The final class to create is the ViewModel. This class will act as the data context for the view. To do this, right-click on the Data folder, select Add ➤ New Item ➤ Class. Name the file ViewModel.cs. The ViewModel will use an instance of the data repository interface to get the necessary data (we well as to make any updates), so we add a class-level variable to hold the instance. Open ViewModel.cs and add a member variable of type IDataRepository<Customer>:

```
IDataRepository<Customer> _data;
```

To get an instance of the repository into the ViewModel, we will use constructor injection. The constructor takes an IDataRepository and initializes the local variable as follows:

```
public ViewModel(IDataRepository<Customer> data)
{
    _data = data;
}
```

Implementing INotifyPropertyChanged

In this example, we want the ViewModel to to implement INotifyPropertyChanged instead of the model. Add the interface INotifyPropertyChanged to the class and create a PropertyChanged event (this is the only item in INotifyPropertyChanged).

```
public class ViewModel:INotifyPropertyChanged
{
  public event PropertyChangedEventHandler PropertyChanged;
}
```

You will need to add a using for System.ComponentModel as follows:

```
using System.ComponentModel;
```

The common implementation is to create a method to encapsulate the raising of the PropertyChanged event. To do this, create a new method called RaisePropertyChange(). Add the following code:

```
private void RaisePropertyChanged(string fieldName)
{
  if (PropertyChanged != null)
  {
    PropertyChanged(this, new PropertyChangedEventArgs(fieldName));
  }
}
```

This method checks to make sure there is a listener for the event and then fires it with the fieldName as the event argument. New in .NET 4.5 (and later) is the ability for a method to extract the method that called it using the CallerMemberNameAttribute. This will become more important as we develop the rest of the ViewModel, but for now, update the method signature to the following. Note that the CallerMemberName requires the parameter to have a default value.

```
private void RaisePropertyChanged(
    [CallerMemberName] string fieldName = "")
```

The following code shows the current status of the ViewModel:

```
public class ViewModel:INotifyPropertyChanged
{
  IDataRepository _data;
  public ViewModel(IDataRepository data)
  {
    _data = data;
  }
  public event PropertyChangedEventHandler PropertyChanged;
  private void RaisePropertyChanged(
    [CallerMemberName] string fieldName = "")
  {
    if (PropertyChanged != null)
    {
      PropertyChanged(this,
        new PropertyChangedEventArgs(fieldName));
    }
  }
}
```

Adding the Public Properties

There are two public properties in the ViewModel: SelectedItem and Customers. We can't use automatic properties because we want to leverage the PropertyChanged notification system. So we have to use property statements with backing fields.

The first property to create is SelectedItem. Add the following code to ViewModel.cs:

```
private Customer _selectedItem;
public Customer SelectedItem
{
  get
  {
    return this._selectedItem;
  }
  set
  {
    if (value != _selectedItem)
    {
      _selectedItem = value;
      RaisePropertyChanged();
    }
  }
}
```

In the Setter, if the value has been changed, then the RaisePropertyChanged method is called. The CallerMemberName attribute allows you to avoid writing this code the old way:

```
RaisePropertyChanged("SelectedItem");
```

The next property is Customers, which is an ObservableCollection of the Customer class. Before adding this property, be sure to add the using for System.Collections.ObjectModel:

```
using System.Collections.ObjectModel;
```

Then, add the property:

```
private ObservableCollection<Customer> _customers;
public ObservableCollection<Customer> Customers
{
  get
  {
    return _customers;
  }
  set
  {
    _customers = value;
    RaisePropertyChanged();
  }
}
```

Go on to create an async method to load the data:

```
public async void Initialize()
{
  Customers = await _data.Load();
}
```

Finally, we are ready to implement the CRUD operations, delegating the work to the repository. We do this as follows:

```
internal void AddCustomer(Customer cust)
{
  _data.Add(cust);
}
internal void DeleteCustomer(Customer cust)
{
  _data.Remove(cust);
}
```

That's it for the ViewModel class. By using a repository, we keep the ViewModel simple, clean, and reusable with different storage approaches.

Local Data

Local Data files include any data in your app, including data that the user entered and should be persisted. One option is to persist this data in the local or roaming settings as discussed in the previous section. This can be less than ideal, especially with large amounts of data.

Another option is to store the data in a file located in a folder under the signed-in user's name. This is not the same as using LocalSettings. The LocalSettings is a dictionary object that is stored in the registry, and as such, is limited in size. Local and Roaming folders are stored alongside the app on the disk.

Using JSON to Format Data

Before getting into the meat of reading and writing data files, we need to consider the different storage formats available. Local data files are text files, and as such, all of the data stored will be simple strings. There was a time that XML was the predominant format for string data. However, XML is heavy with all of the tags and can be difficult to work with.

The current leader in textual data is JSON—JavaScript Object Notation. Initially championed by the web for its lightweight format and its ease of conversion between text and an object graph, JSON is winning the format war, and most Windows 8 developers are using JSON for local storage of text.

The leading package with which C# developers can work with JSON data is Json.NET. One way to add Json.NET to your project is to download the package from http://json.codeplex.com/, install (or unzip based on the download), and reference the correct assemblies. An easier way to add it is to use NuGet to quickly and easily add JSON to your project. See the sidebar for more information.

USING NUGET TO INSTALL JSON.NET

Instead of downloading the Json.NET package from `http://json.codeplex.com`, you can install it through NuGet. To install Json.NET through NuGet, click on Tools ➤ Library Package Manager ➤ Package Manager Console. This will open the console window at the bottom of your screen, providing you the Package Manager prompt (PM>). Then, enter the command to load Json.NET:

```
PM> Install-Package Newtonsoft.Json
```

Remember to include the hyphen between `Install` and `Package`. A few seconds later, the package will have been installed.

As we discussed in the chapter on tooling, you can also use the GUI for NuGet, which includes a nice search feature. Instead of having to know the exact package name, you can search for JSON and the pick the correct package.

Local Data Containers

Just like the settings containers, there are three local data containers that can be used for local storage: local, roaming, and temporary. Local is stored on the device and persists across app launches. Roaming is also stored locally but will sync across devices based on the currently logged in user. Temporary is, again, temporary. It can be deleted by the system at any time.

Creating the File Repository

The actual storage of the file is pretty simple, but we're going to build out a fully reusable repository model based on the interface we created earlier. Using the interface as the base allows us to reapply the same pattern to other storage approaches later. We begin with the data file itself. To keep things simple, I'll stay with the idea of storing and retrieving customer data.

To create the file repository, first add a new Class file to the Data directory by right-clicking the directory, selecting Add ➤ New Item ➤ Class. Name the class `FileRepository`.

Next, add the `IDataRepository<Customer>` interface to the class and the required members. The class will look like this:

```
public class FileRepository:IDataRepository<Customer>
{
  public Task Add(Customer customer)
  {
    // TODO: Implement this method
    throw new NotImplementedException();
  }

  public Task<ObservableCollection<Customer>>Load()
  {
    // TODO: Implement this method
    throw new NotImplementedException();
  }
```

```
public Task Remove(Customer customer)
{
  // TODO: Implement this method
  throw new NotImplementedException();
}

public Task Update(Customer customer)
{
  // TODO: Implement this method
  throw new NotImplementedException();
}
}
```

Finally, add the required usings for System.Collections.ObjectModel and Windows.Storage:

```
using System.Collections.ObjectModel;
using Windows.Storage;
```

Following this, we need to add the member variables of a string for the file name of our specific storage file, an observable collection of Customer, and a StorageFolder referencing the LocalFolder using the following code:

```
string _filename = "customers.json";
ObservableCollection<Customer> _customers;
StorageFolder _folder = ApplicationData.Current.LocalFolder;
```

The constructor calls the Initialize method, which in this example does nothing. The Initialize method will be used when we cover SQLite later in this chapter.

```
public FileRepository()
{
  Initialize();
}
private void Initialize()
{
}
```

Next, create two helper methods in the FileRepository class to save and read the collection of customer data to and from disk. We first need to add the following using statements:

```
using Newtonsoft.Json;
using Windows.Storage;
```

The first helper method serializes the collection of customers and then

```
private Task WriteToFile()
{
  return Task.Run(async () =>
  {
    string JSON = JsonConvert.SerializeObject(_customers);
    var file = await OpenFileAsync();
    await FileIO.WriteTextAsync(file, JSON);
  });
}
```

```
private async Task<StorageFile> OpenFileAsync()
{
  return await _folder.CreateFileAsync(_fileName,
    CreationCollisionOption.OpenIfExists);
}
```

Notice that WriteToFile converts the customers collection to JSON, then asynchronously opens the file to write to, and then finally writes to the file, again asynchronously. To open the file, we add the helper method OpenFileAsync. Notice that when opening the file, we handle CreationCollisions by saying that we want to open the file if it already exists.

Now it's time to add the methods that handle the adding, removing, and updating the customers in the list. The Add method adds a customer (passed in as a parameter) to the customers collection and then calls WriteToFile:

```
public Task Add(Customer customer)
 {
     customers.Add(customer);
     return WriteToFile();
 }
```

The Remove method removes a customer (passed in as a parameter) from the customers collection and then calls WriteToFile as such:

```
public Task Remove(Customer customer)
 {
     customers.Remove(customer);
     return WriteToFile();
 }
```

The third interface method is Update. Here, we have slightly more work to do: we must find the record we want to update and if it is not null then we remove the old version and save the new.

```
public Task Update(Customer customer)
{
  var oldCustomer = customers.FirstOrDefault(
    c => c.Id == customer.Id);
  if (oldCustomer == null)
  {
    throw new System.ArgumentException("Customer not found.");
  }
  customers.Remove(oldCustomer);
  customers.Add(customer);
  return WriteToFile();
}
```

READING AND WRITING THE ENTIRE FILE

So why remove the old record and add the new one? While JSON is a very efficient storage and transport mechanism for text, it is not a relational database. It is much more efficient to simply remove the old record and replace it with the new one than to loop through all of the properties and update the record. Since there isn't any concept of an autoincrement ID (or any other relational database concept for that matter), we don't lose anything, and gain only speed.

A similar question can be asked as to why save the entire file each time there is a change instead of just updating the individual record. The answer is pretty much the same: The time and effort it would take to replace/add/change individual records compared to writing the entire file on each change makes writing the file each time a much faster and less fragile option.

What if you have a really-large text file? Then I would suggest looking at a more database-centric solution, such as SQLite, discussed later in this chapter.

Finally, we come to Load. Here, we create our file asynchronously and if it is not null, we read the contents of the file into a string. Then, the string is deserialized into a list of customers and added into the class's ObservableCollection<Customer>. Prior to flushing out the Load method, we need to add a using for System.Collection.Generic as follows:

```
using System.Collections.Generic;
```

If the Load method isn't marked as async, you will need to do that now. Then add the following code into the Load method:

```
public async Task<ObservableCollection<Customer>>Load()
{
  var file = await _folder.CreateFileAsync(
    _fileName, CreationCollisionOption.OpenIfExists);
  string fileContents = string.Empty;
  if (file != null)
  {
    fileContents = await FileIO.ReadTextAsync(file);
  }
  IList<Customer> customersFromJSON =
    JsonConvert.DeserializeObject<List<Customer>>(fileContents)
    ?? new List<Customer>();
  _customers = new ObservableCollection<Customer>(
    customersFromJSON);
  return customers;
}
```

We then deserialize the customer from the string of JSON into an IList of Customer and create an ObservableCollection of customer from that IList. Now that the repository is complete, it's time to create the view.

143

Creating the View

The view that we create will be very simple. It will consist of four text boxes with labels to add a new record with the list of current customers following the data entry section. It is not an award-winning UI, but enough to show the concepts of this chapter. The last piece of UI is a command bar to hold the Add and Delete command buttons. The UI is shown in Figure 6-2.

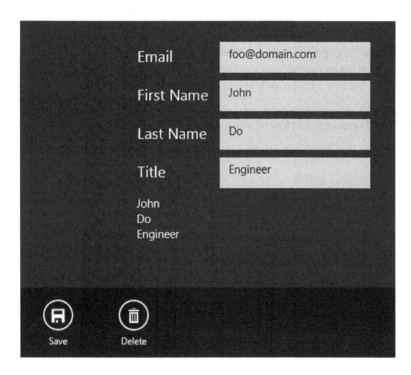

Figure 6-2. *UI for the local data example*

Open up `MainPage.xaml` and add the following styles to the `Page.Resources` section:

```xml
<Page.Resources>
    <Style TargetType="TextBlock">
        <Setter Property="FontSize"
                Value="20" />
        <Setter Property="Margin"
                Value="5" />
        <Setter Property="HorizontalAlignment"
                Value="Right" />
        <Setter Property="Grid.Column"
                Value="0" />
        <Setter Property="Width"
                Value="100" />
        <Setter Property="VerticalAlignment"
                Value="Center" />
    </Style>
```

```
    <Style TargetType="TextBox">
        <Setter Property="Margin"
                Value="5" />
        <Setter Property="HorizontalAlignment"
                Value="Left" />
        <Setter Property="Grid.Column"
                Value="1" />
    </Style>
</Page.Resources>
```

Next, add a `CommandBar` to the `BottomAppBar` as well as the Save and Delete buttons:

```
<Page.BottomAppBar>
  <CommandBar>
    <CommandBar.SecondaryCommands>
      <AppBarButton x:Name="cmdSave" Label="Save"
        Click="cmdSave_Click" Icon="Save"/>
      <AppBarButton x:Name="cmdDelete" Label="Delete"
        Click="cmdDelete_Click" Icon="Delete"/>
    </CommandBar.SecondaryCommands>
  </CommandBar>
</Page.BottomAppBar>
```

Then, we create a set of stack panels to gather the data and a `ListView` to display the data as follows:

```
<StackPanel Margin="150">
  <StackPanel Orientation="Horizontal">
    <TextBlock Text="Email" Margin="5" />
    <TextBox Width="200" Height="40"
      Name="Email" Margin="5" />
  </StackPanel>
  <StackPanel Orientation="Horizontal">
    <TextBlock Text="First Name" Margin="5" />
    <TextBox Width="200" Height="40"
      Name="FirstName" Margin="5" />
  </StackPanel>
  <StackPanel Orientation="Horizontal">
    <TextBlock Text="Last Name" Margin="5" />
    <TextBox Width="200" Height="40"
      Name="LastName" Margin="5" />
  </StackPanel>
  <StackPanel Orientation="Horizontal">
    <TextBlock Text="Title" Margin="5" />
    <TextBox Width="200" Height="40"
      Name="Title" Margin="5" />
  </StackPanel>
  <ScrollViewer>
    <ListView Name="xCustomers"
      ItemsSource="{Binding Customers}"
      SelectedItem="{Binding SelectedItem, Mode=TwoWay}"
      Height="400">
```

```
    <ListView.ItemTemplate>
      <DataTemplate>
        <StackPanel>
          <TextBlock Text="{Binding FirstName}" />
          <TextBlock Text="{Binding LastName}" />
          <TextBlock Text="{Binding Title}" />
        </StackPanel>
      </DataTemplate>
    </ListView.ItemTemplate>
  </ListView>
 </ScrollViewer>
</StackPanel>
```

Notice the binding both for the ItemsSource and the SelectedItem.

The code behind is straightforward. The first thing we do is to instantiate an IDataRepository and declare the ViewModel:

```
public sealed partial class MainPage : Page
{
  private IDataRepository data = new FileRepository();
  private ViewModel _vm;
```

This requires adding the namespace for the Data folder:

```
using LocalFolderSample.Data;
```

In the constructor, we create the ViewModel passing in the repository, then call initialize on the VM, and finally set the VM as the DataContext for the page:

```
public MainPage()
{
  this.InitializeComponent();
  _vm = new ViewModel(data);
  _vm.Initialize();
  DataContext = _vm;
}
```

All that is left is to implement the two event handlers as such:

```
private void cmdSave_Click(object sender, RoutedEventArgs e)
{
  Customer cust = new Customer
  {
    Email = Email.Text,
    FirstName = FirstName.Text,
    LastName = LastName.Text,
    Title = Title.Text
  };
  _vm.AddCustomer(cust);
}
```

```
private void cmdDelete_Click(object sender, RoutedEventArgs e)
{
    if (_vm.SelectedItem != null)
    {
        _vm.DeleteCustomer(_vm.SelectedItem);
    }
}
```

When you run the application, you are presented with the view shown earlier in Figure 6-1. Fill in an entry, right-click (or swipe up from the bottom) to bring up the app bar, and click Save. It immediately appears in the list box.

Once you have saved at least one record, your file, `Customers.json`, has been saved in application data. You can find it by searching under AppData on your main drive, which for most people is the C drive (see Figure 6-3).

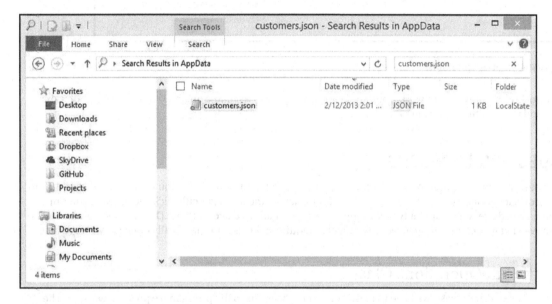

Figure 6-3. *The data file in AppData*

Double-click on that file to see the JSON you've saved:

```
[{"Id":0,"Email":"john@domain.com","FirstName":"John","LastName":"Doe","Title":"Scientist"}]
```

Roaming

To change from storing your data in local storage to roaming storage, you must change *one line* of code. Back in `FileRepository.cs,` change the LocalFolder to a RoamingFolder (see Figure 6-4).

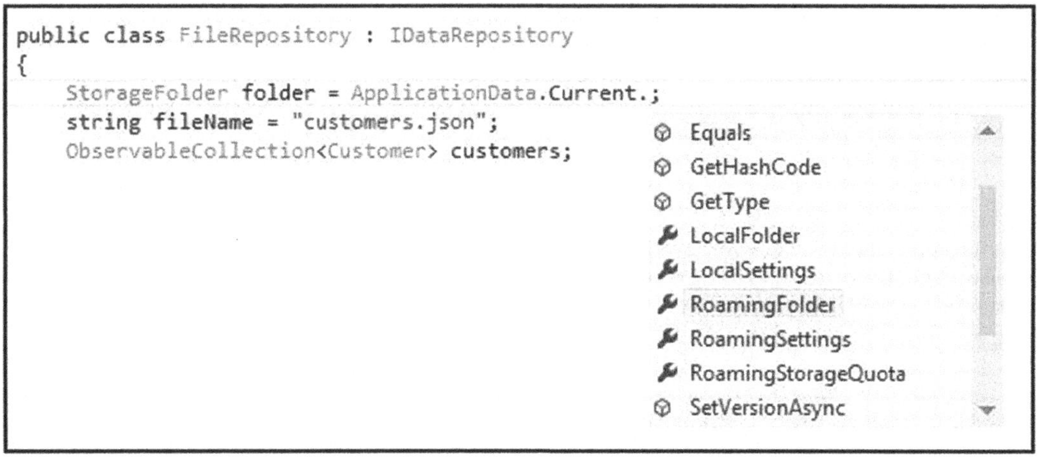

```
public class FileRepository : IDataRepository
{
    StorageFolder folder = ApplicationData.Current.;
    string fileName = "customers.json";
    ObservableCollection<Customer> customers;
```

    ⊙ Equals
    ⊙ GetHashCode
    ⊙ GetType
    🔧 LocalFolder
    🔧 LocalSettings
    🔧 RoamingFolder
    🔧 RoamingSettings
    🔧 RoamingStorageQuota
    ⊙ SetVersionAsync

Figure 6-4. *Available settings options*

Hey! Presto! Without any further work, your application data is now available on any Windows 8 computer that you log on to and also has the application installed.

User-Specified Locations

Local and roaming files are a valid solution for storing application data; but sometimes you want to write your data to a more well-known location. You can do so in Windows 8.1 by having the user explicitly pick a location at run time.

In Windows 8.0, there was a capability in the App Manifest that allowed access to the Documents Library. This has been removed in favor of the stronger security model of requiring the user to specifically open and/or save files.

Creating the FileOperations Class

To create the FileOperations class, we have to make some modifications to the program we previously wrote. The interface remains the same, but the implementation of the DataRepository changes a bit, and we add another class to encapsulate the utilization of the file pickers.

Start by adding a new class to the DataModel folder named FileOperations and add three static class-level variables:

```
static ApplicationDataContainer _settings =
  ApplicationData.Current.LocalSettings;
private static string _mruToken;
private static string _tokenKey = "mruToken";
```

We need to add a method to create the file if it doesn't exist:

```
private static async Task<StorageFile> CreateFile(string fileName)
{
  FileSavePicker savePicker = new FileSavePicker();
  savePicker.SuggestedStartLocation =
    PickerLocationId.DocumentsLibrary;
  savePicker.SuggestedFileName = fileName;
```

```
  savePicker.FileTypeChoices.Clear();
  savePicker.FileTypeChoices.Add("
    JSON", new List<string>() { ".json" });
  var file = await savePicker.PickSaveFileAsync();
  return SaveMRU(file);
}
```

Once the user has selected a file, we want to save the file into the MostRecentlyUsedList. This list remembers that the user gave permission to open the file and therefore that the files that are stored in the list are accessible on successive loads. The code to accomplish this is as follows:

```
private static StorageFile SaveMRU(StorageFile file)
{
  if (file != null)
  {
    _mruToken = StorageApplicationPermissions
      .MostRecentlyUsedList.Add(file);
    _settings.Values["mruToken"] = _mruToken;
    return file;
  }
  else
  {
    return null;
  }
}
```

We also use a FileOpenPicker to enable loading a file off the computer in case the MRUToken isn't available:

```
private static async Task<StorageFile> GetFile()
{
  FileOpenPicker openPicker = new FileOpenPicker();
  openPicker.SuggestedStartLocation =
    PickerLocationId.DocumentsLibrary;
  openPicker.ViewMode = PickerViewMode.List;
  // Filter to include a sample subset of file types.
  openPicker.FileTypeFilter.Clear();
  openPicker.FileTypeFilter.Add(".json");
  // Open the file picker.
  var file = await openPicker.PickSingleFileAsync();
  return SaveMRU(file);
}
```

If the MRUToken does exist, we can greatly simplify getting the file by doing the following:

```
private static async Task<StorageFile> GetFileFromMRU()
{
  return
  await StorageApplicationPermissions
    .MostRecentlyUsedList.GetFileAsync(_mruToken);
}
```

Finally, we create the entry method into the FileOperations:

```
public static async Task<StorageFile> OpenFile(string fileName)
{
  _mruToken = (_settings.Values[_tokenKey] != null) ?
  _settings.Values[_tokenKey].ToString() : null;
  if (_mruToken != null)
  {
    return await GetFileFromMRU();
  }
  var file = await GetFile();
  if (file != null)
  {
    return file;
  }
  else
  {
    return await CreateFile(fileName);
  }
}
```

With the FileOperations class built, there are just a few changes to make to the FileRepository class. At the top of the FileRepository class, we need to delete the instantiation of the StorageFolder:

```
StorageFolder folder = ApplicationData.Current.RoamingFolder;
```

Then, we update the OpenFileAsync to the following:

```
private async Task<StorageFile> OpenFileAsync()
{
  return await FileOperations.OpenFile(fileName);
}
```

Finally, we update the Load method by deleting the first line,

```
var file = await folder.CreateFileAsync(
  fileName, CreationCollisionOption.OpenIfExists);
```

and replacing it with this one:

```
var file = await FileOperations.OpenFile(fileName);
```

Adding the File Association for JSON Files

To add a file association for JSON files, open the Package.appxmanifest file and click on the Declarations tab. Open the drop-down list for the available declarations, select File Type Associations, and click Add, as shown in Figure 6-5.

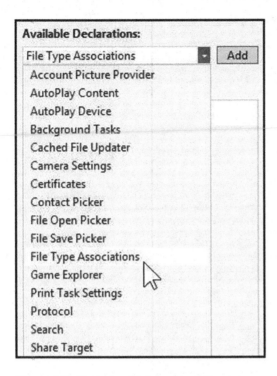

Figure 6-5. *Declaring file type associations*

Once you have added the file type association, you must also fill in a number of fields in the right rail as follows:

- *Display name*: json files
- *Name*: json
- *Content type*: text/plain
- *File type*: `.json`
- *Open is safe*: checked

The filled out form is shown in Figure 6-6.

Declarations   Packaging

properties.

Description:

Registers file type associations, such as .jpeg, on behalf of the app.

Multiple instances of this declaration are allowed in each app.

More information

Properties:

Display name: json files

Logo: ×   ...

Info tip:

Name: json

Edit flags

☑ Open is safe

☐ Always unsafe

Supported file types

At least one file type must be supported. Enter at least one file type; for example, ".jpg".

Supported file type	Remove
Content type: text/plain	
File type: .json	

Figure 6-6. *Declarations*

After adding in the file type association declaration, your app can load `*.json` files from File Explorer, as shown in Figure 6-7.

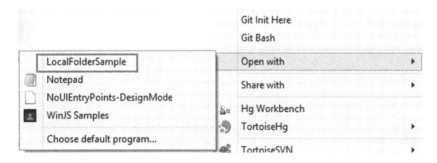

Figure 6-7. *Opening .json files with the app*

SQLite

One of the main benefits of using a repository as we have is that we can swap in SQLite for our data store. We create a new repository based on the `IDataRepository` interface, and the rest of our code largely remains intact. In fact, the ViewModel remains unchanged, while `Customer.cs` and `MainPage.xaml.cs` just receive a tiny tweak. To see this in action, create a new project based on the Blank App template named SQLiteSample.

We must install SQLite and the SQLite Visual Studio Extension. As of this writing, this extension isn't available from the Visual Studio Extensions and Updates screen. You can locate the installer for the Visual Studio Extension from the SQLite.org home page (`www.sqlite.org`). Then click Download and look for the version that works with VS2013 and Windows 8.1. (At the time of this writing, it is `sqlite-winrt81-3080403.vsix`). Alternativley, you can download it from the Visual Studio Gallery (`http://visualstudiogallery.msdn.microsoft.com/`). Either one will work, but I tend to rely on the Visual Studio gallery as my main source for extensions since I only have to remember one URL.

Once in the gallery, search for "SQLite for Windows Runtime" by clicking on Tools ➤ Extensions and Updates, and you will see the options listed in Figure 6-8. Then click on Online and type "SQLite for windows runtime" into the search box. When Search returns, you will see the link for the Windows 8.1 version (as shown in Figure 6-8). Clicking the link will take you to the download page, which will run the VSIX package (Visual Studio Installer for Extensions).

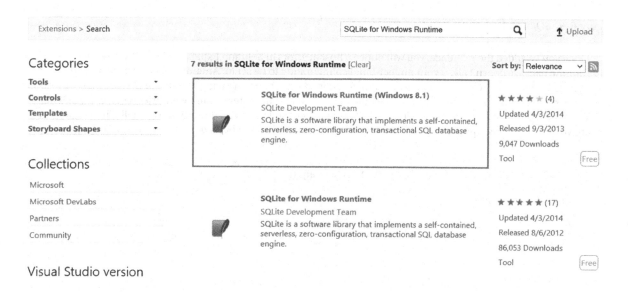

Figure 6-8. *The SQLite extension*

Once that is installed, you might have to restart Visual Studio. (If you do, Visual Studio will prompt you.) Next, add the references for SQLite for Windows Runtime (Windows 8.1) and Microsoft Visual C++ 2013 Runtime Package for Windows, as shown in Figure 6-9.

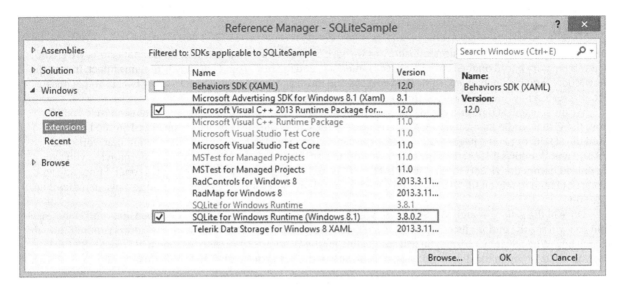

Figure 6-9. *SQLite references for Windows 8.1*

Once you've added the reference, you will notice a host of errors in Solution Explorer. This is because the C++ runtime package doesn't allow your project-build configuration to be set to "AnyCpu." You must go into the Configuration Manager by clicking on Build ➤ Configuration Manager and changing it to x86, or x64, or ARM, whichever you are using (see Figure 6-10). This is due to the different C++ operating system runtime libraries required by SQLite, one for each platform. At the time of this writing, there isn't a mechanism for creating any CPU install. This doesn't prevent you from creating a package for all CPU types; it just means you can't build *one* package for all CPU types.

Figure 6-10. *Changing the target platform*

Finally, you'll want to install the SQLite-net NuGet package. This time, rather than using the console, click on Tools ➤ Library Package Manager ➤ Manage NuGet Packages for Solution, which brings up the NuGet GUI. From there, you can search for and install SQLite, as shown in Figure 6-11.

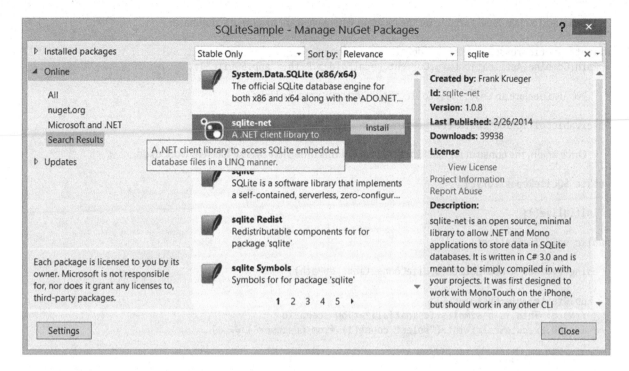

Figure 6-11. *SQLite-net NuGet Package*

Just like our earlier example, create a folder named Data, and add the IDataRepository, ViewModel, and Customer classes from the LocalFolder sample. Because we can leverage the fact that SQLite is a database engine, we are going to add some Data Annotations for the Customer class. Open Customer.cs and add the PrimaryKey and AutoIncrement attributes (shown in bold) to the Id property as follows:

```
public class Customer
{
    [PrimaryKey, AutoIncrement]
    public int Id { get; set; }
    public string Email { get; set; }
    public string FirstName { get; set; }
    public string LastName { get; set; }
    public string Title { get; set; }
}
```

Create a new class in the Data directory named SQLiteRepository, and implement the IDataRepository interface. Start by adding a using for Windows.Storage and the System.Collections.ObjectModel:

```
using Windows.Storage;
using System.Collections.ObjectModel;
```

Next, add a class-level variable for the location where we want to store the database:

```
private static readonly string _dbPath =
  Path.Combine(ApplicationData.Current.LocalFolder.Path, "app.SQLite");
```

We also declare an ObservableCollection<Customer> as follows:

```
ObservableCollection<Customer> _customers;
```

Once again, the constructor calls Initialize, but this time Initialize has real work to do.

```
public SQLiteRepository()
{
  Initialize();
}
public void Initialize()
{
  using (var db = new SQLite.SQLiteConnection(_dbPath))
  {
    db.CreateTable<Customer>();
    //Note: This is a simplistic initialization scenario
    if (db.ExecuteScalar<int>("select count(1) from Customer") == 0)
    {
      db.RunInTransaction(() =>
      {
        db.Insert(new Customer()
            { FirstName = "Phil", LastName = "Japikse" });
        db.Insert(new Customer()
            { FirstName = "Jon", LastName = "Galloway" });
        db.Insert(new Customer()
            { FirstName = "Jesse", LastName = "Liberty" });
      });
    }
    else
    {
      Load();
    }
  }
}
```

The first step in Initialize is to "use" the SqlLiteConnection. The using statement, of course, ensures that this resource will be released the moment we're done with it. SQLite is built using COM and other unmanaged resources, so it's extremely important to make sure all of the resources are disposed of.

We then call dbCreateTable<Customer>, which, using Sqlite.net creates our Customer table based on the Customer class.

If we don't have any customers in the table, we insert three "seed" customers to start; otherwise, we call Load.

Load's job is to make a connection to the database and to extract all the customers as such:

```
public async Task<ObservableCollection<Customer>>Load()
{
  var list = new ObservableCollection<Customer>();
  var connection = new SQLiteAsyncConnection(_dbPath);
```

```
  _customers = new ObservableCollection<Customer>(
    await connection.QueryAsync<Customer>("select * from Customer"));
  return _customers;
}
```

Similarly, the Add and Remove methods make a connection to the database and insert or delete (respectively) the customer, while also updating the in-memory customers collection.

```
public Task Add(Customer customer)
{
  _customers.Add(customer);
  var connection = new SQLiteAsyncConnection(_dbPath);
  return connection.InsertAsync(customer);
}
public Task Remove(Customer customer)
{
  _customers.Remove(customer);
  var connection = new SQLiteAsyncConnection(_dbPath);
  return connection.DeleteAsync(customer);
}
```

Next, the Update method, much as it did in the previous cases, finds the original value for the customer and then removes the old value and replaces it with the new value. It then does an update on the customer in the database.

```
public Task Update(Customer customer)
{
  var oldCustomer = _customers.FirstOrDefault(
    c => c.Id == customer.Id);
  if (oldCustomer == null)
  {
    throw new System.ArgumentException("Customer not found.");
  }
  _customers.Remove(oldCustomer);
  _customers.Add(customer);
  var connection = new SQLiteAsyncConnection(_dbPath);
  return connection.UpdateAsync(customer);
}
```

Finally, copy the XAML after the Page directive from MainPage.xaml in the previous example into MainPage.xaml in this example. Also, copy all of the code from MainPage.xaml.cs starting with public-sealed partial class from the previous example and paste it into MainPage.xaml.cs in this example. Copying the XAML and the C# code in this way preserves the namespaces and usings in the files. We then just need to update one line of code where we instantiate the IDataRepository. The update line should read like this:

```
private IDataRepository data = new SQLiteRepository();
```

You can see that we were able to carry the repository pattern that we used in the first example all the way forward to the SQLite example successfully, saving us a lot of rethinking and redesign. You have a number of choices for where and how you store user data, but none of them is terribly difficult to implement.

Summary

There are a variety of options to choose from when your app needs to store data locally on the device. Simple data can be stored in application settings or in files on the device. More complex data can be stored in SQLite. One noticeably absent item from the list is the SQL Server. The SQL Server doesn't run on ARM devices or under WinRT.

If your app needs to access the SQL Server, it must be done through a service. In the next chapter, we will look into accessing remote data.

CHAPTER 7

■ ■ ■

Remote Data and Services

WHAT'S NEW IN WINDOWS 8.1

The good news is that not much has changed in Windows 8.1 from Windows 8 in how you need to handle Remote Data. The only change is that the package needed to consume Windows Communication Foundation (WCF) and OData (Open Data Protocol) has been updated (see www.microsoft.com/en-us/download/details.aspx?id=39373).

This is a book on Windows 8.1, and we are building client-side applications. So, why do we care about remote data and services? Because experience says that any nontrivial application will deal with data, and that data is most useful when it can be shared outside of the local application.

Retrieving data from or saving data to a remote service fulfills one of the key aspects of Microsoft's recommended data goals for Windows 8.1 applications: *Be connected*. There is good reason for this directive: A connected application is far more valuable to the end user because the application has now broken the boundaries of the box it is running on and is connected to the terabytes of information available worldwide.

In addition, once you can exchange data with a server you can share data between devices all running the same application. The server acts as a central switch, taking in and dispensing data to various instances of your application.

The ability to share data among instances of your application can be extended to the ability to share data among users in a controlled and secure manner. This includes everything from games (like the popular Words with Friends) to line-of-business applications like banking or sales force automation.

With remote data, you also have the opportunity to back up local data to the cloud, and cloud storage can be far more secure and reliable than local storage.

Many popular applications (such as Twitter and Facebook) have a public API (application programming interface) that you can access through remote data calls from Windows 8.1, greatly extending the services your app can offer.

Remote Data Services

A remote data service is exactly what its name implies—a service where a remote client can access (and possibly change) data. The communication with the client needs to be as reliable and secure as the business rules dictate. What does this mean? Simply put, if you are trying to show a Twitter feed in your app, there isn't much need for reliability (you can stand to miss a few tweets), and if it's display only, there isn't any need for security.

However, if you are writing a banking application that will allow your user to transfer data from his account to that of someone else, the need for secure-and-reliable messaging goes up significantly.

There are many different ways to create a remote data service. Using Microsoft-based tools alone, we have had a lot of choices over the years, including ASMX web services, remoting, and WCF. Some of these methods have required that the client use the same technology as the service (such as remoting) and some were more technology agnostic

(ASMX Web Services and WCF) because they use the Simple Object Access Protocol (SOAP). SOAP is based on XML and can be very verbose. Vendor lock-in and verbose messaging are both issues in developing mobile applications in which there is a wide-playing field of device operating systems and network bandwidth can be at a premium.

REST to the Rescue

REST, short for representational state transfer, is an architectural style that was first described in Roy Fielding's doctoral dissertation. Roy was one of the principle authors of the HTTP specification. Roy's dissertation covers quite a bit and there are numerous books about REST, so I am just going to cover the concepts that relate to our goals for developing Windows 8.1 apps.

In the context of web services, REST focuses on a few key concepts:

- Service calls map to resources (nouns) like users, products, and orders.

- HTTP verbs (e.g., GET, POST, PUT, DELETE) describe the actions you're taking on these resources.

- Resources can be represented in different formats (XML, JSON, CSV, text, image, etc.). Rather than have different service endpoints for each format type, the same resource is requested with an HTTP accept header that states the requested response type.

- Interactions are stateless—no state is maintained between successive calls. Each interaction is self-descriptive.

- URLs are important. The URL for a request should look like a directory (e.g., /products/electronic/5) rather than a server-side technology mouthing off (e.g., /products.aspx?catid=204&productid=5).

- REST-ful services should be navigable as hypermedia. For instance, a category would have links to products, which would have links to services that can be performed against the products.

Sounds a lot like very simple HTTP, doesn't it? That's some of the beauty of REST— its brutal simplicity. (REST can get much more complicated, but for our needs, we can keep it dead simple). We can also use whatever messaging format that both ends agree on. SOAP is supported, but the current thinking is to use JSON (JavaScript Object Notation) due to its ubiquity and its lightweight nature.

REST-ful services can be written in any technology as long as they follow the rules of REST and all sides agree on the data-transport format. This eliminates vendor lock-in and enables all sides to agree on a much-more-concise packet.

You should view REST as one of many respected and time-proven patterns in software development. It's recommended because it's been found to work pretty well, and if you follow it other software developers will have an easier time understanding your code. But like any software development pattern, it exists to serve you. The only real test your code needs to meet is in the user experience it provides to your users.

Common API Formats

Just as web servers and browsers communicate via HTML, APIs use some common media formats (like XML or JSON) to communicate. If you're using the ASP.NET Web API on the server and the ASP.NET Web API Client (HttpClient) in your Windows Store Application, they'll automatically negotiate the format for you. But it is still important to have an understanding of the two most common formats, XML and JSON.

XML

XML (eXtensible Markup Language) has been used by services for a while.

```
<album>
  <artist>The Beatles</artist>
  <title>Meet the Beatles!</title>
  <year>1964</year>
</album>
```

It has some benefits:

- As the name implies, it's extensible. New tags can be created to define properties as needed.

- It's human readable and usually pretty self-descriptive.

There's optional support for document validation. An XML document can include a data type definition (DTD) or an XML schema definition (XSD), which define the elements and types the document is expected to contain.

Because there are common formats for defining documents, there are some common industry-standard document types. This is especially useful in fields like finance, business, and health care in which companies interoperate via APIs, and both sides need to be able to ensure that a document is valid. Additionally, common syndication formats like RSS and ATOM have been built on top of XML.

Since XML is pretty tightly structured, there are specifications that allow programs to query, parse, format, and otherwise manipulate XML.

There are two main downsides to XML:

- It's verbose. The start and end tags frequently use as many characters as the actual data they contain. That's partly mitigated by the fact that since the tags are very repetitive, XML documents compress pretty well and can further be reduced by using attributes instead of all elements. But there are still a lot of angle brackets!

- The rigid structure of XML (especially with a schema or definition) is useful, as already described. However, over time some programmers have become tired of all the structure, and question the actual real-world value.

JSON

JavaScript Object Notation (JSON) has recently become very popular as an alternative to XML. For example, if we have an object that has artist, title, and year properties, an instance can be represented as such:

```
{
  "artist" : "The Beatles",
  "title" : "Meet the Beatles!",
  "year" : "1964"
}
```

Its benefits:

- It's very terse and "lightweight."

- While JSON has outgrown its JavaScript roots, it began life as a lightweight format for serializing simple JavaScript objects. Because of that, it can be easily deserialized into JavaScript objects.

- JSON has a simple grammar that isn't concerned with document validity. Those who are tired of XML's structure usually prefer JSON.

The cons:

- Since there are no surrounding tags, JSON isn't as self-descriptive as XML.

- Since JSON isn't as structured and doesn't address document validity, it requires that client code knows more about the API structure. This means that API documentation is a manual process, JSON messages can't be automatically validated, and so forth.

ASP.NET Web API

ASP.NET Web API is a framework for building HTTP services that reach a variety of clients, from browsers to mobile and desktop applications. ASP.NET Web API has been designed to work well as a REST-ful web service. As discussed in the previous section, REST-ful services are very capable of getting data from your app as well as sending data to it, making the ASP.NET Web API a great candidate to create remote data services for our Windows 8.1 apps.

If you've used Windows Communication Foundation (WCF) in the past, you can think of ASP.NET Web API as a streamlined version of WCF that's easier to use (both as a service provider and consumer) because it's optimized for the most common scenarios— communicating using XML or JSON over HTTP. That doesn't mean it's dumbed down, though. It's been very carefully designed to give you easy access to extend and customize it if you need to; you just shouldn't need to very often.

Building a Service with ASP.NET Web API

One of the best and most effective ways to see how to interact with a web service is to build one and to build a Windows 8.1 client to interact with it.

To get started, create a new ASP.NET web application by selecting File ➤ New ➤ Project ➤ Visual C# ➤ Web ➤ ASP.NET web application. Change the Framework to .NET Framework 4.5.1 and name the application ContactManager, as shown in Figure 7-1. Depending on the source control option selected, your dialog might say, "Add to source control" instead of "Create GIT Repository." Don't worry about the differences—the examples don't depend on either TFS or GIT.

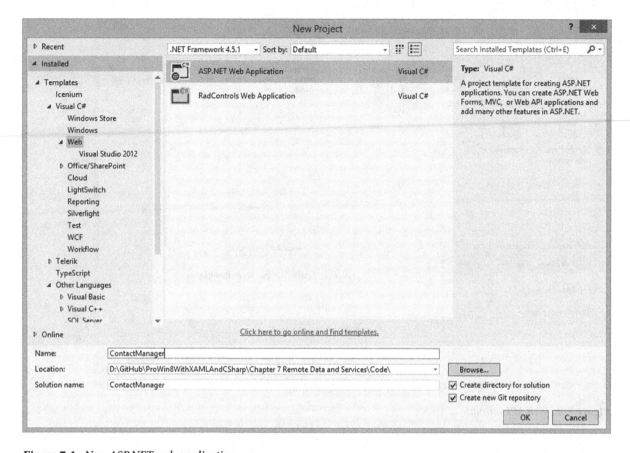

Figure 7-1. *New ASP.NET web application*

After clicking OK, select the Web API template, as shown in Figure 7-2. For this example, we will not be creating a unit test project. While I believe that every real project should have unit tests, adding them into this example would obfuscate what I am trying to show, so I will not include them here.

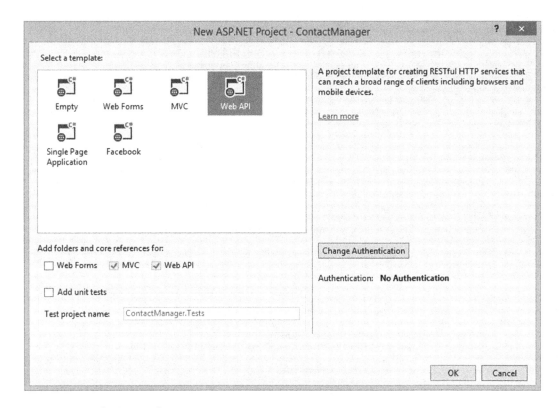

Figure 7-2. *Web API template*

■ **Note**   With Visual Studio 2013, there is just one ASP.NET. The template for ASP.NET web applications allows you to choose ASP.NET WebForms, ASP.NET MVC, and/or ASP.NET Web API all in the same project. For this example, we will select the ASP.NET Web API option, which includes ASP.NET MVC.

This is a book on Windows 8.1 app development, and not meant to be a tome on developing applications with ASP.NET Web API, so I'm going to keep everything simple and to the point.

■ **Note**   For detailed coverage of the ASP.NET Web API, see the following books: *Practical ASP.NET Web API* by Badrinarayanan Lakshmiraghavan (Apress, 2013) and *Pro ASP.NET Web API* by Tugberk Ugurlu, Alexander Zeitler, and Ali Kheyrollahi (Apress, 2013).

Creating the Model

The first step is to create a class that will represent the data of our app, commonly referred to as the model. To do this, make a class named Contact in the Models directory. We're building a simple contact manager, and the Contact class will be the fundamental data that we'll use on both the server and the client.

■ **Note** This example is loosely based on the Microsoft Contact Manager sample for ASP.NET Web API, which shows web, Windows Phone, and a more complex Windows 8.1 client sample. It's available here: `www.asp.net/web-api/samples`.

Right-click on the Models folder that was created for you and add a `Contact.cs` class as shown in the following code. You can combine the attributes for `ContactId` into one set (separated by commas) if you prefer. They are broken out here for readability.

```
public class Contact
{
  [ScaffoldColumn(false),Key]
  [DatabaseGenerated(DatabaseGeneratedOption.Identity)]
  public int ContactId { get; set; }
  [Required]
  public string Name { get; set; }
  public string Address { get; set; }
  public string City { get; set; }
  public string State { get; set; }
  public string Zip { get; set; }
  public string Email { get; set; }
  public string Twitter { get; set; }
}
```

You will see a red squiggly line under `ScaffoldColumn` and `Required`. As usual, pressing Ctrl-Period will bring up Intellisense and you can thus add the following using statements:

```
using System.ComponentModel.DataAnnotations;
using System.ComponentModel.DataAnnotations.Schema;
```

There are two data annotation attributes used in this class. The first, `ScaffoldColumn`, indicates that the `ContactId` is controlled by the application and should not be set externally. The `Required` attribute indicates that, at a minimum, a contact must have a name.

We are ready to create a controller, but to do so we must first build the application so that the `Contact` model class will be available.

Creating the Controller

Now that we have the model that we will be using, we need to create the controller for our views. Visual Studio has an excellent set of templates that you can leverage to speed the development of your application.

1.   Right-click on the Controllers folder and select Add ➤ Controller.

2.   Select the Web API 2 Controller with Actions, Using the Entity Framework, as in Figure 7-3.

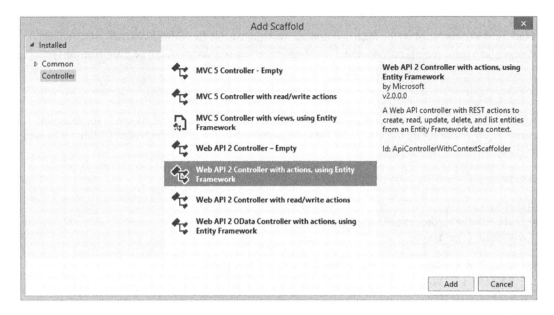

Figure 7-3. *Web API 2 Controller with Entity Framework*

3. After clicking Add, you will see the Add Controller screen. Name the controller
    ContactsController.

4. Drop down the Model class list. From the drop-down list, select Contact (ContactManager.
    Models).

■ **Note**   If the Contact class is not on the list of available models, you will need to build your project, so cancel this
dialog and build the project. In Visual Studio 2012, if you didn't build your project, you couldn't see your class in the list of
available models. In Visual Studio 2013, you can see the class; the problem doesn't surface until later in the wizard, so you
really want to make sure that you have built your project after adding a class and before starting the Add Controller wizard.

---

5. Drop down the data context class list and select New Data Context. Name the new context
    ContactManager.Models.ContactManagerContext, as shown in Figure 7-4.

Figure 7-4. *New Data Context dialog*

6.   Your Add Controller dialog should now be filled in as shown in Figure 7-5. Click the Add button.

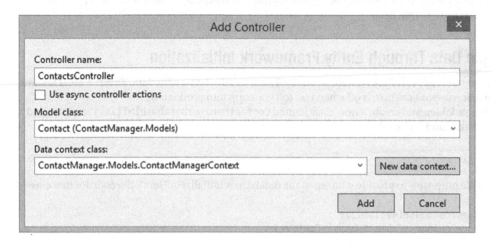

Figure 7-5. *Add Controller dialog*

A new ContactsController class is created. If you get an error stating that the scaffolding couldn't locate the Contact class, this is due to not building your project before starting the add-new-control process.

The new class inherits from ApiController and includes some working default code with the following methods:

- **GetContacts:** This will return all contacts.

- **GetContact(int id):** This will find the contact with the matching ID and return it. If none is found, it will return an HTTP 404 (not found) response—the same HTTP response your browser would encounter if you browsed to a nonexistent web URL.

- **PutContact(int id, Contact contact):** This allows you to replace an existing contact by ID.

- **PostContact(Contact contact):** This allows you to create a new contact.

- **DeleteContact(int id):** This deletes a contact by ID.

Web API Convention over Configuration

The ASP.NET Web API (like ASP.NET MVC) uses conventions to simplify code while conforming to HTTP standards. As you can see, all of the controller action methods are named using HTTP verbs (GET, PUT, POST, DELETE), and ASP.NET Web API will automatically route HTTP requests to the appropriate method based on name without any additional configuration or annotations on your part. Thus, an HTTP GET request to /api/contacts will automatically route to the ContactsController's GetContacts method, simply by following the naming conventions. If you want to change how the Web API works, you certainly can do that through configuration options, but it is not only is a manual process, and will confuse developers who have to maintain the code after you.

Entity Framework

At this point, we have a functioning web service that uses the Entity Framework (EF) to handle data persistence! We're using Entity Framework Code First (EFCF), which lets us model our database using standard .NET classes (our previous Contact class). It will automatically create our database—complete with tables based on our entity classes—when the service is first accessed.

EFCF uses a lot of conventions as well, and for more detail than is provided here, see
http://msdn.microsoft.com/en-us/data/jj679962.

EF also provides a method for inserting a sample or initial data into our database when it's created, known as a
database initializer. We'll make use of that here.

Creating the Sample Data Through Entity Framework Initialization

EF provides a mechanism to not only create your database on the fly but to initialize it with data. This is a great feature
during development, but just remember to turn it off when you roll your app into production!

Right-click on the Models folder, and create a new class named ContactManagerDatabaseInitializer. We need
to add a using for System.Data.Entity, as follows:

```
using System.Data.Entity;
```

This class has one simple purpose—to provide data when the database is initialized. Here's the code for that class:

```csharp
public class ContactManagerDatabaseInitializer :
  DropCreateDatabaseIfModelChanges<ContactManagerContext>
{
  protected override void Seed( ContactManagerContext context )
  {
    base.Seed( context );
    context.Contacts.Add(
      new Contact
      {
        Name = "Jon Galloway",
        Email = "jongalloway@gmail.com",
        Twitter = "jongalloway",
        City = "San Diego",
        State = "CA"
      });
    context.Contacts.Add(
      new Contact
      {
        Name = "Jesse Liberty",
        Email = "jesseliberty@gmail.com",
        Twitter = "jesseliberty",
        City = "Acton",
        State = "MA"
      });
    context.Contacts.Add(
      new Contact
      {
        Name = "Philip Japikse",
        Email = "skimedic@gmail.com",
        Twitter = "skimedic",
        City = "West Chester",
        State = "OH"
      });
  }
}
```

Let's look at this in a bit of detail. The first thing to notice is the base class, DropCreateDatabaseIfModelChanges <ContactManagerContext>. This is one of two standard base classes, the other is DropCreateDatabaseAlways.

The ContactManagerContext was created for you and is used when overriding the Seed method (as we just did). When you register the initializer (see the following section), the initializer will be called by Entity Framework when it creates the database, and it will call your overridden Seed method.

The context Contacts collection that you are adding to in the code is of type DbSet<Contact>, which was created for you when you selected to create a new data context. You can see that collection in ContactManagerContext.cs (within the Models folder):

```
public DbSet<Contact> Contacts { get; set; }
```

Registering the Database Initializer

We need to register this database initializer in Global.asax.cs. We do so in the Application_Start method.

```
Database.SetInitializer(new ContactManagerDatabaseInitializer());
```

You'll need to add using statements to reference the System.Entity and your ContactManagerDatabaseInitializer's namespaces, as shown in Figure 7-6.

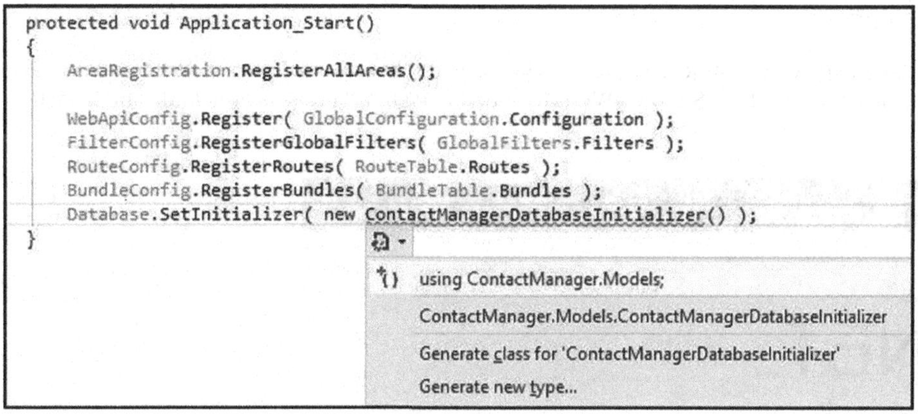

```
protected void Application_Start()
{
    AreaRegistration.RegisterAllAreas();

    WebApiConfig.Register( GlobalConfiguration.Configuration );
    FilterConfig.RegisterGlobalFilters( GlobalFilters.Filters );
    RouteConfig.RegisterRoutes( RouteTable.Routes );
    BundleConfig.RegisterBundles( BundleTable.Bundles );
    Database.SetInitializer( new ContactManagerDatabaseInitializer() );
}
```
```
    using ContactManager.Models;

    ContactManager.Models.ContactManagerDatabaseInitializer

    Generate class for 'ContactManagerDatabaseInitializer'

    Generate new type...
```

Figure 7-6. *Application Start*

With that, our server is ready to provide data to our Windows 8.1 client. We won't deploy the server (that is another chapter in itself), but we'll run it locally as you'll see shortly.

Database Connection Strings

ASP.NET Web API is configured to use LocalDB, which is a streamlined version of SQL Express. If SQL Express was *not* installed when you installed Visual Studio, LocalDB will be used automatically by your project. However, if you do have SQL Express installed, LocalDB will not be the default, and the sample that we just created won't run correctly.

The good news is that the fix is very easy. Open up the Web.Config and look for this line in the Connection Strings section (it will read as one line in the config file but is shown here with line breaks for printability):

```
<add name="ContactManagerContext"
  connectionString="Data Source=(LocalDB)\v11.0;
    Initial Catalog=ContactManagerContext-20131125234122;
    Integrated Security=True; MultipleActiveResultSets=True;
    AttachDbFilename=|DataDirectory|
    ContactManagerContext-20131125234122.mdf"
  providerName="System.Data.SqlClient" />
```

Then, change (LocalDB)\v11.0 in the DataSource parameter to the instance of your SQL Express install. On my development machine, it is "SQL2012Exp," so my connection string looks like this:

```
<add name="ContactManagerContext"
  connectionString="Data Source=.\SQL2012EXP;
    Initial Catalog=ContactManagerContext-20131125234122;
    Integrated Security=True; MultipleActiveResultSets=True;
    AttachDbFilename=|DataDirectory|
    ContactManagerContext-20131125234122.mdf"
  providerName="System.Data.SqlClient" />
```

Testing the Web Service

To test the ASP.NET Web API service, run the project. What you will see is the "hello world" page of ASP.NET MVC, as in Figure 7-7 (remember that in One ASP.NET, ASP.NET MVC is included in Web API projects by default, and in fact, can't be removed).

Figure 7-7. ASP.NET MVC/Web API starter page

Click on the API menu link in the top navigation bar, and you will get a page showing all of your API methods, as in Figure 7-8. There is more information on the page below the Contacts API methods, but we won't be needing them for this example.

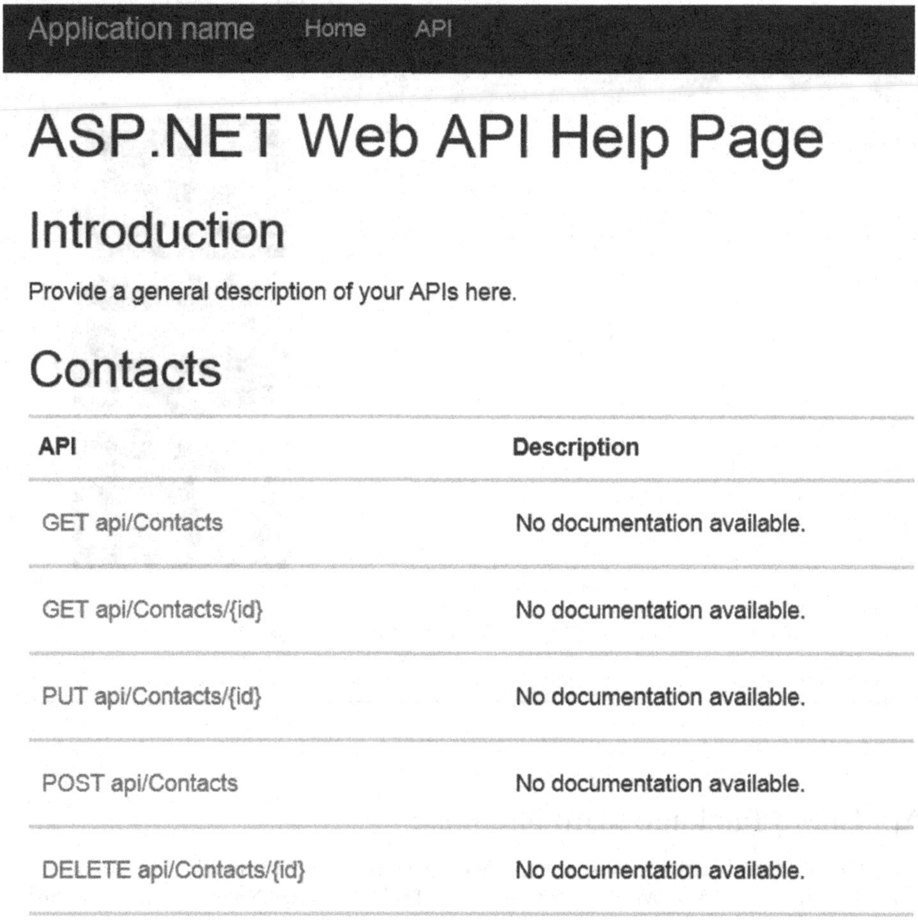

Application name   Home   API

ASP.NET Web API Help Page

Introduction

Provide a general description of your APIs here.

Contacts

API	Description
GET api/Contacts	No documentation available.
GET api/Contacts/{id}	No documentation available.
PUT api/Contacts/{id}	No documentation available.
POST api/Contacts	No documentation available.
DELETE api/Contacts/{id}	No documentation available.

Figure 7-8. *API Help Page*

Accessing the ASP.NET Web API Service from a Windows 8.1 Client

We are ready now to create a Windows 8.1 project that will use the data supplied by the Web API project we've just completed. Right-click on the solution and choose Add New Project. Select Windows Store in the left column, and Grid App in the right column. Name your application ContactManager.WindowsStore, as shown in Figure 7-9.

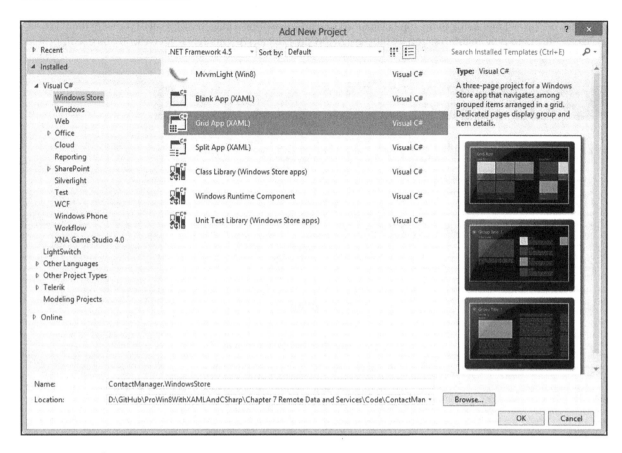

Figure 7-9. *Grid project*

Adding the Web Api Client Package from NuGet

We'll need the Web API client package to work with the Web API application we've built. Fortunately, this can be installed through NuGet. To do this, right-click your Windows 8.1 project and select Manage Nuget Packages. In the dialog, make sure Online is selected, and then search for Web API. Select Microsoft ASP.NET Web API 2.1 Client Libraries, as in Figure 7-10. Note, this package is updated fairly frequently. At the time of this writing, the version is 2.1.

Figure 7-10. Installing Web API Client NuGet package

NuGet not only installs the package that you select but will also install all of the required dependencies in the entire dependency chain. You might see a dialog asking you to accept an end-user license for some of the packages, as shown in Figure 7-11. You also might be prompted to upgrade NuGet. If so, just follow the prompts as directed.

Figure 7-11. License Acceptance dialog

▪ **Note** The NuGet installation can also be performed via the Package Manager console.

Adding the Contact Class

We need to share the Contact class in the Server class as well as in the client. At the risk of making experienced developers feel light-headed, we're going to copy and paste the class into the client project.

To do this, right-click on the DataModel folder and create a new class named Contact. The code will be the same as the Contact class from the ContactManager project without the attributes. The entire code is as follows:

```
public class Contact
{
    public int ContactId { get; set; }
    public string Name { get; set; }
    public string Address { get; set; }
    public string City { get; set; }
    public string State { get; set; }
    public string Zip { get; set; }
    public string Email { get; set; }
    public string Twitter { get; set; }
}
```

Editing the SampleDataSource Class

Within the ContactManager.WindowsStore project, open the SampleDataSource.cs file in the DataModel folder. Add the following function to the end of the SampleDataSource class:

```
public static async Task<SampleDataGroup> LoadDataAsync(
  bool clear = true)
{
}
```

This function will be calling into our service. In the current example application, the service runs on LocalHost, but on a specific port. To find the port number, scroll up to the ContactManager project and double-click on the Properties as shown in Figure 7-12.

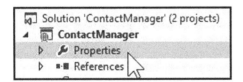

Figure 7-12. *Clicking on Properties*

When the Properties display opens, click on Web (in the left column) to open the Web tab. About halfway down the page you'll find the Servers section, as shown in Figure 7-13. Within that section, find the Project Uri for IIS Express and note the port number.

Figure 7-13. *Finding the port number*

Now that we know the port number, we can open `SampleDataSource.cs` and in the `LoadDataAsync` method add a constant as follows:

```
// Load this from configuration
const string serviceUrl = "http://localhost:35795/";
```

We've included a Boolean parameter (`clear`) that is defaulted to true. If it is indeed true, it will clear the data source before fetching data from the web service. In this case, we do want to have sample data available for design-time support, but we don't want to have the sample data flash on the screen when run by end users, so we'll leave the default set to true.

```
if (clear)
{
  _sampleDataSource.Groups.Clear();
}
```

We will need to add the following using statement for the next block of code. Go to the top of the file to add the statement:

```
using System.Net.Http;
```

We then instantiate an `HttpClient` object and set its `BaseAddress`. We use that to get the contacts asynchronously. They are returned as JSON data that we can then read into a collection of `Contact` objects.

```
HttpClient client = new HttpClient();
client.BaseAddress = new Uri(serviceUrl);
HttpResponseMessage response = await client.GetAsync("api/contacts");
Contact[] contacts = await response.Content.ReadAsAsync<Contact[]>();
```

Surprisingly, this is all you need to do to call a web service that returns JSON data. The `HttpClient` object will make the request, wait asynchronously for the response, and deserialize the result to an array of `Contact` objects.

Finally, we create a new `DataGroup` an ID of `ContactsGroup` and a display value of "My Contacts." We're using another web service for our avatars, `avatars.io`. This site takes a handle and tries to find the best avatar image from popular social networking sites like Twitter and Facebook.

```
SampleDataGroup contactsGroup = new SampleDataGroup(
  "ContactsGroup", "My Contacts", null, null, null);
foreach (Contact contact in contacts)
{
```

```
  contactsGroup.Items.Add(new SampleDataItem(
    contact.ContactId.ToString(),
    contact.Name,
    GetContactInfo(contact),
    new Uri("http://avatars.io/auto/" + contact.Twitter +
        "?size=large", UriKind.Absolute).AbsoluteUri,
        null,
        null));
}
_sampleDataSource.Groups.Add(contactsGroup);
return contactsGroup;
```

Here is the entire method:

```
public static async Task<SampleDataGroup> LoadDataAsync(
  bool clear = true)
{
  // Load this from configuration
  const string serviceUrl = "http://localhost:35795/";
  if (clear)
  {
    _sampleDataSource.Groups.Clear();
  }
  HttpClient client = new HttpClient();
  client.BaseAddress = new Uri(serviceUrl);
  HttpResponseMessage response = await client.GetAsync("api/contacts");
  Contact[] contacts = await response.Content.ReadAsAsync<Contact[]>();
  SampleDataGroup contactsGroup = new SampleDataGroup(
    "ContactsGroup", "My Contacts", null, null, null);
  foreach (Contact contact in contacts)
  {
    contactsGroup.Items.Add(new SampleDataItem(
    contact.ContactId.ToString(),
    contact.Name,
    GetContactInfo(contact),
    new Uri("http://avatars.io/auto/" + contact.Twitter +
      "?size=large", UriKind.Absolute).AbsoluteUri,
    null,
    null));
  }
  _sampleDataSource.Groups.Add(contactsGroup);
  return contactsGroup;
}
```

Add another function named GetContactInfo to format some of the Contact properties into a string for display.

```
static string GetContactInfo(Contact contact)
{
  return string.Format(
    "{0}, {1}\n{2}\n@{3}",
    contact.City ?? "City?",
```

```
    contact.State ?? "State?",
    contact.Email ?? "Email?",
    contact.Twitter ?? "Twitter?");
}
```

Calling LoadDataAsync

Finally, we'll need to call the LoadDataAsync method from App.xaml.cs. To do so, add the line

```
SampleDataSource.LoadDataAsync();
```

above the call to Window.Current.Content = rootFrame,

```
protected override async void OnLaunched(LaunchActivatedEventArgs args)
{
  Frame rootFrame = Window.Current.Content as Frame;
  // Do not repeat app initialization when the Window already has content,
  // just ensure that the window is active
  if (rootFrame == null)
  {
    //...
    SampleDataSource.LoadDataAsync();
    // Place the frame in the current Window
    Window.Current.Content = rootFrame;
  }
}
```

To Await or Not to Await

Typically when you see an async method (such as our LoadDataAsync), you would "await" it. However, this code runs when the application launches, and the store will reject your app if it takes too long to load the first page. To follow in the fast and fluid concept, we add the await keyword like this:

```
await SampleDataSource.LoadDataAsync();
```

In a non-async scenario, the first page won't show until all of the data is loaded. If we us async as we did in this example, the data will continue to load and then appear as if by magic in the page. That is one of the beautiful features designed into Windows 8.1. There isn't any need to call Refresh() or any methods like that to have the data show when it's loaded asynchronously.

Running the Client

To run the client, right-click on the ContactManager solution, and choose Set Startup Projects. This will launch the Property Pages for the solution, as in Figure 7-14. Make sure "Multiple startup projects" is selected, and set the Start action for both projects. Moving ContactManager up in the list will launch the Service first (which is what we want).

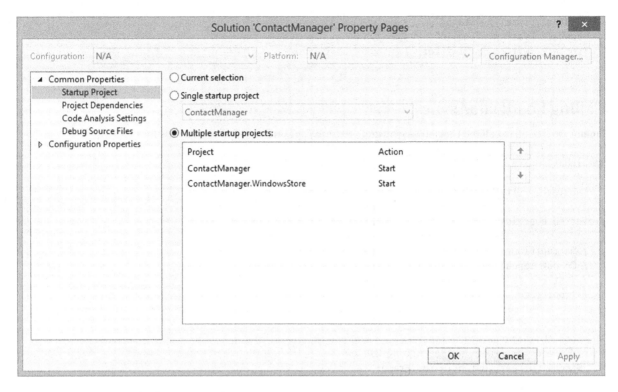

Figure 7-14. *Setting multiple startup projects*

Then, run the applications. You should see the three contacts we created in the sample data displayed in the GridView, as shown in Figure 7-15.

Figure 7-15. *Running application*

Consuming OData in Windows 8.1

Web API will use JSON or XML. However, if you wish to communicate with a public OData source, you'll need to write your code somewhat differently.

OData is a data-focused web protocol that layers data-centric activities like querying and updates on top of existing formats like Atom (an XML syndication format previously mentioned) and JSON. It was originally developed by Microsoft but has been submitted as an open standard.

OData support wasn't included in the first release of ASP.NET Web API. Since then, a NuGet package has been made available that includes partial support for OData. As OData server support is still evolving, we'll focus on accessing OData API's in a Windows Store application.

Accessing a Public OData Service Using the OData Client Tools

To see OData at work, create a new Windows 8.1 Blank Application and name it OData. Be sure to install the WCF Data Service 5.6.0 RTM Tools Installer from the Microsoft Download Center: www.microsoft.com/en-us/download/details.aspx?id=39373.

We will need to add a service reference. To do this, right-click the project and select Add Service Reference, or right-click on the References and select Add Service Reference. The latter method is shown in Figure 7-16.

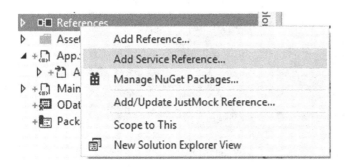

Figure 7-16. *Adding a service reference*

You will then see the Add Service Reference dialog as shown in Figure 7-17. Enter the following values into the dialog, as shown in the figure:

- *Address*: https://api.datamarket.azure.com/Data.ashx/data.gov/Crimes

- *Namespace*: CityCrimes

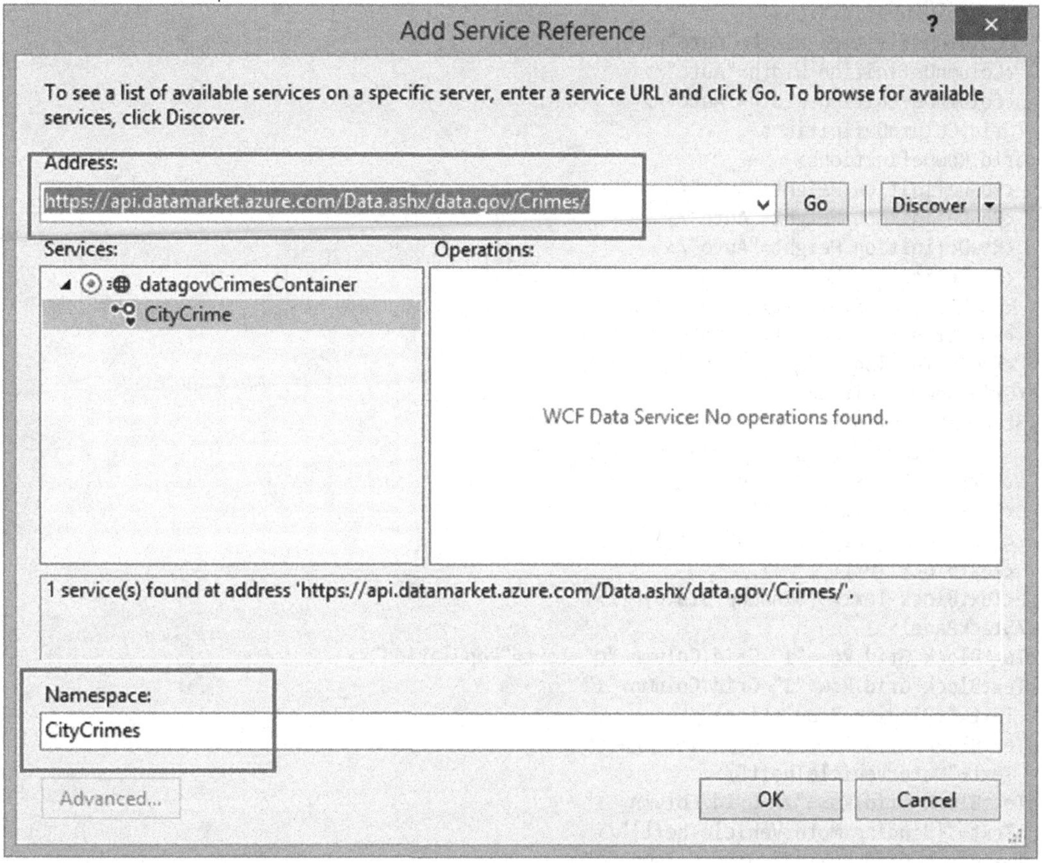

Figure 7-17. *Adding a service reference*

First, fill in the address, and then click Go. That will populate the Services list so you can verify that the URI is correct. Once the services are filled in, update the namespace to CityCrimes and click OK.

In this case, we'll be querying the CityCrime OData service as documented by Microsoft: http://archive.msdn.microsoft.com/datamarketwebapp. While not the most cheerful data, it is a public OData API that doesn't require registration, so it makes a great sample to use to demonstrate consuming OData in Windows 8.1 applications.

The CityCrimes API allows you to (among other queries) request the crime statistics for a city and state. It returns a lot of data, and we are only going to display a subset of the data in a very simple grid. The GridView's datasource will be a CollectionViewSource.

Add the following XAML into your MainPage.xaml:

```
<Page.Resources>
  <CollectionViewSource x:Name="cvs" IsSourceGrouped="False" />
</Page.Resources>
<Grid Background="{StaticResource ApplicationPageBackgroundThemeBrush}">
  <GridView x:Name="myGridView"
    ItemsSource="{Binding Source={StaticResource cvs}}">
    <GridView.ItemTemplate>
      <DataTemplate>
        <StackPanel>
          <Grid>
```

```xml
            <Grid.ColumnDefinitions>
              <ColumnDefinition Width="Auto"/>
              <ColumnDefinition Width="Auto"/>
              <ColumnDefinition Width="Auto"/>
            </Grid.ColumnDefinitions>
            <Grid.RowDefinitions>
              <RowDefinition Height="Auto"/>
              <RowDefinition Height="Auto"/>
              <RowDefinition Height="Auto"/>
              <RowDefinition Height="Auto"/>
              <RowDefinition Height="Auto"/>
              <RowDefinition Height="Auto"/>
              <RowDefinition Height="Auto"/>
            </Grid.RowDefinitions>
            <StackPanel Grid.Row="0" Grid.Column="0"
              Grid.ColumnSpan="3" Orientation="Horizontal">
              <TextBlock Text="{Binding Year}"/>
              <TextBlock Text=" "/>
              <TextBlock Text="{Binding City}" />
              <TextBlock Text="," />
              <TextBlock Text="{Binding State}" />
            </StackPanel>
            <TextBlock Grid.Row="1" Grid.Column="0" Text="Population"/>
            <TextBlock Grid.Row="1" Grid.Column="1"
              Text="{Binding Population}"/>
            <TextBlock Grid.Row="2" Grid.Column="0"
              Text="MotorVehicleTheft"/>
            <TextBlock Grid.Row="2" Grid.Column="1"
              Text="{Binding MotorVehicleTheft}"/>
            <TextBlock Grid.Row="3" Grid.Column="0"
              Text="LarcenyTheft"/>
            <TextBlock Grid.Row="3" Grid.Column="1"
              Text="{Binding LarcenyTheft}"/>
            <TextBlock Grid.Row="4" Grid.Column="0" Text="Burglary"/>
            <TextBlock Grid.Row="4" Grid.Column="1"
              Text="{Binding Burglary}"/>
            <TextBlock Grid.Row="5" Grid.Column="0"
              Text="PropertyCrime"/>
            <TextBlock Grid.Row="5" Grid.Column="1"
              Text="{Binding PropertyCrime}"/>
            <TextBlock Grid.Row="6" Grid.Column="0" Text="Robbery"/>
            <TextBlock Grid.Row="6" Grid.Column="1"
              Text="{Binding Robbery}"/>
          </Grid>
        </StackPanel>
      </DataTemplate>
    </GridView.ItemTemplate>
  </GridView>
</Grid>
```

To actually get the data, we have to make a few calls in the code behind page. Open up `MainPage.xaml.cs`, and if the service requires a user ID and account key, add the following variables to hold your user ID and account key. (The CityCrimes service doesn't require authentication, so we don't need to use them.)

```
// place your Live ID here - for example, "Bugger120"
//private const string USER_ID = "YourLiveID";
// paste your account key here - for example, "dDkr8cCKWOu8q34fdja3894faMOlekr=="
//private const string SECURE_ACCOUNT_KEY = "YourAzureDataMarketAccountKey";
```

Set up a local variable to hold the URI. We will only use this once, so you can certainly add the URI inline, but to make maintenance easier it's preferable to isolate the dependencies.

```
private const string SERVICE_ROOT_URI =
  "https://api.datamarket.azure.com/Data.ashx/data.gov/Crimes/";
```

Next, create the context that will be used to retrieve the data:

```
private datagovCrimesContainer _context;
```

For the final class-level variable, create a `DataServiceCollection` that will be populated by the service and then used as the data source for the `GridView`. The `DataServiceCollection` extends the `ObservableCollection` class that can take a context in its constructor.

```
private DataServiceCollection<CityCrime> _data;
```

The complete arrangement is shown here:

```
private const string SERVICE_ROOT_URI =
  "https://api.datamarket.azure.com/Data.ashx/data.gov/Crimes/";
private datagovCrimesContainer _context;
private DataServiceCollection<CityCrime> _data;
```

You also need to add the following two `using` statements to the top of your file for this code to compile:

```
using System.Data.Services.Client;
using OData.CityCrimes;
```

Now, create a new method called `LoadData` that will load the data from the service, populate the `DataServiceCollection`, and set the DataSource for the DataGrid.

The first line creates a URI and creates a new Container from the URI as the context. Then the credentials are added to the context.

```
Uri serviceUri = new Uri(SERVICE_ROOT_URI);
_context = new datagovCrimesContainer(serviceUri);
```

If the service needs credentials, they would be set on the context (as in the following code snippet). This example is for the purpose of information only, since the CityCrimes service doesn't require any credentials.

```
_context.Credentials = new NetworkCredential(USER_ID, SECURE_ACCOUNT_KEY);
```

Next, we pass the context into the `DataServiceCollection`:

```
_data = new DataServiceCollection<CityCrime>(_context);
```

And then create a query to select the desired data:

```
IQueryable<CityCrime> query = from c in _context.CityCrime
  where c.City == "Chicago" && c.State == "Illinois"
  orderby c.State, c.Year
  select c;
```

Finally, call `LoadAsync` and set the data source for the `GridView` as follows:

```
_data.LoadAsync(query);
cvs.Source = _data;
```

The complete `LoadData` method is listed here:

```
internal async void LoadData()
{
  Uri serviceUri = new Uri(SERVICE_ROOT_URI);
  _context = new datagovCrimesContainer(serviceUri);
  //_context.Credentials = new NetworkCredential(
    USER_ID, SECURE_ACCOUNT_KEY);
  _data = new DataServiceCollection<CityCrime>(_context);
  IQueryable<CityCrime> query = from c in _context.CityCrime
    where c.City == "Chicago" && c.State == "Illinois"
    orderby c.State, c.Year
    select c;
  _data.LoadAsync(query);
  cvs.Source = _data;
}
```

Finally, in the constructor for the view, call `LoadData();` as follows:

```
public MainPage()
{
  this.InitializeComponent();
  LoadData();
}
```

Running the project shows three years of crime data for the city of Chicago, as shown in Figure 7-18.

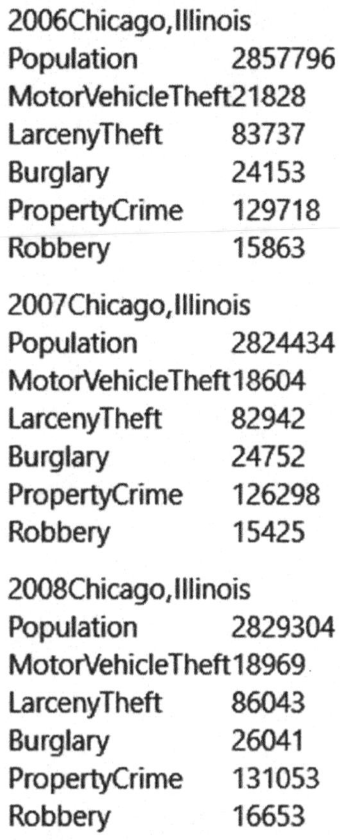

2006Chicago,Illinois
Population   2857796
MotorVehicleTheft21828
LarcenyTheft   83737
Burglary   24153
PropertyCrime   129718
Robbery   15863

2007Chicago,Illinois
Population   2824434
MotorVehicleTheft18604
LarcenyTheft   82942
Burglary   24752
PropertyCrime   126298
Robbery   15425

2008Chicago,Illinois
Population   2829304
MotorVehicleTheft18969
LarcenyTheft   86043
Burglary   26041
PropertyCrime   131053
Robbery   16653

Figure 7-18. *Crime stats for Chicago*

Summary

Windows 8.1 is capable of making very compelling local applications. But to make your app really come alive and be truly useful, you need to connect to data from various services. The remote data capabilities open up a very large array of possibilities to utilize Windows 8 devices in the enterprise.

CHAPTER 8

■ ■ ■

Search and Share Contracts

Windows 8.1 has significantly changed the way Search works. Searching in the Charms bar will allow the user to look for files (local and OneDrive), apps, and settings. The user can also select to narrow the search.

Microsoft has also backed off of the "No Chrome" stance somewhat and also introduced a `SearchBox` control. If you recall from the Windows 8.0 guidance, all chrome (as in buttons, tabs, etc.) was to be moved into the `AppBar`. The new guidance allows some flexibility in the UI, but the goal is still content over chrome. The third sample illustrates how to use the new `SearchBox`.

Windows 8.1 has also brought changes to the Share functionality, including the ability to provide multiple formats for the data, increasing the number of accessible Share Targets. The Uri is replaced by the `WebLink` and `ActionLink` (now separate data points). The share responsiveness can be increased by calling the `DismissUI` method.

When there are multiple apps on the screen, Windows 8.1 displays the charms with the context set for the last app that had focus.

For the first time in the history of Windows, there is a way built into the operating system to search many locations as well as to share data from one app to another.

■ **Note** Windows 7 had a search box on the Start menu that would search for installed applications, but as you will soon see, the Windows 8.1 search is much more involved. You can also tie into the search capabilities in Windows 8.1 through the search contracts, which was not possible in Windows 7.

Search and Share (as well as devices and settings) are presented to the user in the Charms bar, which is brought forward by swiping in from the right-hand side (or pressing Windows-C), as shown in Figure 8-1.

Figure 8-1. *Charms bar*

This chapter focuses exclusively on Search and Share, starting with Search.

Seaching

Clicking the Search button (the magnifying glass) on the Charms bar (or pressing Windows-Q) brings up the Search menu. At the top of the Search menu, the user can choose between searching Everywhere, Settings, Files, Web images, or Web videos (as shown in Figure 8-2).

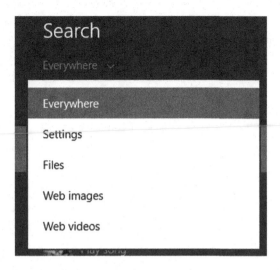

Figure 8-2. *Specifying Search location*

Support for searching (as well as all of the charms) is implemented with contracts. A contract establishes the relationship between your application and the charm service (e.g., searching).

■ **Note**   In-app search is also supported in Windows 8.1 (this is a change from Windows 8.0), and will be covered later in this chapter.

A NOTE ABOUT SEARCH ACTIVATION

As you will discover in Chapter 10 ("Application Life Cycle"), there are different ways an application can be activated. Search is one way an application can be activated from a nonrunning state. A deep understanding of the app life cycle isn't required to integrate a charms-based search, but since an app can respond to Search when it is running as well as when it is not, the recommended software patterns cover activation scenarios. I will make sure to call those out to make it clear in the code.

Adding a Charms-Based Search to an App

To see how to add a charms-based search to an app, let's create an application that will simply retrieve the Search term from the search box. To begin, create a new Windows Store project using the Blank App (XAML) template and call it Searching1. Double-click on the Package.appxmanifest and click on the Declarations tab. Drop down the available declarations and select Search, and then Add, as shown in Figure 8-3.

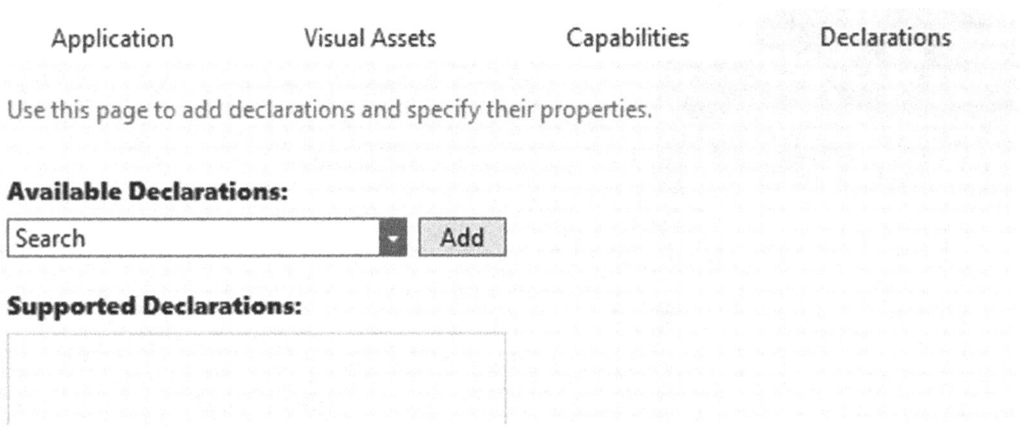

Application	Visual Assets	Capabilities	Declarations

Use this page to add declarations and specify their properties.

Available Declarations:

Search ▾	Add

Supported Declarations:

Figure 8-3. *Adding a search declaration*

Creating the UI

Let's add a TextBlock to MainPage.xaml that will serve to display the search term:

```
<TextBlock Name="StatusBlock"
    FontSize="40"
    Margin="50"
    Text="Ready..." />
```

Search is captured in App.xaml.cs, not the current page. App.xaml.cs needs to be able to call into the methods in the MainPage class, and the easiest way to do this is to assign the current instance of the MainPage to a public static variable. Open MainPage.xaml.cs, create a static variable for this scenario:

```
public static MainPage Current;
```

In the constructor, assign the current MainPage to Current:

```
public MainPage()
{
  this.InitializeComponent();
  Current = this;
}
```

Finally, add a method called ShowQueryText that will display a message in the text block as follows:

```
public void ShowQueryText( string queryText )
{
  StatusBlock.Text = "Query submitted: " + queryText;
}
```

Reacting to Search

In App.xaml.cs, we need to override the virtual method OnSearchActivated. This method is called by the operating system when a charms-based search is executed and is targeting this app. This method takes one argument, of the type SearchActivatedEventArgs. For this example, we will only be looking at the QueryText property of the SearchActivatedEventArgs.

This method first makes sure the application is properly loaded. In this simple example, the call to EnsureMainPageActivatedAsync is commented out because we are handling a charms-based search in a currently running app.

Next, the app determines whether there is a search string in the query, and if so, sends it to the correct process. In a "real" app, the query text would probably get sent to a special search-results page, or get passed into the MainPage in a way that your application knows that the page is getting loaded as a result of a search. In our case, it will simply call the ShowQueryText method on the MainPage.

```
async protected override void OnSearchActivated(
  SearchActivatedEventArgs args )
{
  //Commented out for this sample
  //await EnsureMainPageActivatedAsync( args );
  if ( args.QueryText == "" )
  {
    // navigate to landing page.
  }
  else
  {
    // display search results.
    MainPage.Current.ShowQueryText( args.QueryText );
  }
}
```

Run the application and bring up the Search charm. Notice that the Search defaults to the currently running application (marker 1 in Figure 8-4). Then, type some text into the search box (marker 2) and click on the magnifying glass, and the app will react to the search and display the query text (marker 3).

Figure 8-4. Query submitted

If you are working with multiple monitors, you might need to select the Searching1 app from the Search charm as in Figure 8-5.

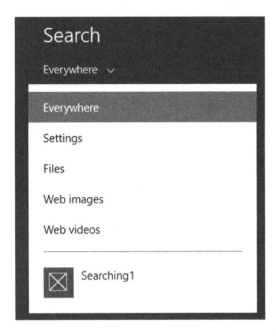

Figure 8-5. *Selecting the Searching1 app from Search charm*

Matching Search Terms

Retrieving the Search term is only half the battle; the other half is returning a match that is appropriate for your application.

The search contract specifies that you must be able to make search suggestions (on partial matches) and search recommendations on full matches. Search suggestions are illustrated in Figure 8-6 and search recommendations in Figure 8-7.

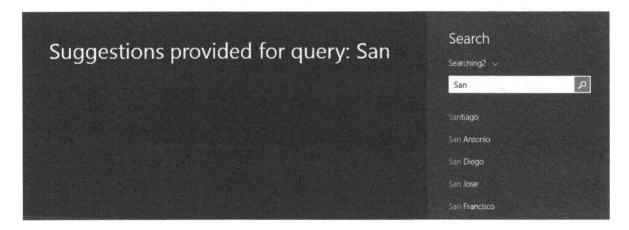

Figure 8-6. *Search suggestions*

Figure 8-7. Search recommendations

Building the Sample to Match Search Terms

Now that we have covered the basics, let's build a sample that leverages the search capabilities to return suggestions based on what the user enters into the search box.

Start by creating a new Blank Application called Searching2. Copy in the changes that we made to `MainPage.xaml`, `MainPage.xaml.cs`, and the App Manifest. You don't need to add the code to `App.xaml.cs`, as we'll be handing the search pane events in `MainPage.xaml.cs`. This also allows us to delete the variable declaration for `Current` from `MainPage.xaml.cs` and the assignment for `Current` in the constructor (although they won't hurt anything in our sample).

```
public static MainPage Current; //at the top of the class
Current = this; //in the constructor
```

■ **Note**   You could copy and paste the entire project, but then there are a lot of little items that need to be updated. It is truly easier to copy in the changes from the first section than to update the App Manifest, the temporary license, and everything else.

In this example, all of the work to accomplish this is in `MainPage.xaml.cs`. In a typical application, this page would most likely be in a separate location than the entry page for the application. This is not an absolute rule, as you should always do what makes the most sense for your particular app.

Adding Data To Be Searched

We need data to search when the user enters search criteria. Normally, we'd retrieve this data from a database or a web service. For now, we'll hard code this data into a static array of strings in `MainPage.xaml.cs` as in the following:

```
private static readonly string[] suggestionList =
{
  "Shanghai", "Istanbul", "Karachi", "Delhi", "Mumbai", "Moscow", "São Paulo", "Seoul", "Beijing",
"Jakarta","Tokyo", "Mexico City", "Kinshasa", "New York City", "Lagos", "London", "Lima", "Bogota",
"Tehran", "Ho Chi Minh City","Hong Kong", "Bangkok", "Dhaka", "Cairo", "Hanoi", "Rio de Janeiro",
"Lahore", "Chonquing", "Bangalore", "Tianjin","Baghdad", "Riyadh", "Singapore", "Santiago",
"Saint Petersburg", "Surat", "Chennai", "Kolkata", "Yangon", "Guangzhou", "Alexandria", "Shenyang",
"Hyderabad", "Ahmedabad", "Ankara", "Johannesburg", "Wuhan", "Los Angeles", "Yokohama", "Abidjan",
"Busan", "Cape Town", "Durban", "Pune", "Jeddah", "Berlin", "Pyongyang", "Kanpur", "Madrid",
"Jaipur", "Nairobi", "Chicago", "Houston", "Philadelphia", "Phoenix", "San Antonio", "San Diego",
```

```
"Dallas", "San Jose", "Jacksonville", "Indianapolis", "San Francisco", "Austin", "Columbus",
"Fort Worth", "Charlotte", "Detroit", "El Paso", "Memphis", "Baltimore", "Boston",
"Seattle Washington", "Nashville", "Denver", "Louisville", "Milwaukee", "Portland", "Las Vegas",
"Oklahoma City", "Albuquerque", "Tucson", "Fresno", "Sacramento", "Long Beach", "Kansas City",
"Mesa", "Virginia Beach", "Atlanta", "Colorado Springs", "Omaha", "Raleigh", "Miami", "Cleveland",
"Tulsa", "Oakland", "Minneapolis", "Wichita", "Arlington", " Bakersfield", "New Orleans",
"Honolulu", "Anaheim", "Tampa", "Aurora", "Santa Ana", "St. Louis", "Pittsburgh", "Corpus Christi",
"Riverside", "Cincinnati", "Lexington", "Anchorage", "Stockton", "Toledo", "St. Paul", "Newark",
"Greensboro", "Buffalo", "Plano", "Lincoln", "Henderson", "Fort Wayne", "Jersey City",
"St. Petersburg", "Chula Vista", "Norfolk", "Orlando", "Chandler", "Laredo", "Madison",
"Winston-Salem", "Lubbock", "Baton Rouge", "Durham", "Garland", "Glendale", "Reno", "Hialeah",
"Chesapeake", "Scottsdale", "North Las Vegas", "Irving", "Fremont", "Irvine", "Birmingham",
"Rochester", "San Bernardino", "Spokane", "Toronto", "Montreal", "Vancouver", "Ottawa-Gatineau",
"Calgary", "Edmonton", "Quebec City", "Winnipeg", "Hamilton"
};
```

Supporting Search Suggestions and Matches

Search suggestions and matches are shown below the search box in an area called the search pane. To access the search pane, use the SearchForCurrentView method off the SearchPane class (in the Windows.ApplicationModel. Search namespace). Then, open up MainPage.xaml.cs and add a constant value for how many suggestions we'll show.

Add these lines after the definition of the Current static variable,

```
private SearchPane searchPane;
internal const int SEARCH_PANE_MAX_SUGGESTIONS = 5;
```

In the constructor, set the searchPane to be the result of calling the static method GetForCurrentView.

```
public MainPage()
{
  this.InitializeComponent();
  searchPane = SearchPane.GetForCurrentView();
}
```

The OnNavigatedTo event is fired when a page is loaded into the foreground. In this sample, there is only one page, so when the app loads, MainPage.xaml.cs is automatically navigated to. There are three events that we need to listen for:

- The query was submitted.

- Suggestions have been requested.

- A result suggestion has been chosen.

Open up MainPage.xaml.cs and add the following code:

```
protected override void OnNavigatedTo(
  NavigationEventArgs e )
{
  SearchPane.GetForCurrentView().QuerySubmitted +=
    new TypedEventHandler<SearchPane,
    SearchPaneQuerySubmittedEventArgs>(OnQuerySubmitted);
  searchPane.SuggestionsRequested +=
```

```
    new TypedEventHandler<SearchPane,
    SearchPaneSuggestionsRequestedEventArgs>
    ( OnSearchSuggestionsRequested );
  searchPane.ResultSuggestionChosen +=
    OnSearchSuggestionChosen;
}
```

Query Submitted

The event handler for query submitted (OnQuerySubmitted) simply passes the query text to a helper method that calls NotifyUser. NotifyUser replaces ShowQueryText from the last example and is more versatile (and more accurately named) than the narrow focused ShowQueryText. In the case when a Query is submitted, the text of the query is displayed in MainPage.xaml.

```
internal void OnQuerySubmitted(
  object sender, SearchPaneQuerySubmittedEventArgs args )
{
  ProcessQueryText( args.QueryText );
}
internal void ProcessQueryText( string queryText )
{
  NotifyUser( "Query submitted: " + queryText );
}
public void NotifyUser( string strMessage )
{
  StatusBlock.Text = strMessage;
}
```

OnSearchSuggestionChose

The more interesting work is done in the other event handlers. The simpler of these is OnSearchSuggestionChosen, which simply notifies the user of which recommendation was selected.

```
void OnSearchSuggestionChosen(
  SearchPane sender,
  SearchPaneResultSuggestionChosenEventArgs args)
{
  NotifyUser("Recommendation picked: " + args.Tag);
}
```

OnSearchSuggestionsRequested

Finally, we turn to OnSearchSuggestionsRequested. Here, we have a good bit of work to do, determining how much of a match, if any, we have and displaying the results accordingly. We first check to see whether the search string is empty, and if it is, we notify the user to use the search pane. The code is as follows:.

```
private void OnSearchSuggestionsRequested(
  SearchPane sender,
  SearchPaneSuggestionsRequestedEventArgs e)
```

```
{
  var queryText = e.QueryText;
  if (string.IsNullOrEmpty(queryText))
  {
    NotifyUser("Use the search pane to submit a query");
  }
}
```

If the query text is not null or empty, set a local variable to the search request (a property of the SearchPageSuggestionsRequestedEventArgs). We initialize a Boolean isRecommendationFound to false. If there is an exact match, we won't continue looking for suggestions. We also initialize a variable to hold our app image. Continuing to modify the OnSearchSuggestionRequested event handler, add the following code:

```
var request = e.Request;
bool isRecommendationFound = false;
```

To determine if there is an exact match, we use the power of LINQ. In our example, we are merely searching a list of strings. In a real application, you would be searching the data source of record.

```
var match = suggestionList
  .Where(x => x.CompareTo(queryText) == 0)
  .Select(x => x).FirstOrDefault();
```

If we get a match, we add an icon to the search result. For this example, we are using a simple Windows icon, which is available in the downloaded code that accompanies this chapter. (Make sure that the image is added to the Assets directory, and is included in the project.)

We set the isRecommendationFound to true, and then populate the results.

```
if (match != null)
{
  RandomAccessStreamReference image =
    RandomAccessStreamReference.CreateFromUri(
    new Uri("ms-appx:///Assets/windows-sdk.png"));
  isRecommendationFound = true;
  string item = match.ToString();
  request.SearchSuggestionCollection
    .AppendResultSuggestion(
      item, // text to display
      item, // details
      // tags usable when called back by
      //ResultSuggestionChosen event
      item,
      image, // image if any
      "image of " + item);
}
```

If we do not get an exact match, we look for a partial match and add it to the SearchSuggestionCollection:

```
else
{
  var results = suggestionList
    .Where(x => x.StartsWith(
      queryText,
      StringComparison.CurrentCultureIgnoreCase))
      .Select(x => x).Take(SEARCH_PANE_MAX_SUGGESTIONS);
  foreach (var itm in results)
  {
    request.SearchSuggestionCollection
      .AppendQuerySuggestion(itm);
  }
}
```

Finally, we indicate a match from the recommendations with an asterisk in the message text and then call NotifyUser with the matching recommendation from the suggestions. If there isn't a match, we notify the user of that fact. The code is as follows:

```
if (request.SearchSuggestionCollection.Size > 0)
{
  string prefix = isRecommendationFound ? "* " : "";
  NotifyUser(prefix
    + "Suggestions provided for query: "
    + queryText);
}
else
{
  NotifyUser("No suggestions provided for query: "
    + queryText);
}
```

Doing a Search Using the SearchBox

One of the new controls in Windows 8.1 is a SearchBox control. As I mentioned in the "What's New in Windows 8.1" section, Microsoft has altered the UI guidance. Instead of removing all chrome (such as buttons, links, etc.) from the UI, *some* chrome is now acceptable in places where it makes sense.

One of those places it is Search. With the complete overhaul of how Search works in Windows 8.1, it might make sense to add Search directly into your application. While it's a nice thought that we can remove Search completely from our apps and let the operating system handle it, it turns out that users just didn't like it.

Fortunately for us, the code is almost exactly the same as using charms-based search. Start with a new Blank App named Searching3. Copy all of the code from MainPage.xaml.cs in Searching2 into MainPage.xaml.cs in the new project. You can delete the variable for the SearchPane and the initializer in the constructor, as we won't need to interact with the Search charm. We will have a couple of other changes to make as well due to some differences in naming of the search event arguments. It's as simple as replacing SearchPane with SearchBox and adding a using statement as follows:

```
using Windows.UI.Xaml.Controls;
```

The complete MainPage.xaml.cs is shown here (minus all of the data strings for brevity):

```
public sealed partial class MainPage : Page
{
  internal const int SEARCH_PANE_MAX_SUGGESTIONS = 5;
  private static readonly string[] suggestionList =
  {
    //Omitted for brevity
  };
  public MainPage()
  {
    this.InitializeComponent();
  }
  internal void OnQuerySubmitted(object sender,
    SearchBoxQuerySubmittedEventArgs args)
  {
    ProcessQueryText(args.QueryText);
  }
  internal void ProcessQueryText(string queryText)
  {
    NotifyUser("Query submitted: " + queryText);
  }
  public void NotifyUser(string strMessage)
  {
    StatusBlock.Text = strMessage;
  }
  void OnSearchSuggestionChosen(
    SearchBox sender,
    SearchBoxResultSuggestionChosenEventArgs args)
  {
    NotifyUser("Recommendation picked: " + args.Tag);
  }
  private void OnSearchSuggestionsRequested(
    SearchBox sender,
    SearchBoxSuggestionsRequestedEventArgs e)
  {
    var queryText = e.QueryText;
    if (string.IsNullOrEmpty(queryText))
    {
      NotifyUser("Use the search pane to submit a query");
    }
    else
    {
      var request = e.Request;
      bool isRecommendationFound = false;
      var match = suggestionList
        .Where(x => x.CompareTo(queryText)==0)
        .Select(x => x).FirstOrDefault();
      if (match != null)
      {
        RandomAccessStreamReference image =
          RandomAccessStreamReference.CreateFromUri(
```

```csharp
      new Uri("ms-appx:///Assets/windows-sdk.png"));
    isRecommendationFound = true;
    string item = match.ToString();
    request.SearchSuggestionCollection
      .AppendResultSuggestion(
      item, // text to display
      item, // details
      item, // tags usable when called
      //by ResultSuggestionChosen event
      image, // image if any
      "image of " + item);
  }
  else
  {
    var results = suggestionList
      .Where(x =>
        x.StartsWith(queryText,
          StringComparison.CurrentCultureIgnoreCase))
      .Select(x => x)
      .Take(SEARCH_PANE_MAX_SUGGESTIONS);
    foreach (var itm in results)
    {
    request.SearchSuggestionCollection
    .AppendQuerySuggestion(itm);
    }
  }
  if (request.SearchSuggestionCollection.Size> 0)
  {
    string prefix = isRecommendationFound ? "* " : "";
    NotifyUser(prefix
      + "Suggestions provided for query: "
      + queryText);
  }
  else
  {
    NotifyUser("No suggestions provided for query: "
      + queryText);
  }
  }
  }
 }
}
```

You also don't need to update the App Manifest of the new project, since app Search is no longer launched from the operating system. We can also delete the event handler for OnNavigatedTo, since the page will already be loaded when the user invokes a search.

Main Page with SearchBoxControl

The final change that we will make is to add the following XAML to the `MainPage.xaml`. We have added another row to the grid, leaving the `TextBlock` from the first two examples exactly where it was, and adding a `SearchBox` in the new row. The XAML is as follows:

```
<Grid.RowDefinitions>
  <RowDefinition Height="Auto"/>
  <RowDefinition Height="*"/>
</Grid.RowDefinitions>
<TextBlock Grid.Row="0" Name="StatusBlock"
  FontSize="40" Margin="50" Text="Ready..." />
<SearchBox Grid.Row="1" Height="35" Margin="50" Width="400"
  HorizontalAlignment="Left" VerticalAlignment="Top"
  SuggestionsRequested=
    "OnSearchSuggestionsRequested"
  QuerySubmitted="OnQuerySubmitted"
  ResultSuggestionChosen="OnSearchSuggestionChosen" />
```

Testing the Application

When you run the application, you see a search box just below the message. The UI is the same as the charms-based search box. When the user starts typing into the search box, suggestions are displayed in a flyout that closely resembles a drop-down list, as in Figure 8-8.

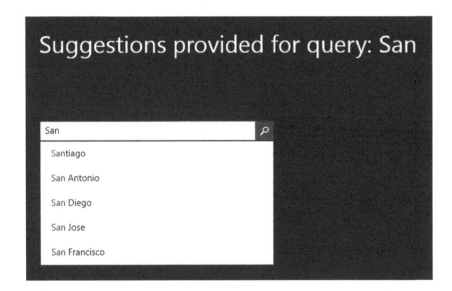

Figure 8-8. *Search suggestions with a search box*

When a match is made, it shows in the search pane for the search box, as shown in Figure 8-9 (looks familiar, doesn't it?).

Figure 8-9. *Search match*

Sharing

Everybody loves to share. Prior to the Sharing charm in Windows 8 and 8.1, if you wanted to add the ability for the user to send an e-mail, you needed to write a significant amount of code. And if you wanted to add additional ways to share, you needed to know all of the options at design time.

Windows 8.1 provides a Share contract, where an app can be a Share Source or a Share Target. By following the standard patterns provided, an app that is a Share Source can share its information with *any* Share Target. Likewise, an app that is a Share Target can receive data from any app that is a Share Source.

Architecture

The process of sharing *sounds* complicated, but the programmer's role is pretty straightforward, and made even easier by the sharing target contract that we'll talk about in the next section.

The Share Source app provides information by registering with the DataTransferManager and exposing data in a predefined format. When the user wants to share, the Share Source receives an event that it responds to by filling a DataPackage.

The (invisible, behind-the-scenes) ShareBroker filters the list of target apps that can handle the types of data you are sharing. The user selects the target app of choice and that application is activated. The target processes the data package contents and reports the action as complete.

Implementation

Creating a Sharing source is incredibly easy. You just create a new Blank App and call it ShareSource. In MainPage.xaml, add a simple TextBlock. This isn't used by the app, but it's more comforting than a blank screen!

```
<Grid Background=
  "{ThemeResource ApplicationPageBackgroundThemeBrush}">
  <TextBlock FontSize="20" Text="Welcome to Sharing!" />
</Grid>
```

In MainPage.xaml.cs, override the OnNavigatedTo event. Here is where we need to get a reference to the DataTransferManager (in the Windows.ApplicationModel.DataTransfer namespace) as well as wire up the event to respond to user requesting to share data.

```
protected override void OnNavigatedTo(
  NavigationEventArgs e)
{
  DataTransferManager dtm =
    DataTransferManager.GetForCurrentView();
  dtm.DataRequested += dtm_DataRequested;
}
```

This example is a single-page app, but in more complex apps, you will want to disconnect the event in the OnNavigatedFrom method.

```
 protected override void OnNavigatedFrom(
  NavigationEventArgs e)
{
  DataTransferManager dtm =
    DataTransferManager.GetForCurrentView();
  dtm.DataRequested -= dtm_DataRequested;
}
```

In the DataRequested event handler, we first get the deferral for the request. This example is trivial, so the deferral's really not needed, but in real applications, it's best to make sure that it is set. The deferral ensures that all work is complete before the search pane opens. Make sure to use a try-catch-finally block to make sure that the Complete method is called on the deferral; otherwise the app (and the Search charm) might be hung up indefinitely.

```
void dtm_DataRequested(DataTransferManager sender, DataRequestedEventArgs args)
{
  DataRequestDeferral deferral = args.Request.GetDeferral();
  try
  {
  }
  catch (Exception ex)
  {
  }
  finally
  {
    deferral.Complete();
  }
}
```

The DataRequestedEventArgs has a property called Request that represents the operating system's request to share data. The Request has a Data property that gets shared with the chosen Share Target. There are many different properties that you can set on the data, and you can even send files and binary data. In this example, we set just a few, but at a minimum, you should set the title, description, and the text of the message.

We start by setting a convenience variable for the request data. Most of the properties that we will access are in the Properties collection of the data object. In the try block (added just after the code to get a references to the deferral), set the Title, Description, and ContentSourceWebLink properties as follows:

```
DataPackage requestData = args.Request.Data;
requestData.Properties.Title =
  "My data from my application";
requestData.Properties.Description =
```

```
"Description of my data from my application";
//requestData.SetApplicationLink();
requestData.Properties.ContentSourceWebLink =
  new Uri("http://www.apress.com");
```

To set the body of the message, we can simply call SetText on the data, or use HTML by calling SetHtmlFormat. If using HTML, the HtmlFormatHelper is extremely useful to make sure the format is correctly set in the data package.

```
requestData.SetText("This is text from my source");
args.Request
  .Data.SetHtmlFormat(
  HtmlFormatHelper.CreateHtmlFormat(
    "<b>Important</b> data from  my application "
    + "placed in <i>HTML</i>"));
```

> ■ **Note**   A very helpful app for testing Share Source code is the MSDN sample Share Target app, which can be downloaded here: http://code.msdn.microsoft.com/windowsapps/Sharing-Content-Target-App-e2689782.

That's it! You can now run your application, and when it starts, swipe to bring in the charms. Click on Share and you will be presented with a list of all the applications registered on your computer that can handle the data types you are presenting (text and HTML), as shown here in Figure 8-10. If you don't install the Share Target samples from MSDN, your list will be shorter (perhaps just Mail).

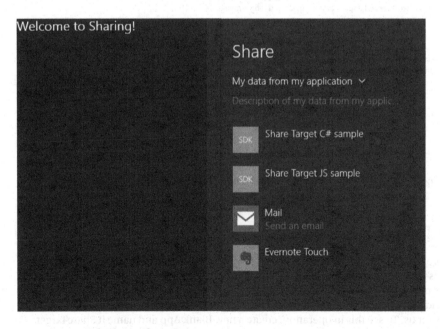

Figure 8-10. *Selecting a Share Target*

Select the Share Target C# sample notice saying that the properties that we set in the example are displayed in the Share Target as in Figure 8-11.

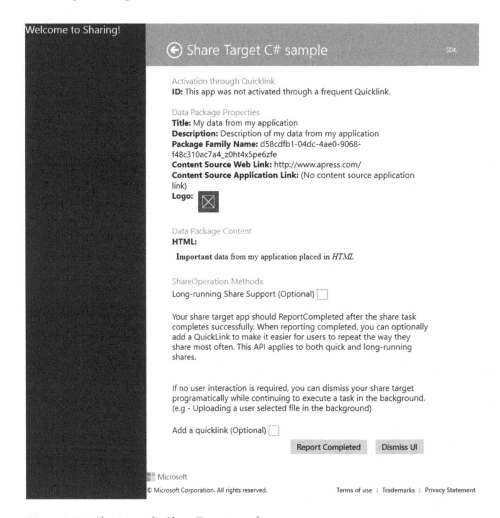

Figure 8-11. *Sharing to the Share Target sample*

Creating a Sharing Target

Creating a Share Target is a bit more complex. In addition to registering with the OS, the target needs to be able to potentially handle multiple formats for the share payload from a Share Source. Fortunately Visual Studio provides a template that greatly simplifies the process.

By using the template, we avoid having to set the package appxmanifest and we avoid having to muck about in App.xaml.cs. All that work is done for us. To see this in operation, create a new Blank App and name it ShareTarget.

Right-click on the project in Solution Explorer, and choose Add ➤ New Item. From the list, select *Share Target Contract* and use the default name. You will be prompted that there are required files that Visual Studio can add for you, as shown in Figure 8-12. Click Yes.

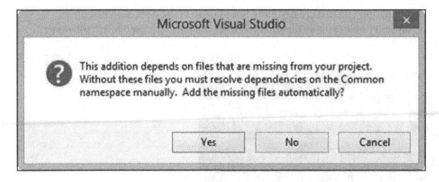

Figure 8-12. *Additional files message*

Wait a few seconds and you'll see that a number of files have been added to the Common directory and that
ShareTargetPage1.xaml has been added to your project.

That's it! You now have a target. The sample page provides all of the needed information, including the ability to
add a comment.

To see this at work, run the program once (to register it) and then stop the new target program. Remember that
targets don't have to be running to be in the target list; if the user selects your target application, it will be started
for you.

Return to the Share Source application that we built in the previous section and start that up. Swipe to bring in
the charms and click the Sharing charm. Notice that the list of target applications now includes your new application,
as shown in Figure 8-13.

Figure 8-13. *Source target*

If you click on SharingTarget (the application you just created), the *text* version of the data is picked up as our target currently only supports text (if you try Mail, you'll still see the HTML version). The results are shown in Figure 8-14.

Figure 8-14. *Share Target template*

The ShareTarget application works by listening for the ShareTargetActivated event in App.xaml.cs (this code is added by the template). The event handler calls the Activate method in ShareSearchPage1. The ShareTargetActivatedEventArgs class is in the Windows.ApplicationModel.Activation namespace.

```
protected override void OnShareTargetActivated(
  ShareTargetActivatedEventArgs e)
{
  var shareTargetPage = new ShareTarget.ShareTargetPage1();
  shareTargetPage.Activate(e);
}
```

The Activate method arguments include a ShareOperation property that carries the payload from the ShareSource (in the Data property). Accessing the properties is the reverse of populating them. The ShareTargetPage1 is displayed in the Share charm by setting it to be the Window.Current.Content and then activating it.

```
public async void Activate(ShareTargetActivatedEventArgs e)
{
  this._shareOperation = e.ShareOperation;
  // Communicate metadata about the shared content through the view model
  var shareProperties = _shareOperation.Data.Properties;
  var thumbnailImage = new BitmapImage();
  this.DefaultViewModel["Title"] = shareProperties.Title;
  this.DefaultViewModel["Description"] =
    shareProperties.Description;
  this.DefaultViewModel["Image"] = thumbnailImage;
  this.DefaultViewModel["Sharing"] = false;
```

```
this.DefaultViewModel["ShowImage"] = false;
this.DefaultViewModel["Comment"] = String.Empty;
this.DefaultViewModel["Placeholder"] = "Add a comment";
this.DefaultViewModel["SupportsComment"] = true;
Window.Current.Content = this;
Window.Current.Activate();
// Update the shared content's thumbnail image in the background
if (shareProperties.Thumbnail != null)
{
    var stream =
        await shareProperties.Thumbnail.OpenReadAsync();
    thumbnailImage.SetSource(stream);
    this.DefaultViewModel["ShowImage"] = true;
}
}
```

Note that this new application doesn't do anything with the data you've shared; you'll have to write additional code to integrate that data into your new application.

Summary

Windows 8.0 and Windows 8.1 greatly enhance the developer and the user experience by providing a unified experience for searching applications. By providing operating system search capabilities through the Search charm, the UI is consistent across modern apps. Windows 8.1 has introduced a SearchBox control to allow for in-app searching, providing the same UI (and API) as the charms-based search.

CHAPTER 9

■ ■ ■

Notifications

"If you build it, they will come" might have worked in the movies, but it seldom works for software. In order for your app to be successful, it needs to be used. A good-looking tile induces the user to try your application. Smartly developed live tiles and notifications bring 'em back again and again.

If you are developing a commercial app that you are selling in the store, the more your customers use your application, the happier they will be with it, and the better ratings you'll receive, which in turn will help sell more copies. If your model is in-app purchases, users need to be using your app in order to make purchases. If you are building a line of business apps, the more your app gets used, the better it is for your business. One thing is true regardless of the model of your app: it can't be successful unless people use it.

Display Options for Notifications

There are three ways to tell your users that your application has something interesting going on: live tiles, secondary tiles, and toast notifications.

Live tiles can entice your user to open up your app. Tiles are the entry point into your app, and showing content through live tiles and badges will notify the user that there is new information available. The more your app is used, the more sticky it becomes, and the higher the user will value it.

Secondary tiles allow users to mark an area in the application and create a tile for the Start screen that brings them right back to that area. A classic example would be a secondary tile that follows the weather in a users' favorite city or follows the value of the users' favorite stock. Making customizations like this part of your app will improve the use of your app, which will in turn improve the likelihood that the user will keep your app installed on their system.

Toast notifications are a great way to let the user know that something significant and demanding immediate attention has happened in your program. But *beware* of toast spam—send too much toast and your user will, at a minimum, turn notifications off for your app and, worst case, delete your app entirely.

Each of these toasts is designed to say, "Hey! Look here! Something interesting is going on." You can use all or none in your application, but the important thing to do is strike the right balance. Not enough information and users lose interest. Too much and they will feel nagged and uninstall your app.

Delivery Options for Notifications

In addition to the different mechanisms for showing the notifications just described, there are different options for sending the notifications:

Local notifications are generated directly from your application's code, and are great for displaying information while your application is running. They may happen either while your user is actively using your application (e.g., a game notifying users that they've just hit a new high score or unlocked an achievement) or in the background (e.g., indicating the current song in a music application or that a background report the user has initiated has completed).

There are also three other types of notifications, and they can interact with your user at times when your application may not be running. Fortunately, they all use the same general code structure as local notifications; the only difference is the delivery mechanism. The other notification methods are scheduled, periodic, and push notifications. They are used in the following ways:

- A *scheduled notification* notifies the user at a particular time. An obvious example of this would be an appointment reminder from a calendar application.

- A *periodic notification* updates tiles or badges on a regular basis. An example would be a news or podcast application, which should check regularly for new content. It's important to keep in mind that periodic notifications are not precise and should be used to keep your application's content fresh, not to perform time-critical tasks.

- A *push notification* allows you to send notifications to users from a cloud service at any time, regardless of whether the Windows 8.1 application is running. As an example, users may register with a shopping application to be notified when their favorite brand of shoes go on sale or when their favorite musician releases a new album; the shopping application's server could also send them a notification a month later when the conditions have been met. As long as they still have the application installed, they'll get the notification. Push notifications are sent to your users from a remote server and don't require them to continually poll for updates.

Live Tiles

You can see examples of live tiles just by pressing the Windows key and examining many of the applications that come with Windows 8.1. The Photos application, the News application and many others are all clamoring for your attention by updating their tiles with new images or text. An app can have up to five different data sets for live tiles that can be rotated through.

Tile notifications can contain text and/or images in one of the predefined formats. Windows 8.1 introduced two more tiles, bringing the total to four. There is also a fallback value that can be provided in the data packet so that the tile-notifications data can be understood by Windows 8.0 as well. The four tile sizes are as follows:

- Small (70x70)

- Square (150x150)

- Wide (310x150)

- Large (310x310)

Applications must always include a medium logo in the manifest, and if you want to use a wide tile, it must include a wide logo as well. If you want to use a large square tile (310x310), you must include a wide and large logo as well.

To get started creating live tiles, we'll first create the data for the tile, and then examine what it takes to set up local notification to the tile, which causes the tile to "come alive" on the Start screen. It turns out to be startlingly easy to add a live tile to your application. Microsoft offers a number of different tile templates, some with text and some with images, and some with both. Microsoft has also created a Visual Studio extension that greatly assists with creating tiles. Unfortunately, at the time of this writing, the NuGet version of the extension is targeting Windows 8.0, not Windows 8.1. The good news is that it is available from the "App Tiles and Badges Sample" section on the Microsoft web site: http://code.msdn.microsoft.com/windowsapps/App-tiles-and-badges-sample-5fc49148#content. It is also included in the downloadable source code for this chapter.

Creating the Sample

To begin, create a new Blank App named LiveTile. In order to display wide and large tiles, the manifest needs to have the appropriately sized images specified, so we will start by creating two new images to update the manifest. Alternatively, you can grab the images from the downloadable code that accompanies this chapter.

▪ **Note** You don't have to plan to support all tile sizes to add live tiles to your app. It is up to you and your specific requirements to determine the tile sizes you intend on supporting.

Creating New Images

The easiest way to create new images (at least for a demo app) is to use a free program like paint.net (available here: www.getpaint.net/) to add two images (in PNG format) based on the default images. You need to make one 310x150 pixels and the other 310x310 pixels and place them in the Assets folder of your project. This is because (as previously mentioned) your user can't choose a wide or square tile unless you have the appropriately sized images configured in the App Manifest.

Updating the App Manifest

Once you have added the correctly sized images, open up Package.appmanifest file, and select the Visual Assets tab. On this tab, you can select what sizes you want the App Name to appear for. Enter the Friendly name that will be shown. You can also set the Default Size and Foreground Text (light or dark) as well as the background color. Those settings are the same for all image assets. In the left rail, click on Wide 310x150 Logo and then click on the button with the ellipses under the Scaled Asset control labeled Scale 100. Select the 310x150 image that you created (or copied). Do the same for the Square 310x310 Logo. This is shown in Figure 9-1.

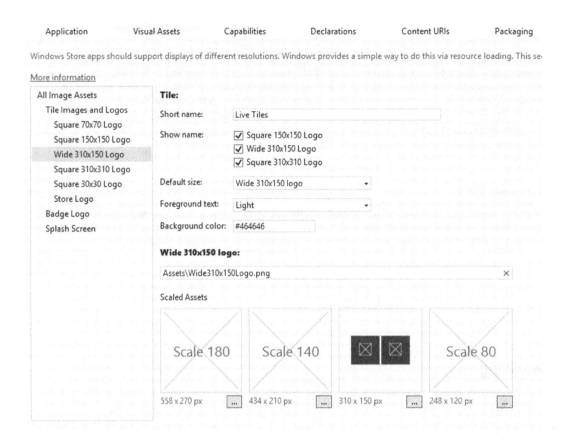

Figure 9-1. *Assigning the Visual Assets*

Deploy the app by selecting Build ➤ Deploy Solution. This compiles your app and places the icon in the apps list. Go to your Start screen (you might have to go into the full app list by clicking on the down arrow or swiping up). Select the icon for the LiveTile app and pin it to start. Go back to the Start screen and select the icon for your app (it will have defaulted to the size that you selected in the App Manifest). You can resize it to all four of the options.

■ **Note**   The default size only works the first time your app is installed and pinned to the Start screen. After that, Windows remembers the last size the user selected, even if you uninstall and reinstall the app. Great feature for users, not so great for developers wanting to test their App Manifest.

Creating the UI for the Samples

The UI for this sample is very simple. There are four buttons for creating/clearing the live tile information and two instances of TextBlock to show the information being sent to the tile. You can see the finished product in Figure 9-2.

Figure 9-2. *Live tile sample*

Open up `MainPage.xaml`, and add in the following XAML. Since the XAML that we are using here is very straightforward, there isn't much to say about it. The interesting parts come in the code in the next section.

```
<Grid Background="{ThemeResource ApplicationPageBackgroundThemeBrush}">
    <Grid.ColumnDefinitions>
        <ColumnDefinition Width="120"/>
        <ColumnDefinition Width="*"/>
        <ColumnDefinition Width="50"/>
        <ColumnDefinition Width="*"/>
    </Grid.ColumnDefinitions>
    <Grid.RowDefinitions>
        <RowDefinition Height="100" />
        <RowDefinition Height="Auto" />
        <RowDefinition Height="*" />
    </Grid.RowDefinitions>
    <StackPanel  Grid.Column="1" Grid.Row="0" Orientation="Horizontal">
        <Button Name="CreateTileWithXML" Content="Create XML"
            Click="CreateTileWithXML_Click"/>
        <Button Name="ClearTilesXML"
            Content="Clear"
            Click="ClearTiles_Click"/>
    </StackPanel>
    <TextBlock Name="TextBasedXML" TextWrapping="WrapWholeWords"
Grid.Column="1" Grid.Row="1"
```

```
Style="{StaticResource BodyTextBlockStyle}"></TextBlock>
    <StackPanel  Grid.Column="3" Grid.Row="0" Orientation="Horizontal">
        <Button Name="CreateTileWithExtensions"
            Content="Create With Extensions"
            Click="CreateTileWithExtensions_Click"/>
        <Button Name="ClearTilesExt"
            Content="Clear"
            Click="ClearTilesExt_Click"/>
    </StackPanel>
    <TextBlock Name="ExtensionBasedXML" TextWrapping="WrapWholeWords"
Grid.Column="3" Grid.Row="1"
Style="{StaticResource BodyTextBlockStyle}"></TextBlock>
</Grid>
```

For each of the buttons, make sure to add the event handlers in the code behind. You can let Visual Studio help you with this, or you can add the following code to MainPage.xaml.cs.

```
private void CreateTileWithXML_Click(object sender, RoutedEventArgs e)
{
}
private void CreateTileWithExtensions_Click(object sender, RoutedEventArgs e)
{
}
private void ClearTiles_Click(object sender, RoutedEventArgs e)
{
}
public void ClearTilesExt_Click(object sender, RoutedEventArgs e)
{
}
```

Adding Live Tiles Manually

Live tile information is specified in XML. There are multiple formats available for each tile size, with various combinations of images and text (wrapping or not). The formats can be found in the TileTemplateType enumeration located on the Microsoft web site (see Note).

■ **Note**   To see all of the formats available, please see the MSDN documentation located here: http://bit.ly/1gvCuzB.

On the web site, start by choosing the template that you want to use. In this example, I selected all text tiles with headings and no wrapping for the content lines:

- TileSquare150x150Text01

- TileWide310x150Text01

- TileSquare310x310Text01

Once you have the templates selected, we can start writing the code. Open up `MainPage.xaml.cs` and add the following using statements to the top of the file:

```
using System.Xml.Linq;
using Windows.UI.Notifications;
using Windows.Data.Xml.Dom;
```

For each of the tiles, the process is the same. Get the XML from the template, update it accordingly, and then use the notification framework to send the XML to the tile.

Creating the Tile Data

The first tile we will create is the 150x150 tile. This is an arbitrary decision, as we will need to create all three sizes and send them together in the payload for the tile, since you don't know what size tile your user will select.

To get the XML, use the `TileUpdateManager` (in the `Windows.UI.Notifications` namespace) to access the `TileTemplateType` enumeration. Assign the XML to an `XmlDocument` variable so we can work with it easier. Add the following code to the `CreateTileWithXML_Click` event handler:

```
XmlDocument tileSquareXML = TileUpdateManager.GetTemplateContent(
    TileTemplateType.TileSquare150x150Text01); //Header, 3 lines (no wrap)
```

The `XmlDocument` for this particular format is shown here:

```
<tile>
    <visual version="2">
        <binding template="TileSquare150x150Text01"
            fallback="TileSquareText01">
            <text id="1"></text>
            <text id="2"></text>
            <text id="3"></text>
            <text id="4"></text>
        </binding>
    </visual>
</tile>
```

The visual version indicates if it's designed for Windows 8 (version 1) or Windows 8.1 (version 2). The binding tells the tile what template there is and if there is a fallback tile for Windows 8.0. Then, there are text nodes to contain the content. Although it isn't indicated in the XML, the first text in this template is a header row, and then text nodes 2-4 are individual and nonwrapping. Since the text doesn't wrap (but gets truncated), you need to be careful how much information is placed in each node.

For this demo, we are going to specify the size of the tile in the heading, and then fill out the lines with a simple "Line 1," "Line 2," and so forth. Add the following code to the same event handler, immediately after the code that we added in the previous step:

```
XmlNodeList tileTextAttributes = tileSquareXML.GetElementsByTagName("text");
tileTextAttributes[0].InnerText = "My Square Tile Header XML";
tileTextAttributes[1].InnerText = "Line 1";
tileTextAttributes[2].InnerText = "Line 2";
tileTextAttributes[3].InnerText = "Line 3";
```

The two remaining templates are exactly the same except that they have more lines of text (the header plus four lines in the wide tile and the header plus nine lines in the large tile). The code to create the next two tiles is listed here:

```
XmlDocument tileWideXML = TileUpdateManager.GetTemplateContent(
    TileTemplateType.TileWide310x150Text01);
    XmlNodeList wideTileTextAttributes = tileWideXML.GetElementsByTagName("text");
wideTileTextAttributes[0].InnerText = "My Wide Tile Header XML";
wideTileTextAttributes[1].InnerText = "Line 1";
wideTileTextAttributes[2].InnerText = "Line 2";
wideTileTextAttributes[3].InnerText = "Line 3";
wideTileTextAttributes[4].InnerText = "Line 4";
XmlDocument tileLargeXML = TileUpdateManager.GetTemplateContent(
    TileTemplateType.TileSquare310x310Text01); //Header, 9 lines (no wrap)
XmlNodeList largeTileTextAttributes = tileLargeXML.GetElementsByTagName("text");
largeTileTextAttributes[0].InnerText = "My Large Tile Header XML";
largeTileTextAttributes[1].InnerText = "Line 1";
largeTileTextAttributes[2].InnerText = "Line 2";
largeTileTextAttributes[3].InnerText = "Line 3";
largeTileTextAttributes[4].InnerText = "Line 4";
largeTileTextAttributes[5].InnerText = "Line 5";
largeTileTextAttributes[6].InnerText = "Line 6";
largeTileTextAttributes[7].InnerText = "Line 7";
largeTileTextAttributes[8].InnerText = "Line 8";
largeTileTextAttributes[9].InnerText = "Line 9";
```

Combining the Tile Data

As previously mentioned, the entire payload needs to be sent in one package. This is done by adding each of the binding nodes as children of the visual node in one of the instances of an XmlDocument. This is simple XML manipulation and is shown here:

```
//Combine all into one payload
IXmlNode squareNode =
        tileLargeXML.ImportNode(
        tileSquareXML.GetElementsByTagName("binding").Item(0),
        true);
IXmlNode wideNode = tileLargeXML.ImportNode(
        tileWideXML.GetElementsByTagName("binding").Item(0), true);
var visual = tileLargeXML.GetElementsByTagName("visual").Item(0);
visual.AppendChild(wideNode);
visual.AppendChild(squareNode);
```

Sending the Notification Binding Payload

To send the information to the tile, use the TileNotification class as well as the TileUpdateManager (both in the Windows.UI.Notifications namespace). The first thing to do is to get an instance of the TileUpdater for the app using the TileUpdateManager.

```
var updater = TileUpdateManager.CreateTileUpdaterForApplication();
```

In order to add multiple tiles, the notification queue must be enabled:

```
updater.EnableNotificationQueue(true);
```

Finally, we create an instance of a TileNotification, passing the XmlDocument that we just created into the Update method of the TileUpdaterForApplication:

```
TileNotification notification = new TileNotification(tileLargeXML);
updater.Update(notification);
```

That's it! Your information will now show on your app's tile on the Start screen. But before we run the app to test it, let's show the XML payload on the screen. We'll use the XDocument class in the System.Xml.Linq namespace to format the XML for easier viewing.

```
TextBasedXML.Text = XDocument.Parse(tileLargeXML.GetXml()).ToString();
```

Testing the App

To test the app, run it and click the Create XML button, and you will see a screen similar to Figure 9-3.

Figure 9-3. *The XML payload*

Running the app installs it on your machine. To see the tile in action, pin it to the Start screen. Wait for a few seconds and the tile will flip to show your data. Figure 9-4 shows all of the different tiles that we created (the smallest size doesn't support live tiles).

Figure 9-4. The live tiles

Removing the Logo from the Tile

The tiles we just looked at show the app icon in the lower-left corner. If you decide that you don't want to show the icon, these can be removed in one of two ways. For all tiles in the payload, you can add the attribute "branding" with the value of "none" to the "visual" element. For individual tiles in the payload, you can add the attribute to the "binding" element. To add the attribute for all three nodes in this example, add the following code after appending the child nodes to the tileLargeXML XmlDocument:

```
//Remove the Icon from the lower-left corner
var bindings = tileLargeXML.GetElementsByTagName("binding");
for (var x=0;x < bindings.Length;x++)
{
    ((XmlElement)bindings[x]).SetAttribute("branding", "none");
}
```

Adding Live Tiles Through the Notifications Extensions

As mentioned in the introduction to this section, Microsoft has developed a project called NotificationsExtensions that greatly assists in the creation of live tiles. Even though (at the time of this writing) the NuGet package is only applicable for Windows 8.0, the project is updated in the MSDN sample (and available through the downloadable code with this chapter).

To take advantage of the NotificationsExtensions project, either add the NotificationsExtensions project to your solution or add a reference to the NotificationsExtensions.winmd file. Open MainPage.xaml.cs and add the following using to the top of the file:

```
using NotificationsExtensions.TileContent;
```

Next, navigate to the CreateTileWithExtensions_Click method. The NotificationsExtensions library adds a series of convenience methods to the process that we just finished manually. Each of the available tile templates are represented by a strongly typed class.

Creating the Tile Data

To create the 150x150 tile, start by getting an instance of the ITileSquare150x150Text01 interface:

```
ITileSquare150x150Text01 square150x150Content =
    TileContentFactory.CreateTileSquare150x150Text01();
```

All of the XML nodes are available as properties on the specific interface for your template. For example, to turn off the logo image for the tile, set the Branding property to the value of TileBranding.None:

```
square150x150Content.Branding = TileBranding.None;
```

For the layouts that have a Header, there is a TextHeading property (instead of populating the text node with an ID="1").

```
square150x150Content.TextHeading.Text = "Square Tile EXT";
```

For the rest of the lines, the rows are numbered accordingly:

```
square150x150Content.TextBody1.Text = "Line 1";
square150x150Content.TextBody2.Text = "Line 2";
square150x150Content.TextBody3.Text = "Line 3";
```

To create the rest of the tile formats, enter the code listed here:

```
 ITileWide310x150Text01 wide310x150Content =
     TileContentFactory.CreateTileWide310x150Text01();
wide310x150Content.Branding = TileBranding.None;
wide310x150Content.TextHeading.Text = "Wide Tile EXT";
wide310x150Content.TextBody1.Text = "Line 1";
wide310x150Content.TextBody2.Text = "Line 2";
wide310x150Content.TextBody3.Text = "Line 3";
wide310x150Content.TextBody4.Text = "Line 4";


ITileSquare310x310Text01 tileContent =
    TileContentFactory.CreateTileSquare310x310Text01();
tileContent.Branding = TileBranding.None;
tileContent.TextHeading.Text = "Large Tile EXT";
tileContent.TextBody1.Text = "Line 1";
tileContent.TextBody2.Text = "Line 2";
tileContent.TextBody3.Text = "Line 3";
tileContent.TextBody4.Text = "Line 4";
tileContent.TextBody5.Text = "Line 5";
tileContent.TextBody6.Text = "Line 6";
tileContent.TextBody7.Text = "Line 7";
tileContent.TextBody8.Text = "Line 8";
tileContent.TextBody9.Text = "Line 9";
```

Combining the Tile Data

Combining the tile data is done by setting properties on the larger tile template. The wide tile has a property for the small tile, and the large tile has a property for the wide tile:

```
// Attach the Square150x150 template to the Wide310x150 template.
wide310x150Content.Square150x150Content = square150x150Content;

// Attach the Wide310x150 template to the Square310x310 template.
tileContent.Wide310x150Content = wide310x150Content;
```

Sending the Notification Binding Payload

Creating the TileUpdaterForApplication is done the same way as it was when we created and updated the XML manually:

```
var updater = TileUpdateManager.CreateTileUpdaterForApplication();
updater.EnableNotificationQueue(true);
```

The only difference is that the interfaces provided by the NotificationsExtensions have a CreateNotification method:

```
updater.Update(tileContent.CreateNotification());
```

Finally, we update the UI to show the generated XML:

```
ExtensionBasedXML.Text = XDocument.Parse(tileContent.GetContent()).ToString();
```

Resetting the Tiles

To remove the live tiles, call the Clear method on the CreateTileForApplication class. There are two buttons on the form. Both will reset all of the live tiles, as well as clear the respective TextBlock. Update the two event handlers for the Clear buttons in MainPage.xaml.cs:

```
private void ClearTiles_Click(object sender, RoutedEventArgs e)
{
    TileUpdateManager.CreateTileUpdaterForApplication().Clear();
    TextBasedXML.Text = "";
}

public void ClearTilesExt_Click(object sender, RoutedEventArgs e)
{
    TileUpdateManager.CreateTileUpdaterForApplication().Clear();
    ExtensionBasedXML.Text = "";
}
```

Secondary Tiles

To see secondary tiles in action, we need to have two pages in our app. We can then have our users pin the second page in the app as a secondary tile and come right back to it.

The example we will create is very simple. The page to be pinned to the Start screen will have a button that starts the process for creating the secondary tile. If successful, the `message` text block will display a success message as in Figures 9-5 and 9-6.

Figure 9-5. *Waiting for user action*

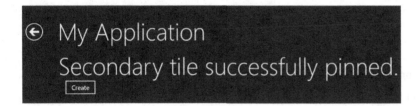

Figure 9-6. *After the secondary tile is created*

Creating the Project

To see this at work, create a new Blank App named SecondaryTiles. Delete the default MainPage.xaml page and add a new Basic Page named MainPage.xaml. Then add a second page Basic Page named PinnedPage. As a reminder, you add Basic Pages by selecting Add ➤ New Item, and selecting Basic Page.

Updating MainPage.xaml

To update MainPage.xaml, open up the page and add a single button to the page inside a StackPanel just before the closing </Grid> tag. This will be used for navigation.

```
<StackPanel Grid.Row="2" Margin="120,0,0,0">
    <Button Name="Navigate" Content="Navigate" Click="Navigate_Click" />
</StackPanel>
```

Open up MainPage.xaml.cs and create the event handler for the button click.

```
public void Navigate_Click(object sender, RoutedEventArgs e)
{
    this.Frame.Navigate(typeof(PinnedPage));
}
```

That's it. Now on to creating a secondary tile.

Creating the UI for PinnedPage

Open PinnedPage.xaml, add a StackPanel, TextBlock, and a Button. Add this before the final closing </Grid> tag.

```
<StackPanel>
    <TextBlock Name="Message" Text="Ready..." FontSize="42" />
    <Button Name="Create" Content="Create" FontSize="20" Click="Create_Click" />
</StackPanel>
```

Open up PinnedPage.xaml.cs and add an empty event handler for the button click:

```
public  void Create_Click(object sender, RoutedEventArgs e)
{
}
```

Creating the Secondary Tile

There are five steps to create a secondary tile:

1. First, create a TILEID.

2. Then, create the Tile Activation Arguments.

3. Define the visual assets for all of the tile sizes to be supported.

4. Create an instance of a SecondaryTile class and assign the correct properties.

5. Call the RequestCreateForSelectionAsync method on the secondary tile.

Creating the Tile ID and Visual Assets

Each secondary tile must have an ID. To add the id for our example, open PinnedPage.xaml.cs and add the following constant:

```
public const string TILEID = "SecondaryTileExample";
```

The visual assets are defined as System.Uris. Copy the additional images from the last sample in the Assets folder and add them to the project (or create additional ones). Next, create the Uris for each of the logos at the top of the event handler that we created for the button click named Create_Click.

```
Uri logo = new Uri("ms-appx:///Assets/Logo-scale-100.scale-100.png");
Uri wideLogo = new Uri("ms-appx:///Assets/Wide310x150Logo.scale-100.png");
Uri largeLogo = new Uri("ms-appx:///Assets/Square310x310Logo.scale-100.png");
```

The activation arguments are passed into the app when it's activated from the secondary tile. For this demo, we'll just use very simple arguments:

```
string tileActivationArguments =TILEID + " WasPinnedAt=" +
    DateTime.Now.ToLocalTime().ToString();
```

Next, we create the secondary tile. There are several overloads for the constructor, and in this example, we are using the tile ID, display name, activation arguments, default logo, and default size.

```
SecondaryTile secondaryTile = new SecondaryTile(TILEID,
    "Title text shown on the tile",
    tileActivationArguments,
    logo,
    TileSize.Square150x150);
```

We then set the properties for the additional tiles to the secondary tile. This gives the user options for different sizes when pinning the tile. We also set RoamingEnabled to be false (if set to true, it will be on all of the user's Start screens).

```
secondaryTile.VisualElements.Wide310x150Logo = wideLogo;
secondaryTile.VisualElements.Square310x310Logo = largeLogo;
secondaryTile.RoamingEnabled = false;
```

Creating the GetElementRect Helper Method

When a secondary tile is requested by an app, a fly-out is created that lets users select which tile size to use as well as cancel if they change their mind. One of the required parameters for the request is a Rect that specifies where the fly-out will be displayed. Create a new method in PinnedPage.xaml.cs and add the following code:

```
public static Rect GetElementRect(FrameworkElement element)
{
    GeneralTransform buttonTransform = element.TransformToVisual(null);
    Point point = buttonTransform.TransformPoint(new Point());
    return new Rect(point, new Size(element.ActualWidth, element.ActualHeight));
}
```

Pinning the Tile

Back in the Create_Click event handler, we add the call RequestCreateForSelectionAsync on the secondary tile. This will create an overlay that allows users to confirm that they want to pin the tile and select which of the tile sizes to pin. The method returns a Boolean value representing whether the tile was pinned or not (e.g., if the user cancelled out of the dialog).

```
bool isPinned = await secondaryTile.RequestCreateForSelectionAsync(
    MainPage.GetElementRect((FrameworkElement)sender),
    Windows.UI.Popups.Placement.Below);
```

Because we are using await in the call, we must add the keyword async to the method declaration:

```
public async void Create_Click(object sender, RoutedEventArgs e)
{
```

Finally, update the TextBlock on the view to indicate if the tile was pinned.

```
if (isPinned)
{
    Message.Text = "Secondary tile successfully pinned.";
}
else
{
    Message.Text = "Secondary tile not pinned.";
}
```

Running the App and Creating the Tile

Run the application, navigate to the second page, and click the button to create the secondary tile. You will see a fly-out on which you can add text for the tile, as shown in Figure 9-7.

Figure 9-7. Notification fly-out

Once you click Pin to Start, the tile will be pinned to your Start screen, as shown in Figure 9-8.

Figure 9-8. *Secondary tile pinned*

Responding to Secondary Tile Launch

Creating a secondary tile doesn't do much good if your app doesn't know when the secondary tile was used to launch your app. Fortunately, this is easy! When an app is launched from a secondary tile, the launch arguments in the secondary tile get passed into the app as the LaunchActivatedEventArgs.

Choosing the Start Page

If your app will load the same page regardless of how it is launched, you don't need to do anything in this code. However, that kind of defeats the advantages of pinning a particular page in your app. You should examine the launch arguments and determine what your app needs to do based on the type of launch and the arguments passed in.

Open App.xaml.cs and navigate to the bottom of the OnLaunched event handler after the block:

```
if (rootFrame == null)
```

And navigate to the one before it:

```
if (rootFrame.Content == null)
```

Add the following code:

```
Type launchType = null;
if (!String.IsNullOrEmpty(e.Arguments))
{
    launchType = typeof(PinnedPage);
}
```

```
else
{
    launchType = typeof(MainPage);
}
```

Since the navigation method requires the type of the page to be loaded, we declare a variable to pass into the navigate method. We then determine if arguments exist, and if so, set the type to PinnedPage. If not, we set the type to MainPage (the default).

Then, we need to change this line:

```
rootFrame.Navigate(typeof(MainPage), e.Arguments);
```

to this one:

```
rootFrame.Navigate(launchType, e.Arguments);
```

Getting the Launch Args

Open PinnedPage.xaml.cs, and navigate to the override for the OnNavigatedTo event.

```
protected override void OnNavigatedTo(NavigationEventArgs e)
{
    base.OnNavigatedTo(e);
}
```

The LaunchActivatedEventArgs get passed into the Main page as the parameter of the NavigationEventArgs. Set the Message TextBlock to the arguments passed in from the tile:

```
if (e != null && e.Parameter != null && !String.IsNullOrEmpty(e.Parameter.ToString()))
{
    Message.Text = e.Parameter.ToString();
}
base.OnNavigatedTo(e);
```

Testing the App

If you pinned the secondary tile to the Start screen in the previous step, go ahead and remove it (right-click on the tile, select Unpin from Start from the command bar).

To test your code, run the app, navigate to the second page, and (re)create the secondary tile. Close the app. Go to your Start screen and launch the app from the secondary tile. You should see something similar to Figure 9-9.

Figure 9-9. *Launched from the secondary tile*

Debugging the Secondary Tile Launch

If you want to debug your app, you need to change a setting on the Build tab of the project properties. To get to the correct tab, go to Debug ➤ SecondaryTiles Properties. Select the option "Do not launch, but debug my code when it starts," as shown in Figure 9-10.

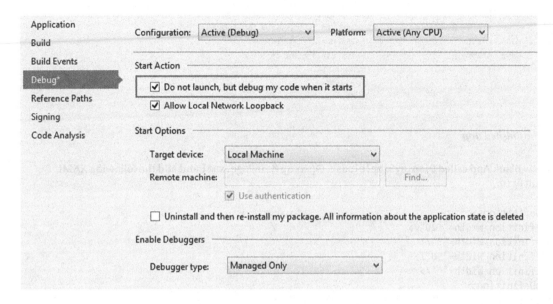

Figure 9-10. *Debugging secondary tile launch*

When that option is selected, running the app will not bring up the UI. Visual Studio will wait for an app activation, and then attach to that process. Set a break point in the OnNavigatedTo event handler, and click on the secondary tile on the Start screen. Visual Studio will break on that line, allowing you to debug your app when started from the secondary tile.

Toast Notifications

A toast notification is a bit of a misnomer, left over from when these notifications used to pop up on the lower-right-hand corner of the user's screen, not unlike toast popping up out of the toaster. Today, toast notifications show up in the right-hand corner as short banners with text and/or images. The user can ignore them (and they will fade away), dismiss them, or click on them to go to the associated program.

Creating the Toast Notification Sample App

To create the toast notification sample app, we'll use a similar sample app as we used for the live tiles demo. The app will create toast notifications manually from the templates as well as use the NotificationsExtensions project from Microsoft. The UI will have two buttons to create toast notifications (one for XML manipulation and the other for the NotificationsExtensions) and two buttons to clear the results panes. The result will be similar to Figure 9-11.

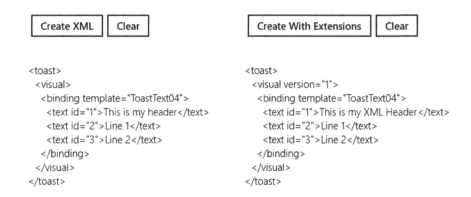

Figure 9-11. *The finished app*

Create a new Blank App called `DisplaySimpleToast`. Open up `MainPage.xaml` and add the following XAML inside the default Grid:

```
<Grid.ColumnDefinitions>
    <ColumnDefinition Width="120"/>
    <ColumnDefinition Width="*"/>
    <ColumnDefinition Width="50"/>
    <ColumnDefinition Width="*"/>
</Grid.ColumnDefinitions>
<Grid.RowDefinitions>
    <RowDefinition Height="100" />
    <RowDefinition Height="Auto" />
    <RowDefinition Height="*" />
</Grid.RowDefinitions>
<StackPanel  Grid.Column="1" Grid.Row="0" Orientation="Horizontal">
    <Button Name="CreateTileWithXML" Content="Create XML"
        Click="CreateToastWithXML_Click"/>
    <Button Name="ClearTilesXML"
        Content="Clear"
        Click="ClearToast_Click"/>
</StackPanel>
<TextBlock Name="TextBasedXML" TextWrapping="WrapWholeWords"
Grid.Column="1" Grid.Row="1" Style="{StaticResource BodyTextBlockStyle}"></TextBlock>
<StackPanel  Grid.Column="3" Grid.Row="0" Orientation="Horizontal">
    <Button Name="CreateTileWithExtensions"
        Content="Create With Extensions"
        Click="CreateToastWithExtensions_Click"/>
    <Button Name="ClearTilesExt"
        Content="Clear"
        Click="ClearToastExt_Click"/>
</StackPanel>
<TextBlock Name="ExtensionBasedXML" TextWrapping="WrapWholeWords"
Grid.Column="3" Grid.Row="1" Style="{StaticResource BodyTextBlockStyle}"></TextBlock>
```

Create the event handlers in `MainPage.xaml.cs`:

```
public void CreateToastWithXML_Click(object sender, RoutedEventArgs e)
{
}
public void ClearToast_Click(object sender, RoutedEventArgs e)
{
}
public void CreateToastWithExtensions_Click(object sender, RoutedEventArgs e)
{
}
public void ClearToastExt_Click(object sender, RoutedEventArgs e)
{
}
```

Updating the Manifest

Windows 8.1 added a manifest setting for toast notifications. To have toast enabled for your app, open the `Package.appxmanifest`, and on the Application tab, select Yes for toast capable, as shown in Figure 9-12.

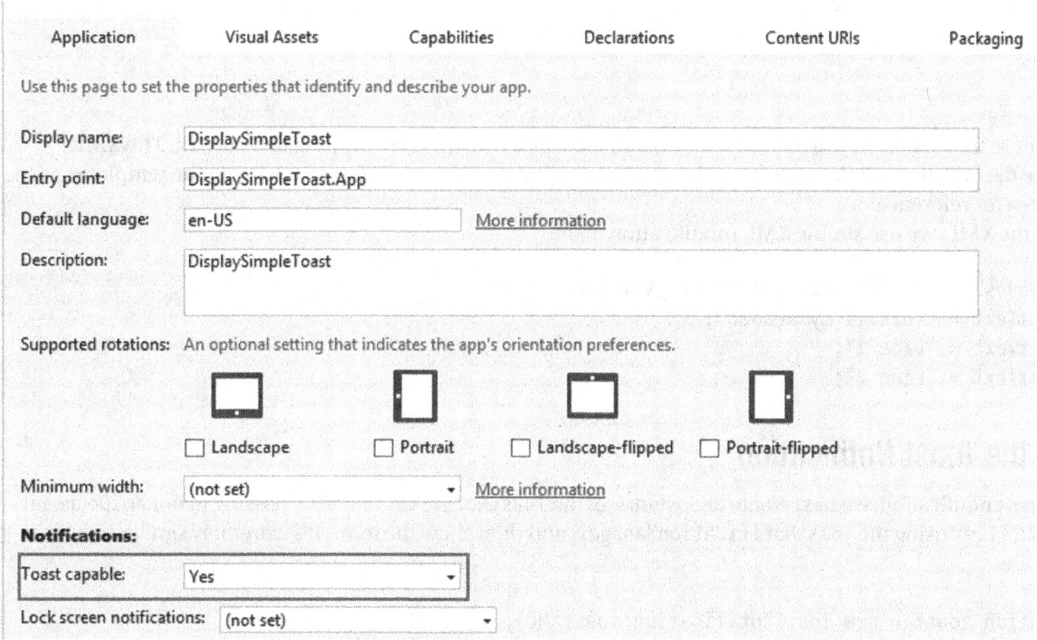

Figure 9-12. Allowing toast in the App Manifest

Creating Toast Notifications Manually

Toast notifications come in a variety of formats, including images and/or text. All of the available options can be found at http://bit.ly/OkFO9S. For these examples, I have chosen to use the `ToastText04` format, which includes one line of bold (header) and two lines of nonwrapping text.

229

Creating the Toast Data

To get the XML for the template, use the ToastNotificationManager (in the Windows.UI.Notifications namespace) and call the GetTemplateContent method. Passing in the desired template (using the ToastTemplateType enumeration) will return an XmlDocument (in the Windows.Data.Xml.Dom.XmlDocument namespace).

Then, add the following namespace to the top of the file:

```
using Windows.UI.Notifications;
using Windows.Data.Xml.Dom.XmlDocument;
```

Now, add the following line to the CreateToastWithXML_Click method:

```
XmlDocument toastXML = ToastNotificationManager.GetTemplateContent(ToastTemplateType.ToastText04);
```

The XML from the template is shown here for your reference:

```
<toast>
    <visual>
        <binding template="ToastText04">
            <text id="1"></text>
            <text id="2"></text>
            <text id="3"></text>
        </binding>
    </visual>
</toast>
```

The first line is the header (it will appear in bold) and the other two are nonwrapping lines of text. The XML doesn't indicate the layouts, so unless you have the templates memorized, you might want to keep the templates page from MSDN open for reference.

To update the XML, we use simple XML modification code:

```
XmlNodeList nodes = toastXML.GetElementsByTagName("text");
nodes[0].InnerText = "This is my header";
nodes[1].InnerText = "Line 1";
nodes[2].InnerText = "Line 2";
```

Launching the Toast Notification

To launch the toast notification, we next create an instance of the ToastNotification class, passing in our XmlDocument, create a ToastNotifier using the ToastNotificationManager, and then show the toast. It's extremely similar to how we created live tiles:

```
ToastNotification toast = new ToastNotification(toastXML);
ToastNotifier notifier = ToastNotificationManager.CreateToastNotifier();
notifier.Show(toast);
```

Then, we display the XML in the left pane of the UI. As a reminder, this has nothing to do with the process of creating a toast notification; it just helps to compare the XML created manually vs. the XML created using the NotificationsExtensions project from Microsoft.

```
TextBasedXML.Text = XDocument.Parse(toastXML.GetXml()).ToString();
```

Finally, we run the app and click on Create XML, where we will see a screen similar to Figure 9-13 (with the excess blank space removed).

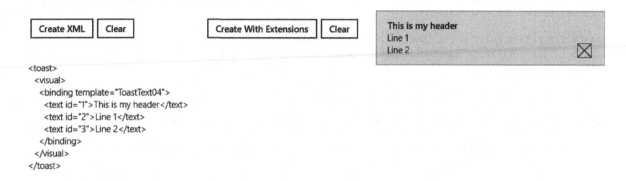

```
<toast>
 <visual>
  <binding template="ToastText04">
   <text id="1">This is my header</text>
   <text id="2">Line 1</text>
   <text id="3">Line 2</text>
  </binding>
 </visual>
</toast>
```

Figure 9-13. *Showing the toast notification and the XML created*

CAN I REMOVE THE LOGO FROM A TOAST NOTIFICATION?

Just like live tiles, you can add a "branding" attribute to the binding node. However, unlike live tiles, this attribute is ignored for toast notifications. So there isn't any way at this time to remove the logo from that toast notification.

Creating Toast Notification Through the Notifications Extensions

Once again, add in the NotificationsExtensions project or the reference to the NotificationsExtensions.winmd (both are provided with the sample code for this chapter). Still in MainPage.xaml.cs, add a using for the ToastContent:

```
using NotificationsExtensions.ToastContent;
```

To create the ToastContent, we use the ToastContentFactory to return an instance of the template that we want to use. Each of the templates has an interface that represents the values and options that can be set. In our case, we are creating an instance of the IToastText04 interface. After creating this instance, add the values to the Heading and the TextBody. Add the following code to the CreateToastWithExtensions_Click method:

```
IToastText04 toastContent = ToastContentFactory.CreateToastText04();
toastContent.TextHeading.Text = "This is my XML Header";
toastContent.TextBody1.Text = "Line 1";
toastContent.TextBody2.Text = "Line 2";
```

Launching the Toast Notification

To launch the toast notification here, we then use the `IToastText04` interface method `CreateNotification` to create the toast notification, and use the `ToastNotificationManager` (just like we did when we created the code manually) to show the toast as follows:

```
ToastNotification toast = toastContent.CreateNotification();
ToastNotifier notifier = ToastNotificationManager.CreateToastNotifier();
notifier.Show(toast);
```

Finally, we display the XML in a friendly format in the UI:

```
ExtensionBasedXML.Text = XDocument.Parse(toastContent.GetContent()).ToString();
```

When you run app and click both buttons, you will get two toast notifications, as in Figure 9-14.

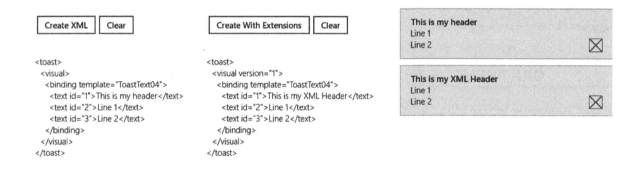

Figure 9-14. *Toast notifications*

Resetting the UI

Since toast notifications don't persist like live tiles, resetting the UI is very simple. All you need to do is clear out all the occurrences of a `TextBlock`:

```
public void ClearToast_Click(object sender, RoutedEventArgs e)
{
    TextBasedXML.Text = "";
}
public void ClearToastExt_Click(object sender, RoutedEventArgs e)
{
    ExtensionBasedXML.Text = "";
}
```

Responding to Toast Notification Launch

Responding to an app activation from toast is very similar to responding to that of an activation from a secondary tile. The `Launch` parameter is passed into the app in the `OnLaunched` event and is then passed to the loaded window as part of the navigation parameters. Well, that's true if the app isn't currently running, the toast was scheduled, or came from the app through a background notification.

When the app is currently running, the OnLaunched event doesn't fire (it's already running) and the OnNavigatedTo event (in our example) doesn't fire because the Main Page is already the loaded page. In this case, we can use the Activated event on the ToastNotifier to wire up an event handler to respond to the user clicking on the toast notification.

Updating the UI

When the toast is clicked, we want to visually show that the notification back to the app was received. We are going to use a simple TextBlock to do this. Open MainPage.xaml and add the following XAML just before the closing <Grid> element:

```
<TextBlock Name="LaunchParameter" Grid.Column="1"
Grid.ColumnSpan="3" Grid.Row="2"
Style="{StaticResource HeaderTextBlockStyle}" />
```

Adding a Launch Parameter

The Launch parameter is an attribute on the root node ("toast") in the XML payload. Adding this is very simple regardless if you are using the raw XML method or the NotificationsExtensions.

Add this to CreateToastWithXML_Click (just before creating the ToastNotification instance) as follows:

```
toastXML.DocumentElement.SetAttribute("launch", "Activated from XML Toast");
```

Add this to CreateToastWithExtensions_Click (just before creating the ToastNotification instance):

```
toastContent.Launch = "Activated from Toast";
```

Adding the Event Handler

The rest of the code is the same regardless of the method you used. Add the following code to both Click events just after creating the ToastNotification:

```
toast.Activated += toast_Activated;
```

Let Visual Studio create the event handler (or add it in manually). Update the method so it's marked async.

```
async void toast_Activated(ToastNotification sender, object args)
{
}
```

The next part takes some background information. Windows was and is a single-threaded UI. We can certainly spin up additional threads and tasks and run them in the background (as we've done many times in this book), but at the end of it all, only a single thread can update the UI.

When a toast notification is clicked on a running application, the thread that notifies the app that the toast was clicked is *not* the UI thread. More often than not, this is OK, as the event handler is probably going to do some work and then navigate to another page. In our example, we are just updating a TextBlock, so we need to marshal the callback to the UI thread.

To do this, we will use the `Dispatcher` (in the `Windows.UI.Core` namespace) and call `RunAsync`. The `RunAsync` method takes two parameters, the first is the priority, the second is the function to be called. For our example, we can set the `Priority` to `Normal` and use an anonymous function to update the UI. Add the following code into the `toast_Activated` method.

```
await Dispatcher.RunAsync(
Windows.UI.Core.CoreDispatcherPriority.Normal,
()=>LaunchParameter.Text =((ToastActivatedEventArgs)args).Arguments);
```

Now when you run the app, create the toast, and the click on the toast, your UI should resemble Figure 9-15.

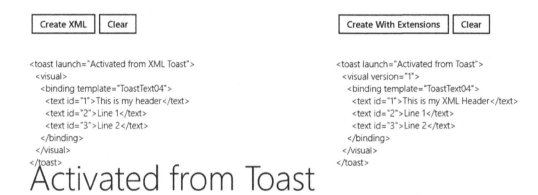

Figure 9-15. *Activated from toast*

Push Notifications with Windows Notification Service (WNS) and Windows Azure Mobile Services (WAMS)

Everything we've shown you so far in this chapter has dealt with local notifications. Push notifications have a few more moving parts than the various local notification types. The key ingredient is the Windows Push Notification Service, or WNS. There are many different services available that can be used to create push notifications, but by far the easiest is to use Windows Azure Mobile Services, or WAMS. For more information, see: `http://bit.ly/1kyPxnL`.

WNS Interaction Overview

The workflow involves six steps (as detailed in Figure 9-16). Following the numbers in the figure, here are the steps:

1. Your application requests a channel from the Notification Client Platform.

2. The Notification Client Platform communicates with the WNS to obtain a notification channel.

3. The Notification Client Platform returns the URI for the channel to your Windows Store application.

4. Your application sends the channel URI to your cloud service, where it is stored until needed.

5. When your cloud service has a notification to send to your user, it will authenticate with WNS, and then send the content and channel URI to WNS.

6. WNS sends the notification to the Notification Client Platform, which will then handle the toast or tile updates.

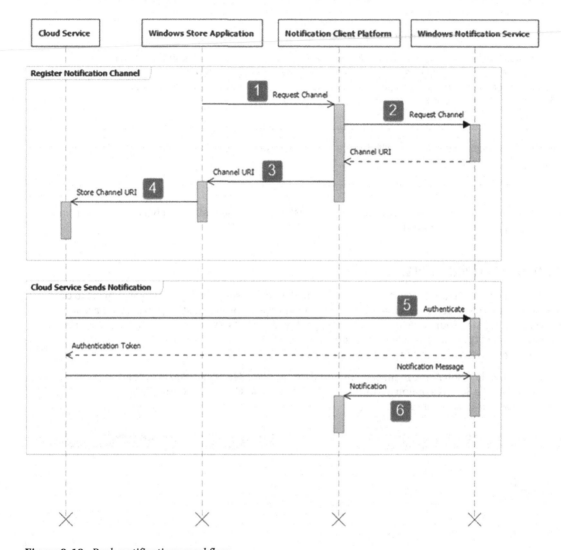

Figure 9-16. *Push notifications workflow*

Why Use WAMS

WAMS is a great way to handle the cloud service portion of a push notification architecture for a number of reasons:

- It handles a lot of the plumbing for you—for example, OAuth2 authentication with WNS.

- It provides a preconfigured, free server infrastructure, whereas WNS requires that you have a backing server.

- It works with other push notification systems, such as SMS.

- It works with other platforms capable of receiving push notifications, such as iOS and Android.

- You can configure notifications using insert scripts on the server, which means you can make changes or enhancements to your notifications without needing to deploy an updated Windows Store client application.

- You can scale with Notification Hubs if needed.

- It is extremely inexpensive for most use cases. MSDN subscribers get a threshold of use in the free tier. At the time of this writing, all of the pricing is being lowered but Microsoft. Actual cost depends on your usage and subscription level. For more information see: http://azure.microsoft.com/en-us/.

■ **Note** The Mobile Services calculator is available here: www.windowsazure.com/en-us/pricing/calculator/?scenario=mobile.

We'll walk through setting up push notifications using WAMS first, and then talk about what's required if you want to host your own cloud service outside of WAMS.

Creating an Azure Mobile Service

If you haven't registered for an Azure account, you'll need to do that first. It should take about five minutes to do. The process requires entering a credit card, but there's an automatic spending cap of $0 applied to your account, so no money will be charged to your credit card until you explicitly remove the spending cap. You can sign up for a free Azure account here: http://aka.ms/progwin8-azure.

Next, you'll create a new Windows Azure Mobile Service.

1. Log into the Microsoft Azure management portal (http://manage.windowsazure.com), click the Mobile Services option in the left rail, and then click "Create a new mobile service," as shown in Figure 9-17.

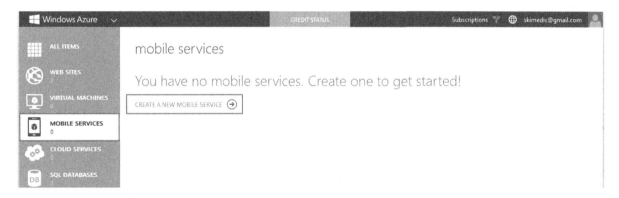

Figure 9-17. *Creating a new mobile service*

2. The Create a Mobile Service dialog requires you to select a subdomain. This is a real, public URL on the Internet, so you'll need to pick something unique. For this example, I'm picking "ProWindows8XAMLNotificationSample"; since I've taken that one, you'll need to come up with something different!

3. Once you've got a working URL, select "Create a free 20MB SQL Database" in the database dropdown (unless you've already got a Windows Azure SQL database configured), and then click the arrow to advance to the next step in the wizard, as shown in Figure 9-18.

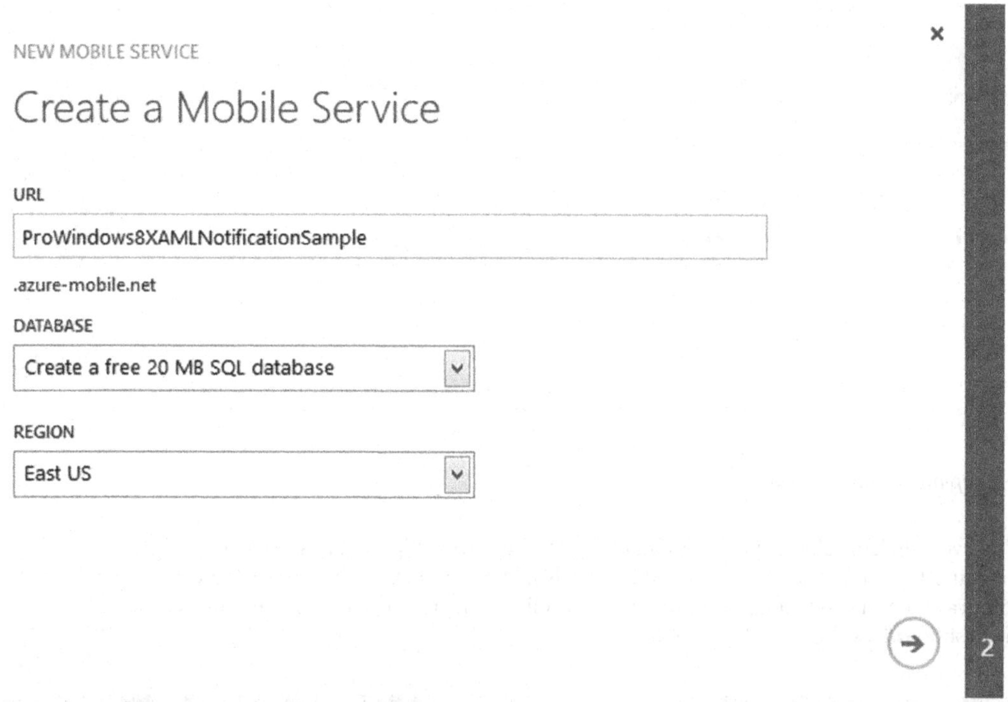

NEW MOBILE SERVICE

Create a Mobile Service

URL

ProWindows8XAMLNotificationSample

.azure-mobile.net

DATABASE

Create a free 20 MB SQL database

REGION

East US

2

Figure 9-18. *Creating a Mobile Service Wizard*

4. The next wizard step requires you to enter the information for the new SQL database, as shown in Figure 9-19.

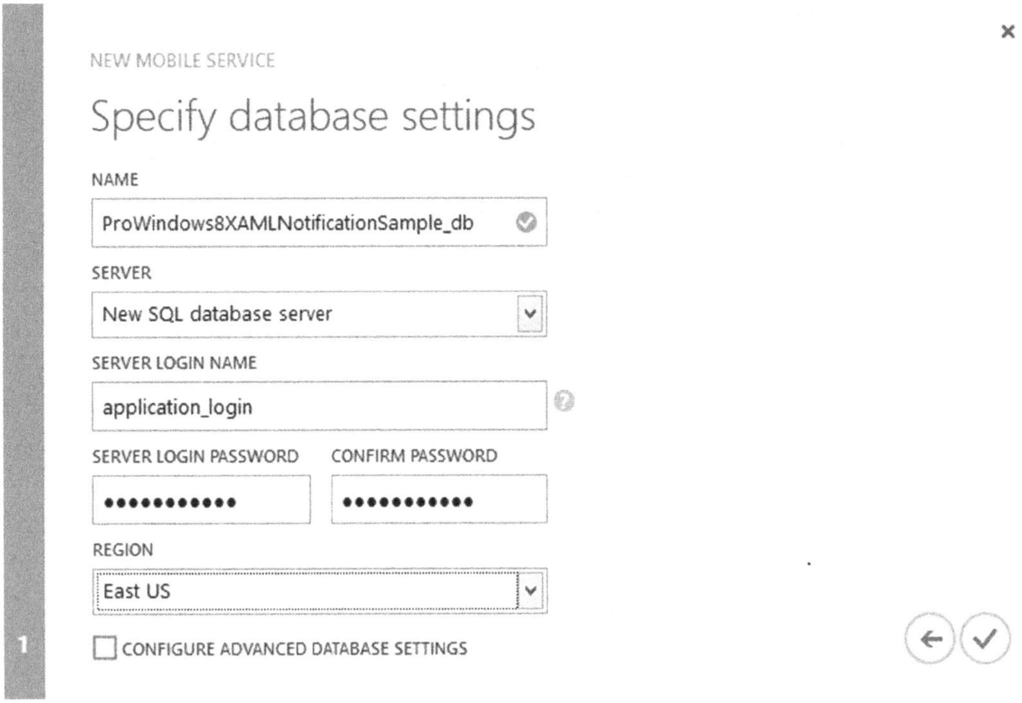

Figure 9-19. *Specifying database settings wizard*

5. When you click the checkmark to indicate you are done, the new WAMS site will be configured. After a short wait (for me it was fairly instantaneous, but based on traffic and other variables it can take up to 20 seconds), you'll see the new mobile service show up in the dashboard, as shown in Figure 9-20.

Figure 9-20. *Mobile services dashboard*

6. Clicking on the name of the mobile service shows the Quick Start screen, as shown in Figure 9-21.

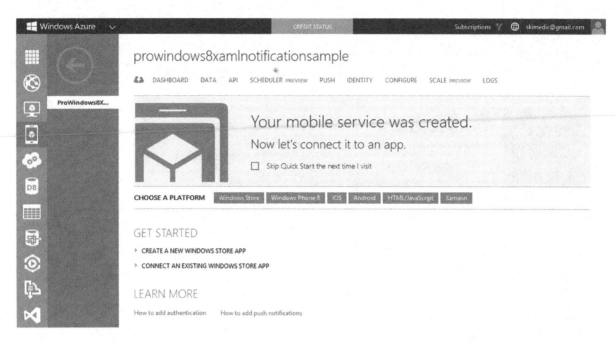

Figure 9-21. Quick Start screen

■ **Note**   The Quick Start screen also shows the necessary steps for connecting to an existing Windows Store application. We've decided to show the new Windows Store application example for two reasons. First, it allows us to focus on notifications and avoid the distraction of repeating the File/New Windows Store application instructions we've already covered multiple times. Second, we recommend that you start with this approach to get familiar with WAMS-based notifications before you move on to adding it to your existing Windows Store applications.

7. For this example, we'll be extending the Todo Quick Start sample to include push notifications. Expand the Create a New Windows Store App section.

■ **Note**   If you've made it this far into this book, you already have Visual Studio installed. If you don't already have Visual Studio installed, you can install it in Step 1 of the Create a New Windows Store app. Microsoft is making every effort to streamline the app generation and notifications process by providing a mechanism to install Visual Studio from the WAMS process.

8. Next, you'll create the TodoItem table. Click the Create TodoItem Table button, as shown in Figure 9-22.

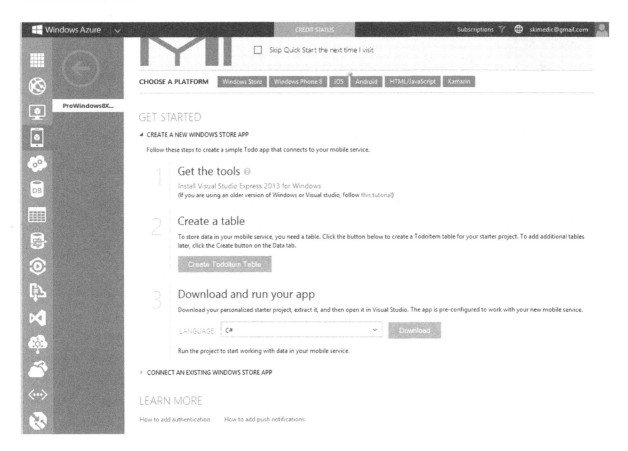

Figure 9-22. *Creating the Todo Item table*

9. Finally, click the Download button to download a Windows Store application that is preconfigured to connect to your Mobile Service instance. This will download a Zip file containing the application code. Before extracting the Zip file, you might need to unblock the file. To do so, right-click the Zip file, select Properties, and click the Unblock button, as shown in Figure 9-23.

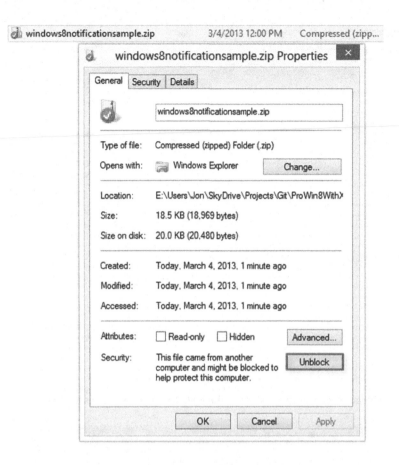

Figure 9-23. *Unblocking the Zip file*

Restoring the Packages

To restore the package, open the Visual Studio project. The first thing you will notice is all of the compile errors. This is because the NuGet packages don't come with the download. The solution is configured to restore the packages after it is downloaded.

This application is preconfigured to work with WAMS but doesn't include notification support yet. Before setting up notifications, we'll take a look at the basic Mobile Services support. To do so, right-click on the project and select Manage NuGet packages. You will see the dialog box shown in Figure 9-24. Notice the top line explaining that some packages are missing from the solution and the button on the right to restore the missing packages.

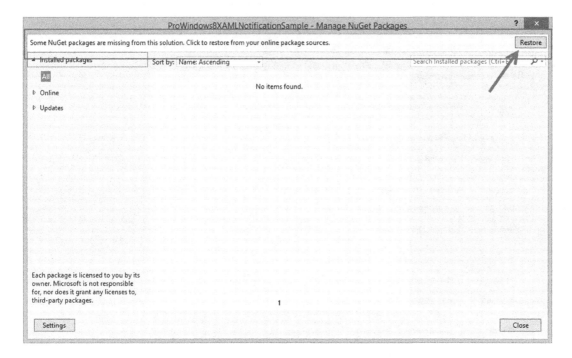

Figure 9-24. *Missing NuGet packages*

After clicking on the Restore button, the installed packages will show in the Installed Packages list, as in Figure 9-25.

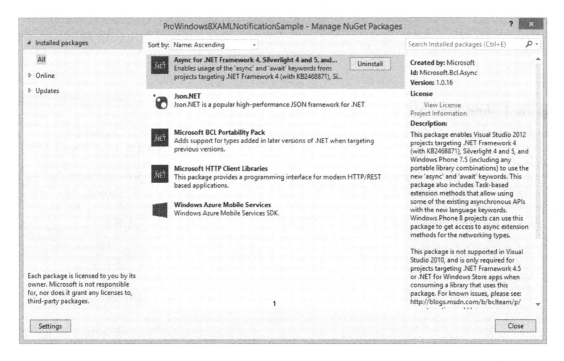

Figure 9-25. *Installed NuGet packages*

Examining the WAMS application

The application contains a single page, `MainPage.xaml`. This page allows you to add a new item to a Todo list, which will be saved in the database on the server. The form appears as shown in Figure 9-26.

WINDOWS AZURE MOBILE SERVICES

ProWindows8XAMLNotificationSample

1 **Insert a TodoItem**
Enter some text below and click Save to insert a new todo item into your database

[   ] Save

2 **Query and Update Data**
Click refresh below to load the unfinished TodoItems from your database. Use the checkbox to complete and update your TodoItems

Refresh

Figure 9-26. *Todo List Form*

■ **Note**   If you are seeing numbers in the upper corners of the screen, open `App.xaml.cs` and comment out the following line to disable the frame rate counter: `this.DebugSettings.EnableFrameRateCounter = true;`

Open `MainPage.xaml.cs`. This page has a simple `TodoItem` class at the top.

```
public class TodoItem
{
    public string Id { get; set; }

    [JsonProperty(PropertyName = "text")]
    public string Text { get; set; }

    [JsonProperty(PropertyName = "complete")]
    public bool Complete { get; set; }
}
```

This is a standard POCO (Plain Old CLR Object), which uses two `DataMember` attributes to map between C# uppercase property names and lowercase names. While not required, this is helpful if you are also working with JavaScript-based applications where the common pattern is to use camel casing on properties, while in C# the common pattern is to use Pascal casing for properties.

WAMS provides a lightweight client that allows you to interact with data on the server as if it were simple local collections. First, the page includes an instance of `IMobileServiceTable<TodoItem>` and a `MobileServiceCollection<TodoItem,TodoItem>`.

```
private MobileServiceCollection<TodoItem, TodoItem> items;
private IMobileServiceTable<TodoItem> todoTable = App.MobileService.GetTable<TodoItem>();
```

This page contains a call to `RefreshItems` in the `OnNavigatedTo` event, which uses a LINQ query to populate the `MobileServicesCollection` with Todo items that have not yet been marked complete.

```
protected override void OnNavigatedTo(NavigationEventArgs e)
{
    RefreshTodoItems();
}
```

```
private async void RefreshTodoItems()
{
    MobileServiceInvalidOperationException exception = null;
    try
    {
        // This code refreshes the entries in the list view by querying the TodoItems table.
        // The query excludes completed TodoItems
        items = await todoTable
            .Where(todoItem => todoItem.Complete == false)
            .ToCollectionAsync();
    }
    catch (MobileServiceInvalidOperationException e)
    {
        exception = e;
    }

    if (exception != null)
    {
        await new MessageDialog(exception.Message, "Error loading items").ShowAsync();
    }
    else
    {
        ListItems.ItemsSource = items;
    }
}
```

The rest of the methods on Main Page just interact directly with the MobileCollectionView, which pushes updates to WAMS using InsertAsync and UpdateAsync calls.

Next, open App.xaml.cs. You'll see that it declares a static instance of the MobileServicesClient, along with your secret application key. You'll want to safeguard this key in your application; that is, don't include it in code that's checked into a public source-code repository. This application key was prepopulated in our generated code, but it's also available in the WAMS portal, and you can reset it there if it's accidentally disclosed.

```
// This MobileServiceClient has been configured to communicate with your Mobile Service's url
// and application key. You're all set to start working with your Mobile Service!
public static MobileServiceClient MobileService = new MobileServiceClient(
    "https://ProWindows8XAMLNotificationSample.azure-mobile.net/",
    "yoursecretapplicationkey"
);
```

That's all there is to it. Run the application and add a Todo item, and then click Save, as shown in Figure 9-27.

WINDOWS AZURE MOBILE SERVICES

ProWindows8XAMLNotificationSample

1

Insert a TodoItem
Enter some text below and click Save to insert a new todo item into your database

| Sample ToDo Item| | ✕ | **Save** |

Figure 9-27. Inserting a Todo item

Now, let's take a look at the data in the Windows Azure portal. View your mobile service and click on the Data tab. You should see one record listed, as shown in Figure 9-28.

Figure 9-28. One item listed

Click on the table name (TodoItem) and you'll see the newly added item values, as shown in Figure 9-29.

Figure 9-29. Examining the table contents

Next, we'll extend it to add support for notifications.

Registering Your Windows Store Application

As we discussed earlier, push notifications require interaction with the Windows Push Notification Service, and that requires registering your Windows Store application. Fortunately, that's a pretty-easy process, but it requires a Windows Store Developer Account. To create an account:

1. Navigate to `http://dev.windows.com`.

2. On your account dashboard, select Submit an App.

3. Click on the App Name icon, as shown in Figure 9-30.

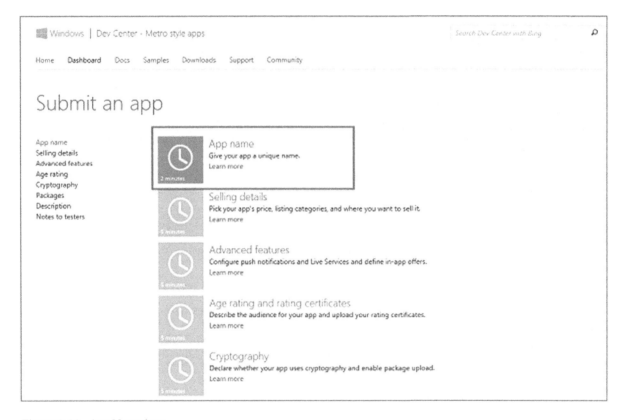

Figure 9-30. *App Name icon*

4. Next, you'll need to enter a (unique) name for your application, as shown in Figure 9-31.

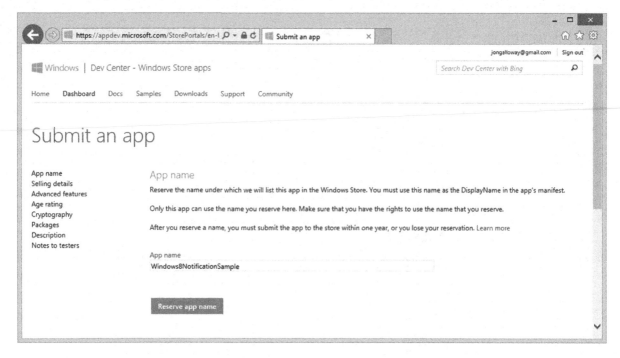

Figure 9-31. Entering a name for your application

    5.   After you've reserved the name, you'll be returned to the App Details view, where you can now click on the Services bar to configure push notifications, as shown in Figure 9-32.

ProWindows8XAMLNotificationSample: Release 1

App name
Selling details
Services
Age rating
Cryptography
Packages
Description
Notes to testers

News

Free Phone developer account
Add Windows 8.1 packages
Increase in app roaming limits
Age ratings
Latest Windows ACK

App name

You reserved an app name.

You can reserve other names for your app to use in different languages or to change your app's name.

Learn more

Complete

Selling details

Pick your app's price, listing categories, and where you want to sell it.

Learn more

5 minutes

Services

Add push notifications, authenticate users, enable cloud storage, and define in-app offers.

Learn more

5 minutes

Age rating and rating certificates

Describe the audience for your app and upload your rating certificates.

Learn more

5 minutes

Cryptography

Declare whether your app uses cryptography and enable package upload.

Learn more

5 minutes

Packages

Upload your app to the Windows Store.
To enable this step, complete the Cryptography page.

Learn more

30 minutes

Description

Briefly describe for your customers what your app does.

Learn more

30 minutes

Notes to testers

Add notes about this release for the people who will review your app.

Learn more

2 minutes

Figure 9-32. *Services*

6. On the Services page, click the push notifications and Live Services link, as shown in
    Figure 9-33.

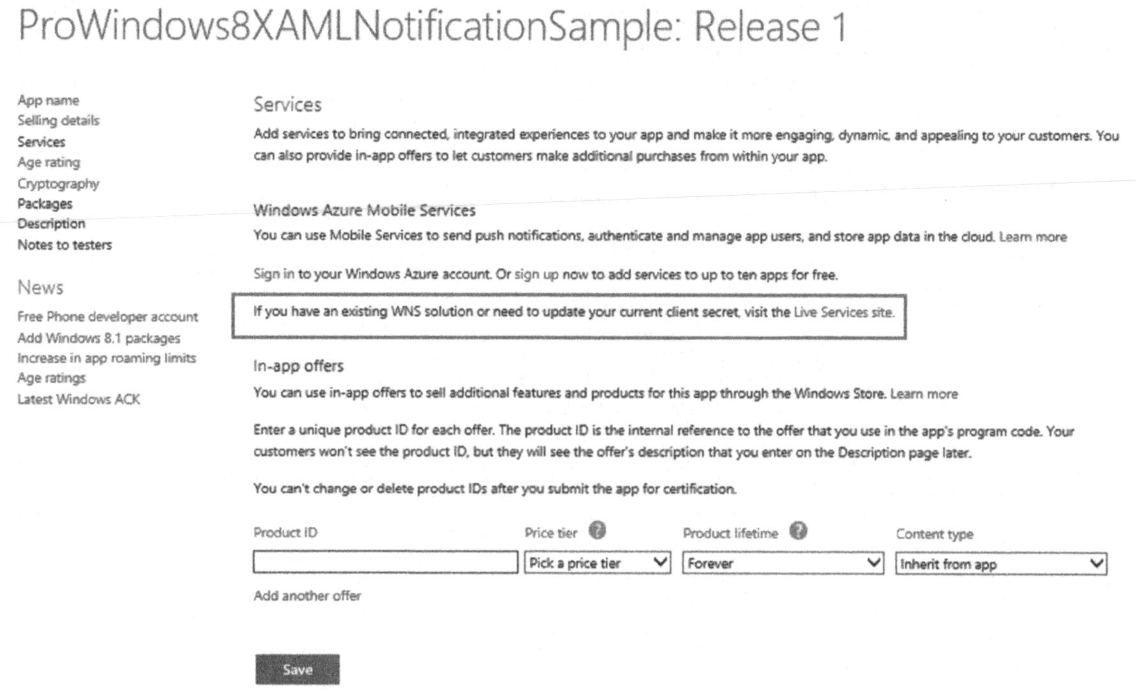

ProWindows8XAMLNotificationSample: Release 1

App name
Selling details
Services
Age rating
Cryptography
Packages
Description
Notes to testers

News

Free Phone developer account
Add Windows 8.1 packages
Increase in app roaming limits
Age ratings
Latest Windows ACK

Services

Add services to bring connected, integrated experiences to your app and make it more engaging, dynamic, and appealing to your customers. You can also provide in-app offers to let customers make additional purchases from within your app.

Windows Azure Mobile Services

You can use Mobile Services to send push notifications, authenticate and manage app users, and store app data in the cloud. Learn more

Sign in to your Windows Azure account. Or sign up now to add services to up to ten apps for free.

If you have an existing WNS solution or need to update your current client secret, visit the Live Services site.

In-app offers

You can use in-app offers to sell additional features and products for this app through the Windows Store. Learn more

Enter a unique product ID for each offer. The product ID is the internal reference to the offer that you use in the app's program code. Your customers won't see the product ID, but they will see the offer's description that you enter on the Description page later.

You can't change or delete product IDs after you submit the app for certification.

Product ID	Price tier ❷	Product lifetime ❷	Content type
	Pick a price tier ▾	Forever ▾	Inherit from app ▾

Add another offer

Save

Figure 9-33. *Services*

7.   On the push Live services info page, click Activate.

Updating Your App's Identity (Associating Your App with the Store)

In order to use Push notifications, you must associate your app with the store. If you have already uploaded your app (which we haven't), this will be done for you. For our example, we will use Visual Studio to make the association.

1.   Right-click on the Project name in the Solution Explorer, and first select Store and then Associate App with the Store, as in Figure 9-34.

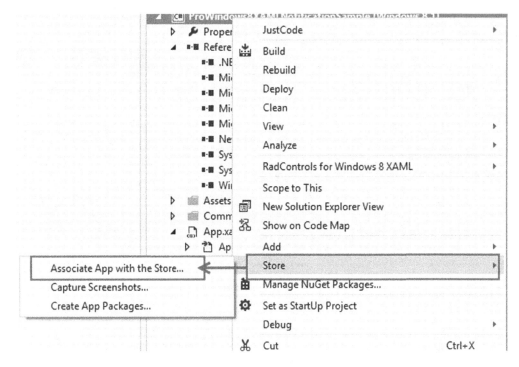

Figure 9-34. *Starting the Association Wizard*

2. The next step in the wizard (Figure 9-35) explains what is going to happen. After reading it, just click Next.

Figure 9-35. *Overview of the association process*

3. The next screen that appears (Figure 9-36) will list all of the registered apps in your Developer account. Note that you might have to log in prior to getting to this screen. Select the correct name (if there is more than one) and click Next.

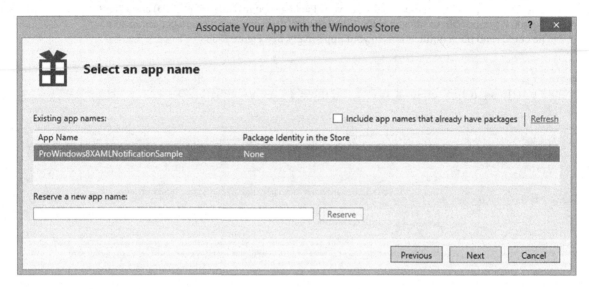

Figure 9-36. *Selecting the correct app*

4. When the screen comes prompting you to associate your app with the Windows store, finish the process by clicking on the Associate button.

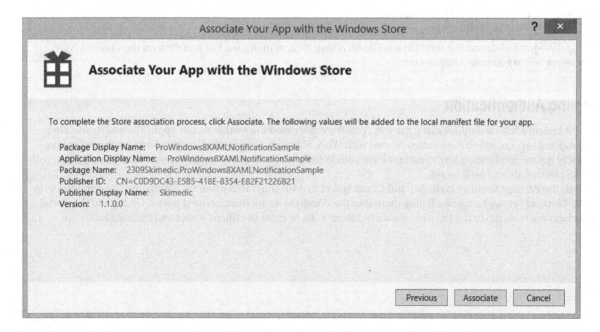

Figure 9-37. *Finalizing the association*

The final step will update the App Manifest with the correct values, specifically the Package Name and Publisher (if necessary) as well as the Version (incrementing the Minor version by 1).

5.   Click on Authenticating Your Service in the left rail or on the link at the bottom of the page. The next screen that comes up will show your Package Security Identifier (SID) and Client Secret. It's important to safeguard the Client Secret; if anyone else were to get access to it, he could send illicit notifications to your app's users. See Figure 9-38.

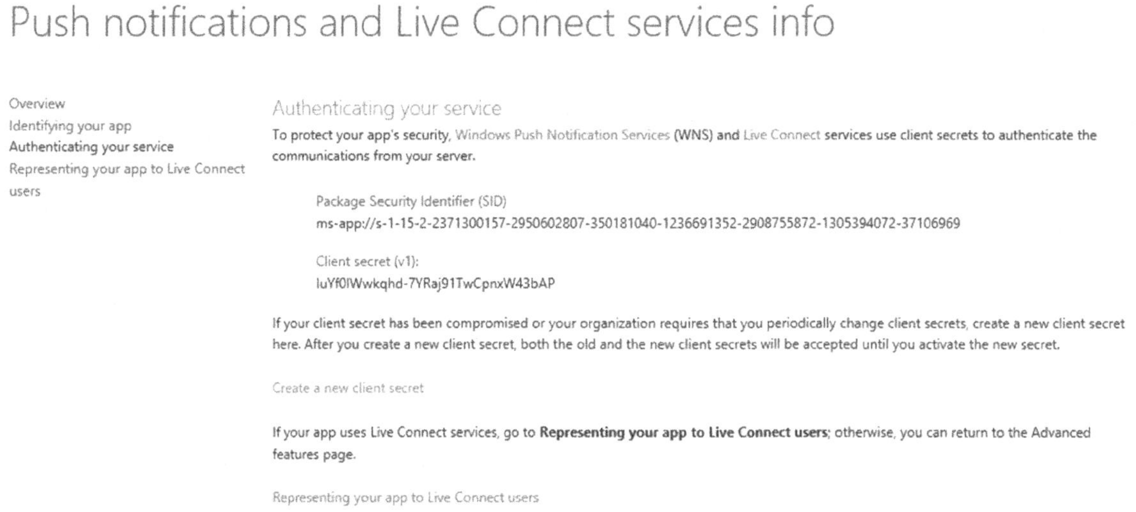

Push notifications and Live Connect services info

Overview
Identifying your app
Authenticating your service
Representing your app to Live Connect users

Authenticating your service

To protect your app's security, Windows Push Notification Services (WNS) and Live Connect services use client secrets to authenticate the communications from your server.

Package Security Identifier (SID)
ms-app://s-1-15-2-2371300157-2950602807-350181040-1236691352-2908755872-1305394072-37106969

Client secret (v1):
luYf0IWwkqhd-7YRaj91TwCpnxW43bAP

If your client secret has been compromised or your organization requires that you periodically change client secrets, create a new client secret here. After you create a new client secret, both the old and the new client secrets will be accepted until you activate the new secret.

Create a new client secret

If your app uses Live Connect services, go to **Representing your app to Live Connect users**; otherwise, you can return to the Advanced features page.

Representing your app to Live Connect users

Figure 9-38. *Package Security ID and Client Secret*

Oops! We just published our secret in a book! All is lost! Well, actually, we can just click on the Create a New Client Secret link to generate a new secret.

Handling Authentication

We've picked up a few credentials along the way. When we discussed the workflow, our application authenticated with the cloud service, which then authenticated with WNS. Since we downloaded the Windows Store application, it's already got the Application Key to authenticate with WAMS. We just need to configure our WAMS application with the WNS credentials and we'll be set.

Grab the Package Security Identifier and Client Secret that we generated when we configured our application in the Live Connect Services page; we'll plug them into the Windows Azure management portal. Go back to the portal and click on the Push tab in the top row, shown in Figure 9-39, to enter the Client Secret and Package SID.

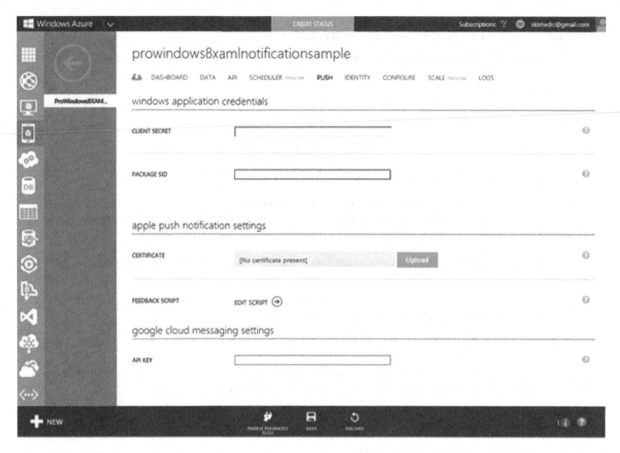

Figure 9-39. *Push tab*

Copy the Client Secret and Package SID values from the Live Services Connect page into the WASM push/Windows Application Credentials section, and click the Save button. The Save button doesn't show up until you make a change on the page.

Updating Your Windows Store App to Use Push Notifications

Now that the plumbing is in place, we can set up two simple push notifications. To do this, we need to do the following steps:

1. Enable toast notifications in the App Manifest.

2. Update the tile as Todo items are added.

3. Display a toast notification for urgent items.

The first step is the same change that we needed to make to enable toast notification earlier in this chapter. Open the Package App Manifest, and on the Application tab, set toast Capable to "Yes."

We'll handle the next two steps using an insert script in WAMS, with a few small changes to our Windows Store application to include the notification channel for each TodoItem.

1. Add the following using statement to App.xaml.cs:

    ```
    using Windows.Networking.PushNotifications;
    ```

2. Then, add the following to the App class in App.xaml.cs:

    ```
    public static PushNotificationChannel CurrentChannel { get; private set; }

    private async void AcquirePushChannel()
    {
        CurrentChannel = await PushNotificationChannelManager
            .CreatePushNotificationChannelForApplicationAsync();
    }
    ```

The AcquirePushChannel method requests a notification channel from the Windows Push Notification Service client.

3. Next, we'll need to call the AcquirePushChannel during application launch. Add the following call to the top of the OnLaunched event handler:

    ```
    AcquirePushChannel();
    ```

At this point, our client Windows Store application has a push channel, but WAMS doesn't know about it yet. We can take care of that by adding a new Channel property to the TodoItem class.

4. In the MainPage.xaml.cs file, add the following namespace declaration to the top of the file:

    ```
    using System.Runtime.Serialization;
    ```

5. Next, add a Channel property declaration to the TodoItem class:

    ```
    [JsonProperty(PropertyName= "channel")]
    public string Channel { get; set; }
    ```

■ **Note** We're taking advantage of a very useful feature of Azure Mobile Services called dynamic schema. This feature is enabled by default, and when enabled, it automatically adds new properties to the backing database. You may decide to have it enabled during initial development and then disable it once you've shifted to postrelease/maintenance mode on your Windows Store application. You can do that in the Configure tab in the Windows Azure management portal; see Figure 9-40.

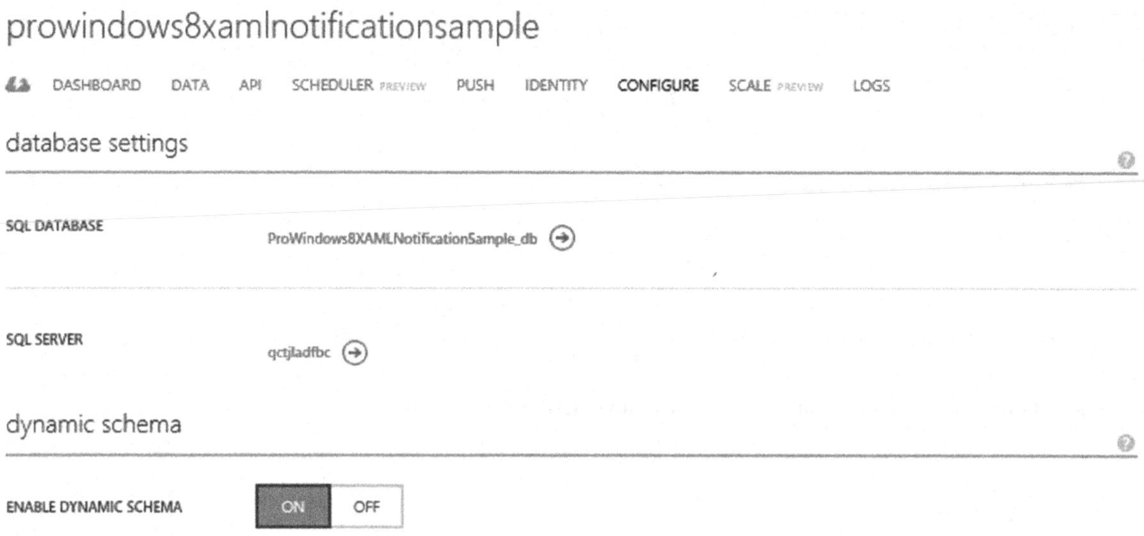
prowindows8xamlnotificationsample
DASHBOARD
DATA
API
SCHEDULER PREVIEW
PUSH
IDENTITY
CONFIGURE
SCALE PREVIEW
LOGS
database settings
SQL DATABASE
ProWindows8XAMLNotificationSample_db
SQL SERVER
qctjladfbc
dynamic schema
ENABLE DYNAMIC SCHEMA
ON
OFF

***Figure 9-40.** Configuration*

6. Next, we'll update the `ButtonSave_Click` event method to include the `Channel` property in in each newly created `TodoItem`:

```
private void ButtonSave_Click(object sender, RoutedEventArgs e)
{
    var todoItem = new TodoItem { Text = TextInput.Text,  Channel =
    App.CurrentChannel.Uri };
    InsertTodoItem(todoItem);
}
```

Sending Notifications Using Data Insert scripts

Now, we're ready to begin sending notifications. The simplest way to handle this is to add an insert script. As you might expect from the name, this script will be executed every time a `TodoItem` is added. What you might not have expected, though, is that this is written in JavaScript.

In the Windows Azure management portal, open your Mobile Service and click on the Data tab, and then click on the table name (`TodoItem`, in this case). This will bring up the table view. Click on the Script tab, as shown in Figure 9-41.

Figure 9-41. *The Script tab*

The default Insert script is displayed, as shown in Figure 9-42.

Figure 9-42. *The default insert script*

We'll make an edit that will do two things: (1) send tile notifications for all updates and (2) send toast notifications for urgent updates. Our selection criteria for urgent updates is very simple—we're just looking for the word *urgent* in the TodoItem text. This word allows you do use a prefix ("URGENT: Remember to breathe!"), a hashtag syntax ("Eliminate zombies. #urgent #undead #doubletap"), and so on. You could, of course, customize this to use whatever logic you'd like.

Replace the insert script with the following:

```
function insert(item, user, request) {
    request.execute({
        success: function() {
            // Insert the data and return, process notifications in background
            request.respond();

            // Use a regular epxression to search for "urgent" - case insensitive
            var regexp = /urgent/i;
```

```
        if(regexp.test(item.text)) {
            // Send the toast notification, then log it
            push.wns.sendToastText04(item.channel, {
                text1: item.text
            });
            console.log("Sent toast:", item.text);
        }

        // All todo items, urgent or not, should send a tile update and log that
        push.wns.sendTileSquareText04(item.channel, {
            text1: item.text
        });
        console.log("Sent tile update:", item.text);
    }
});
}
```

Make sure you save the script before continuing.

This script first saves the newly inserted data and responds, so the notifications happen in the background. Next, it checks for the occurrence of "urgent" in the TodoItem text (using a case-insensitive regular expression) and sends a toast notification if found. Finally, it sends a tile update notification for all items.

You can test this out using the Windows Store application—try inserting several items, some of which include the term "urgent," as shown in Figure 9-43.

Figure 9-43. *Urgent notification*

To see the tile Update, pin the app to your Start screen. After entering an item, you will see that item displayed in your tile (as long as you aren't using the Small tile size), as shown in Figure 9-44.

Figure 9-44. *Live Tile in action*

WAMS Logs

You may have noticed that the insert script included calls to `console.log()`. This is really helpful for tracking and troubleshooting any problems with notifications. You can see the logged output from the previous responses in the Windows Azure management portal, looking in the Logs tab. To get to the log, click on Logs in the WAMS management screen. The logs screen is shown in Figure 9-45.

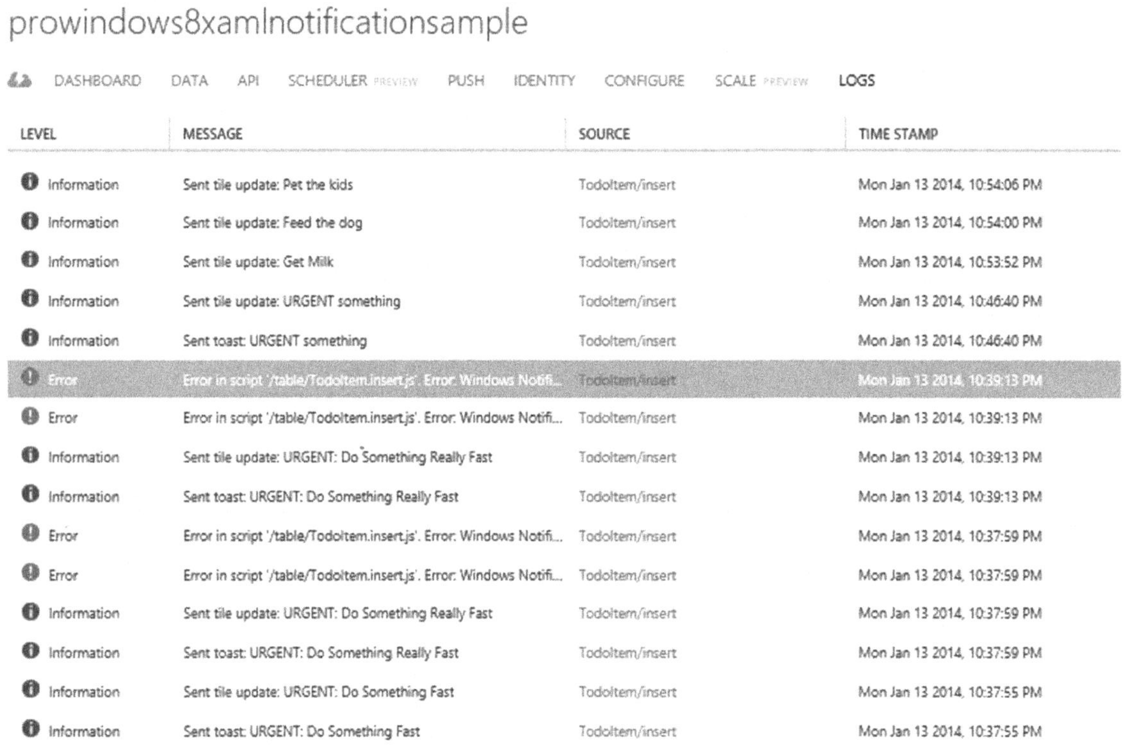

prowindows8xamlnotificationsample

◢◣	DASHBOARD	DATA	API	SCHEDULER PREVIEW	PUSH	IDENTITY	CONFIGURE	SCALE PREVIEW	**LOGS**	

LEVEL	MESSAGE	SOURCE	TIME STAMP
ⓘ Information	Sent tile update: Pet the kids	TodoItem/insert	Mon Jan 13 2014, 10:54:06 PM
ⓘ Information	Sent tile update: Feed the dog	TodoItem/insert	Mon Jan 13 2014, 10:54:00 PM
ⓘ Information	Sent tile update: Get Milk	TodoItem/insert	Mon Jan 13 2014, 10:53:52 PM
ⓘ Information	Sent tile update: URGENT something	TodoItem/insert	Mon Jan 13 2014, 10:46:40 PM
ⓘ Information	Sent toast: URGENT something	TodoItem/insert	Mon Jan 13 2014, 10:46:40 PM
⊘ Error	Error in script '/table/TodoItem.insert.js'. Error: Windows Notifi...	TodoItem/insert	Mon Jan 13 2014, 10:39:13 PM
⊘ Error	Error in script '/table/TodoItem.insert.js'. Error: Windows Notifi...	TodoItem/insert	Mon Jan 13 2014, 10:39:13 PM
ⓘ Information	Sent tile update: URGENT: Do Something Really Fast	TodoItem/insert	Mon Jan 13 2014, 10:39:13 PM
ⓘ Information	Sent toast: URGENT: Do Something Really Fast	TodoItem/insert	Mon Jan 13 2014, 10:39:13 PM
⊘ Error	Error in script '/table/TodoItem.insert.js'. Error: Windows Notifi...	TodoItem/insert	Mon Jan 13 2014, 10:37:59 PM
⊘ Error	Error in script '/table/TodoItem.insert.js'. Error: Windows Notifi...	TodoItem/insert	Mon Jan 13 2014, 10:37:59 PM
ⓘ Information	Sent tile update: URGENT: Do Something Really Fast	TodoItem/insert	Mon Jan 13 2014, 10:37:59 PM
ⓘ Information	Sent toast: URGENT: Do Something Really Fast	TodoItem/insert	Mon Jan 13 2014, 10:37:59 PM
ⓘ Information	Sent tile update: URGENT: Do Something Fast	TodoItem/insert	Mon Jan 13 2014, 10:37:55 PM
ⓘ Information	Sent toast: URGENT: Do Something Fast	TodoItem/insert	Mon Jan 13 2014, 10:37:55 PM

Figure 9-45. *The Logs*

If you don't enable toast notifications, you will get an error like the one shown in Figure 9-46, suggesting that the notification went out, but because you must explicitly enable toast for Windows 8.1 (and I didn't do that originally in this sample), the client dropped the toast.

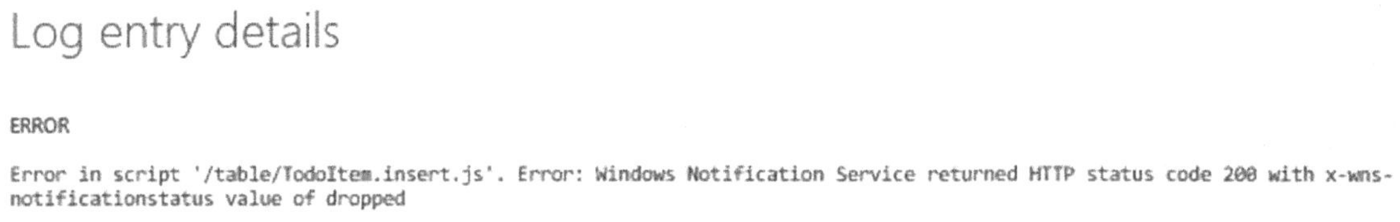

Log entry details

ERROR

```
Error in script '/table/TodoItem.insert.js'. Error: Windows Notification Service returned HTTP status code 200 with x-wns-
notificationstatus value of dropped
```

Figure 9-46. *Error when toast isn't enabled*

Summary

Live tiles, secondary tiles, and push notifications add compelling features to your app. These include features such as creating a secondary tile in the weather app for your hometown (or favorite vacation spot), having those tiles receive notifications of the current weather forecast, and getting toast notifications of weather warnings. Adding such interactive features into your app can make the difference between making sales or fading into obscurity. Yet, you must temper your actions with wisdom. Too much interaction, or live tiles that don't behave the way a user expects, will drive your users (and potential users) away.

CHAPTER 10

■ ■ ■

Application Life Cycle

Windows 8.1 has removed the LayoutAwarePage from the templates. In Windows 8.0, the LayoutAwarePage was the base class for the BasicPage and exposed the events and methods necessary for saving and loading state. The BasicPage in Windows 8.1 declares a local instance of the NavigationHelper class and ties into the navigation events in the page constructor. A Windows 8.0 app retargeted for Windows 8.1 will have issues if it is using the LayoutAwarePage.

The Load and Save event handlers have been cleaned up significantly due to this change. Instead of including the PageState object directly as a parameter, it is now a property of the custom EventArgs used by the Load and Save events. This provides better encapsulation and makes the process more flexible for changes.

In Windows 7, as in all prior versions of Windows (and virtually every other operating system for that matter), the life cycle of an application was largely determined by the user. The user started the application and when done closed the application. The exceptions were crashes and other unforeseen terminations.

For Windows 8.1 modern design apps, the process is very different from that of Windows 7 (or even Windows 8.1 desktop applications). Users can start apps in the usual way by tapping (or clicking) on the app's tile, but they can also start with a number of new methods, including searching and sharing. They can switch from app to app and when they are finished, they typically do not close the application but simply open another one.

The operating system plays a much larger role in the life cycle of each application in the new version. When an app no longer has the focus, Windows 8.1 suspends it. A suspended app is not running in the background but truly idle. This means no processor time at all, and only its state is retained in memory. If the user then brings that app back into the foreground, it once again receives processor time and returns to normal operations.

Suspended apps can also be terminated by the operating system. The most common reason for the termination of an app is memory pressure, although there are some other ways termination can occur. Users also do not know that their apps have been terminated other than the fact it is no longer in the list of running apps.

When developing Windows 8.1 apps, you need to make sure that your app provides a seamless experience regardless of the state of the application. If users open an app that was terminated and it does not bring the state right back to where they left off, it will appear that the app crashed, which can undermine user confidence in your app.

The Three App States

There are three app states: running, suspended, and terminated. As just mentioned, the operating system (and not the user) plays a key role in determining the state of an application. This was done for a number of reasons, but the two that figured most prominently in the decision were 1) to match how users work with mobile devices and 2) to conserve battery power and other resources.

In the case of mobile devices, unlike working with a plugged-in desktop (or laptop), they are designed to be, well, *mobile*! Battery life is a crucial element in deciding which mobile device a consumer selects. Running multiple applications in the background (as users are accustomed to do in Windows 7 or Windows 8 desktop mode) would drain the battery in a very short period of time.

Tablets have been out long enough that the typical usage pattern is well-known. When users have an app on the screen, it is the focus of their attention. When an app is moved to the background, then it is out of sight, out of mind. One of the enhancements to Windows 8.1 is allowing users to have multiple apps in the foreground. Time will tell what number of apps users will find optimal, but as a developer, it is important to be aware of the users' options.

Running

If your user can see your app on his device, it is *running*. Running apps get processor time, memory, access to device hardware, and everything else one would expect. With Windows 8.1, your user can load multiple apps into the foreground, and each will share resources accordingly.

Suspended

When the user moves an app to the background (removes it from view), the app goes into the *suspended* state. As an app moves into the background, it has five seconds to store its state. Once the app is in the background, it is completely isolated from the operating system. Anything in memory in the app will stay there, but it has no access to processor threads or any other resources. Therefore, as a developer, you must treat the suspension event as if your app will be terminated.

The lack of resource utilization minimizes power consumption for apps that are not in the foreground, helping to extend the battery life of the device. It also helps to keep foreground apps much more responsive, as system resources are dedicated to apps in the foreground (which are visible to the user).

By retaining in memory the state of the app, the user can switch back to the app by bringing it into view in a near instant, which gives the illusion that it was running all along in the background.

Terminated

As discussed earlier, the operating system can *terminate* apps when certain conditions exist, most often memory pressure. Since the app does not have access to any system resources (except for the memory that it was using when it moved to suspended), no notification is given when a termination happens.

While the operating system certainly has an algorithm that it follows in determining which apps to terminate, this information is not available to you as a developer, and you must assume that as soon as your app is suspended it will terminate. If you did not save your app's data and state (including session and navigation), it will be lost. The next time a user launches your app, it will appear as if it crashed. And in reality, if your app doesn't handle saving its state on suspend, it did crash.

State Transitions

App state transitions can happen due to user or operating system action. As shown in Figure 10-1, six actions can affect the state of an app: launching, activating, suspending, resuming, terminating, and killing.

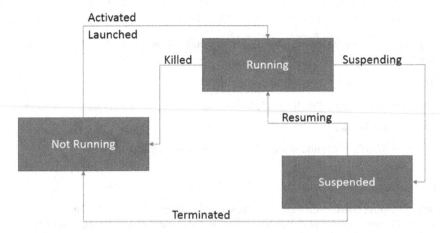

Figure 10-1. *State transitions*

Launching

Launching an app is a user-driven action. It occurs when a user clicks on an app to load it. This places the app in the running state.

Activating

Another way for an app to move to running is activation. Activation occurs through the operating system. Some examples of activation include the Search and Share charms as well as notifications.

During activation, the arguments passed into the OnLaunched event provide information on the previous execution state. This enables you to determine how the app transitioned into the not-running state. If the previous execution state was terminated, then you need to restore the state that was saved during the suspension process.

Suspending

The operating system will suspend an app when it is no longer in the foreground.

Resuming

When a suspended app returns to the foreground, the app is resumed. Since suspended apps maintain state, there is no need to do anything in code to provide the expected user experience.

Terminating

Your app may be terminated by the operating system for any number of reasons, including memory pressure requiring that your app be closed to allow other apps to run, the app taking too long to start, or the app taking too long to suspend.

Killing

An app changes directly from running to not running (skipping the suspended state) only when it is killed. An app can be killed by any of the following conditions:

- The user swiping down from the top of the screen (or pressing Alt-F4)

- The user logging off, shutting down, or restarting the computer

- The user killing the process in Task Manager

- The app freezing, taking longer than five seconds to suspend, or taking longer than fifteen seconds to start

- The app exit being called

If the user performs a close gesture (swiping down from the top of the screen), the app suspends for 10 seconds before it gets killed. This provides a better user experience for an accidental closure of an app. The user can immediately relaunch the app and still maintain the same state.

Working with the Suspension Manager

Microsoft has provided a great deal of readymade code to handle saving state and data for the user in the SuspensionManager utility class. This class (and many other helpful classes) are included in your project after adding a Basic Page template. The SuspensionManager greatly simplifies saving and restoring session and navigation states for each active page.

The BasicPage derives from the LayoutAwarePage class (also included when adding the BasicPage) and contains two virtual events (SaveState and LoadState) that you will use to handle suspension and activation tasks. As we've already seen, the LoadState and SaveState page methods are used in navigation. These methods are also used in restoring and saving page state during the activation and suspension state transitions.

The SuspensionManager class has SaveAsync and RestoreAsync methods that are used for saving and restoring application state during the suspend and activation state transitions. Calling SaveAsync or RestoreAsync also causes the SaveState and LoadState methods to be called on the active page.

The SuspensionManager and LayoutAwarePage classes are included in the Common directory of projects created using the Grid App or Split App templates, but can also be added to projects started using the Blank App template. The easiest way to add the Suspension Manager to a Windows Store app created using the Blank App template is to add a new page using the Basic Page template (Add ➤ New Item ➤ Basic Page).

Using Async Methods

As noted previously, the SuspensionManager class provides two key methods, SaveAsync and RestoreAsync. As you might have guessed from the name, they are asynchronous methods. While this chapter is not meant to be a lesson on the new Async-Await pattern, it is important to note that whenever using the await keyword on a method, the method must be marked with the async keyword. It is a common mistake to forget to change the method signature, so it is worth mentioning here before we get into writing the code in order to handle suspension and activation.

Adding a Suspension Manager to the Blank App

For the sample code in this chapter, we will start with the Blank App template and add a Basic Page.

1. To get started, create a new Blank App project by selecting File ➤ New Project ➤ Visual C# ➤ Windows Store ➤ Blank App (XAML), and setting the name of the project to "LifeCycle" as shown in Figure 10-2.

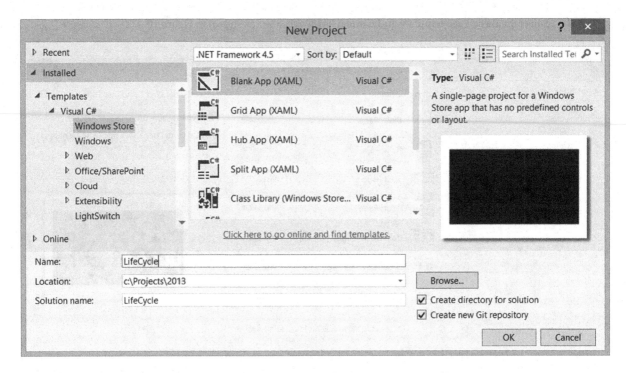

Figure 10-2. *Creating the LifeCycle project*

2. Delete the MainPage.xaml file from the project by right-clicking MainPage.xaml in the project and selecting Delete.

3. Add a New Item to the project by right-clicking on the project and selecting Add ➤ New Item from the context menu as shown in Figure 10-3.

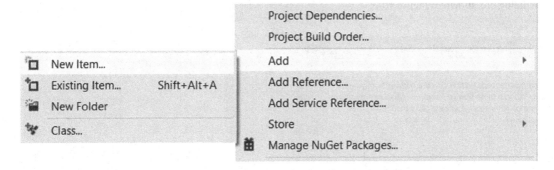

Figure 10-3. *Adding a New Item*

4. Select the Basic Page template and name it `MainPage.xaml` as shown in Figure 10-4.

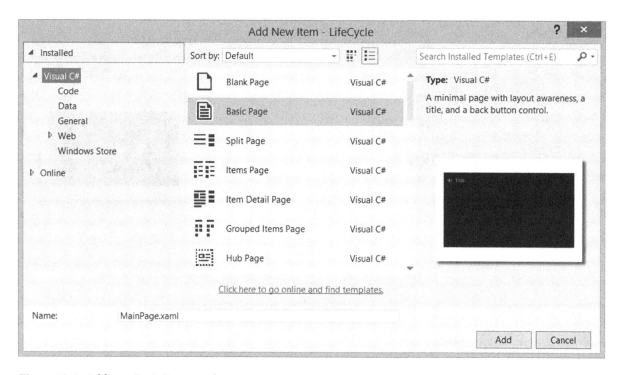

Figure 10-4. *Adding a Basic Page template*

5. Adding a Basic Page template starts a Visual Studio wizard that will add several utility classes (including `SuspensionManager` and `LayoutAwarePage`) into your project under the Common directory, but you must give the wizard permission to do so by clicking Yes on the dialog box shown in Figure 10-5.

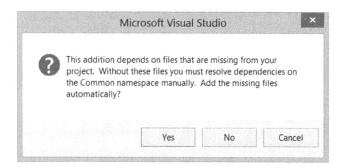

Figure 10-5. *Confirmation dialog box to add SuspensionManager and LayoutAwarePage classes*

Building the Sample App

In order to demonstrate saving and restoring data and state, we need a simple app that has data and more than one page to prove that we can restore data as well as navigation. The Main Page (shown in Figure 10-6) includes a list of tasks that need to be completed. Clicking on the Add button or selecting an item and clicking Edit will bring the user to the Details Page (shown in Figure 10-7), which allows for adding to or editing the list values. This app is very simplistic on purpose because the main goal is to show how to save and restore state and app data.

Figure 10-6. *Main Page of Item Tracker app*

Figure 10-7. *Details Page of Item Tracker app*

Adding the Navigation Parameter Class

When navigating from one page to another, any object can be passed as a parameter to the new page. In our sample app, we need a custom object to pass two values back to the Main Page from the Details Page.

To do so, add a new class to the project named NavigationParameter.cs. In that class, enter the following code:

```
class NavigationParameter
{
    public string OriginalItem { get; set; }
    public string UpdatedItem { get; set; }
}
```

Creating the Details Page

The Details Page allows the user to add or edit tasks. Right-click on the project, add another Basic Page named Details.xaml, and complete the following steps:

1. Open up Details.xaml, and add the following markup just before the closing </Grid> tag:

    ```
    <Grid Row="1" Margin="120">
        <StackPanel>
        <TextBlock FontSize="20">Item Title</TextBlock>
        <TextBox Name="ItemTitle" Text="New Item" />
        <Button Name="Submit" Click="Submit_Click" HorizontalAlignment="Right"
    Margin="0,20,0,0">
            Save</Button>
        </StackPanel>
    </Grid>
    ```

2. Add the stub for the Submit_Click method in Details.xaml.cs:

    ```
    public void Submit_Click(object sender, RoutedEventArgs e)
    {
        var param = new NavigationParameter
        {
            OriginalItem = this.OriginalItem,
            UpdatedItem = ItemTitle.Text
        };

        this.Frame.Navigate(typeof(MainPage), param);
    }
    ```

3. Add a variable to hold the original value if the user is editing an existing list item. Add this code just before the constructor:

    ```
    private string OriginalItem = string.Empty;
    ```

4. Add the following code in the navigation Helper_LoadState method in Details.xaml.cs to handle the parameter data (if any):

    ```
    protected override void navigationHelper_LoadState(object sender, LoadStateEventArgs e)
    {
        if (e.NavigationParameter != null)
    ```

```
        {
            string param = e.NavigationParameter as string;
            if (!string.IsNullOrEmpty(param))
            {
                //Editing an existing item
                OriginalItem = param;
                ItemTitle.Text = param;
            }
            else
            {
                ItemTitle.Text = "Add a new item...";
            }
        }
    }
}
```

Creating the Main Page

The Main Page contains two buttons and a `ListView` control that will be a simple Item Tracker/TODO app.
Open up `MainPage.xaml` and complete the following steps:

1. Open up `MainPage.xaml` from the project previously created. Add the following XAML just
    before the closing `</Grid>` tag:

```xml
<StackPanel Grid.Row="1" Margin="120,30,0,0">
    <StackPanel Orientation="Horizontal">
        <Button Name="Add"
            Content="Add"
            Click="Add_Click" />
        <Button Name="Edit"
            Content="Edit"
            Click="Edit_Click" />
    </StackPanel>
    <ListView Name="ItemsList"/>
</StackPanel>
```

2. Open up `MainPage.xaml.cs` and add the two-button click method handlers and the
    following code:

```csharp
public void Edit_Click(object sender, RoutedEventArgs e)
{
    this.Frame.Navigate(typeof(Details), ItemsList.SelectedValue);
}

public void Add_Click(object sender, RoutedEventArgs e)
{
    this.Frame.Navigate(typeof(Details), string.Empty);
}
```

3. Add starter data to the ListView by copying the following code to the top of the class just before the constructor:

```
string[] _defaultItems = {"Go shopping","Motorcycle maintenance","Build underground lair"};
string[] _items;
```

4. Add a using for Windows.Storage at the top of the file:

```
using Windows.Storage;
```

5. Add an application data container to save the application data:

```
private ApplicationDataContainer _settings = ApplicationData.Current.RoamingSettings;
```

Handling Adding/Editing List Items

The navigationHelper_LoadState method is executed whenever a page is navigated to. The following code first checks to see if there are items in the roaming settings for application data containers, which have been added to the navigationHelper_LoadState method checks to see if a navigaton parameter was passed in. If so, the list gets updated accordingly, the app data is saved in the application data container, and the ItemsSource property for the ListView is set to the Items Collection:

```
private void navigationHelper_LoadState(object sender, LoadStateEventArgs e)
{
    _items = _settings.Values["StoredItems"] as string[] ?? _defaultItems;
    var param = e.NavigationParameter as NavigationParameter;
    if (param != null && !string.IsNullOrEmpty(param.UpdatedItem))
    {
        List<string> items = new List<string>(_items);
        if (!string.IsNullOrEmpty(param.OriginalItem))
        {
            items.Remove(param.OriginalItem);
        }
        items.Add(param.UpdatedItem);
            _items = items.ToArray();
                _settings.Values["StoredItems"] = _items;
    }
    ItemsList.ItemsSource = _items;
}
```

Responding to App Suspension

As previously mentioned, the operating system notifies apps on suspension, but not when killed or terminated. The app must therefore save its state every time the suspended event occurs in case the app eventually terminates. This state includes data on the screen, navigation location and history, and anything else that pertains to the user or session data. The app must complete the suspension event within five seconds, or the operating system will kill the app. This means in addition to saving state on suspension, saving app data should be an ongoing and continual process. For more information on saving app data to local or roaming settings, please refer to Chapter 6.

Registering the Root Frame

The first step to working with the Suspension Manager is to register the root frame of the app. This sets the initial context for the app state, and allows the Suspension Manager to track the state of the app.

1. Open App.xaml.cs

2. In the OnLaunched method, find the line that reads:

    ```
    rootFrame = new Frame();
    ```

3. Immediately after that line add the code to register the root frame:

    ```
    LifeCycle.Common.SuspensionManager.RegisterFrame(rootFrame, "appFrame");
    ```

The OnSuspending Event

If you are using one of the templates provided, the app-suspending event already has a handler called OnSuspending in App.xaml.cs. The out of the box has three lines as shown here:

```
private void OnSuspending(object sender, SuspendingEventArgs e)
{
    var deferral = e.SuspendingOperation.GetDeferral();
    //TODO: Save application state and stop any background activity
    deferral.Complete();
}
```

The call to GetDeferral returns an object of type SuspendingDeferral and it has only one method: Complete. You need to sandwich your work between these two calls if you are working with asynchronous methods. As explained in the "Using Async Methods" section, the SuspensionManager calls are ASYNC calls. When using async, the OnSuspending method will run until you call Complete or the five seconds allocated is exhausted, whichever comes first. There are three steps that need to be handled:

1. Open App.xaml.cs. and navigate to the OnSuspending method.

2. Change the method signature by adding the ASYNC keyword.

3. Add a call to SuspensionManager.SaveAsync.

■ **Note**   SuspensionManager takes on the default namespace of the project.

The complete code is shown here:

```
private async void OnSuspending(object sender, SuspendingEventArgs e)
{
    var deferral = e.SuspendingOperation.GetDeferral();
    await LifeCycle.Common.SuspensionManager.SaveAsync();
    deferral.Complete();
}
```

Saving Session Data

When SaveAsync is called, the active page's navigationHelper_SaveState method gets invoked. It may seem tempting to use this time to save all of your app's data in addition to its state. However, there is only a five-second time-out, and anything but a very trivial app will struggle to save everything in that brief period of time. It is extremely important to save application data very frequently, maybe even every time the data changes, so that the Suspension Manager and the pages only save certain "status" values that focus more on the state of your app than the state of the app data. This might include which information is visible, what is selected, user input data, and so forth.

The Suspension Manager provides a dictionary that can be used to save page state and session information. This is a manual process. In other words, you must decide what gets saved. Saving the navigation state (current page and navigation history) is done as part of the SuspensionManager.SaveAsync call.

For this sample, if the user is currently on the Main Page, then we will save the currently selected item if the user had a selected item, and if the user is currently on the Details Page, we will save the value entered into the text box. The list of items is already saved on every change, as it should be in a production application.

To save the Currect Items list, complete these steps:

1. Open MainPage.xaml.cs.

2. Add the following code to the navigationHelper_SaveState method:

   ```
   _settings.Values["StoredItems"] = _items;
   ```

Saving Session State

The navigationHelper_SaveState and navigationHelper_LoadState methods event args (SaveStateEventArgs and LoadStateEventArgs, respectively) contain a property named PageState that is of type Dictionary<String,Object>. Anything placed in this dictionary will be written to disk during the saving of the app session state. It will then be read from disk and populated by the Suspension Manager, and passed into the page methods for programmatic handling.

Since all of the data is serialized to disk, anything placed in the dictionary must be serializable.

Follow these steps to save the currently selected item (Main Page):

1. Open MainPage.xaml.cs.

2. Add the following code to the navigationHelper_SaveState method (before or after the line just added):

   ```
   e.PageState["SelectedValue"] = ItemsList.SelectedValue;
   ```

To save text box data (Details Page), perform these steps:

1. Open Details.xaml.cs.

2. Add the following code to the navigationHelper_SaveState method to save any data the user had entered before the suspend/terminate state transition:

   ```
   e.PageState["ItemTitle"] = ItemTitle.Text;
   ```

Responding to App Activation

When an app is activated, the OnLaunched event is raised. We have already used this when we registered the root frame of the app with the Suspension Manager. This method is also where app session is restored.

Determining the Previous Application State

The custom event argument for the OnLaunched event (LaunchActivatedEventArgs) contains a property
PreviousExecutionState of type ApplicationExecutionState. The ApplicationExecutionState enumeration
contains values representing the five possible states that an app can be in prior to activation:

- NotRunning

- Running

- Suspended

- Terminated

- ClosedByUser

The only time that app state must be restored is when the previous application state is terminated. If the
PreviousExecutionState is ApplicationExecutionState.Terminated, call the SuspensionManager.RestoreAsync()
method. This reloads the navigation state using the registered frame. It also populates the pageState dictionary parameter
in the Page LoadState method as we will see in the next section. There are three steps to restoring app state, as follows:

1. Open App.xaml.cs, navigate to the OnLaunched event, and find the if statement that
   checks the previous execution state:

   ```
   if (e.PreviousExecutionState == ApplicationExecutionState.Terminated)
   {
       //TODO: Load state from previously suspended application
   }
   ```

2. After the //TODO: comment, add the following line of code:

   ```
   await LifeCycle.Common.SuspensionManager.RestoreAsync();
   ```

3. Since we are using the await keyword, the event handler must be marked async.

   ```
   protected async override void OnLaunched(LaunchActivatedEventArgs e)
   {
   ```

The event handler should look like this now (with the unrelated parts omitted)

```
protected async override void OnLaunched(LaunchActivatedEventArgs e)
{
    Frame rootFrame = Window.Current.Content as Frame;
    if (rootFrame == null)
    {
        rootFrame = new Frame();
        LifeCycle.Common.SuspensionManager.RegisterFrame(rootFrame, "appFrame");
        if (e.PreviousExecutionState ==
            ApplicationExecutionState.Terminated)
        {
            await LifeCycle.Common.SuspensionManager.RestoreAsync();
        }
        Window.Current.Content = rootFrame;
    }
//Omitted for brevity
}
```

Testing the Restoring Navigation State

Visual Studio makes it very easy to test termination and activation. While an app is running, locate the Suspend menu option. It will vary based on customization, but the default location is the left-hand side of the third row of the toolbars. (If it isn't showing, you can enable the toolbar by selecting View ➤ Toolbars ➤ Debug Location.) The Suspend menu gives you the option to suspend, resume, or suspend and shut down the app being debugged. This menu is shown in Figure 10-8.

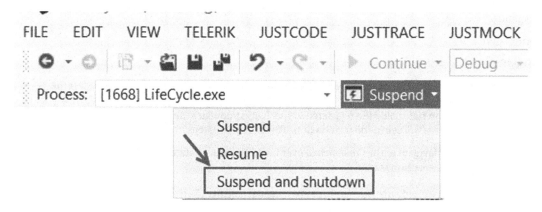

Figure 10-8. *Suspend options in Visual Studio*

Follow these steps to run the test:

1. Run the app.

2. Click Add on the Main Page to navigate to the Details Page.

3. Go back to Visual Studio, and on the Suspend menu, click Suspend and Shutdown. When the app has completed termination, Visual Studio's menu bar returns to the nonrunning state.

4. Run the app again, and the app will load with the Details Page as the current page.

Restoring Session Information

The last step is to restore the session information that we saved in the navigationHelper_SaveState method of the pages. In the navigationHelper_SaveState methods, we saved the currently selected record on the Main Page and the current value in the text box on the Details Page. If the RestoreAsync method was called on the SuspendManager, the pageState dictionary is populated with the values stored in the navigationHelper_SaveState method. If an app is shut down normally and not through the Suspend event, the SaveAsync method isn't called, and the PageState property of the eventargs is null. There are fours steps to completing this:

1. Open MainPage.xaml.cs and navigate to the navigationHelper_LoadState method.

2. Add the following line of code to the end of the navigationHelper_LoadState method:

```
if (e.PageState != null && e.PageState["SelectedValue"] != null)
{
    ItemsList.SelectedValue = e.PageState["SelectedValue"];
}
```

3. Open `DetailsPage.xaml.cs` and navigate to the `navigationHelper_LoadState` method.

4. Add the following code to the end of the `navigationHelper_LoadState` method:

```
if (e.PageState != null && e.PageState["ItemTitle"] != null)
{
    ItemTitle.Text = e.PageState["ItemTitle"] as string;
}
```

Testing the Restoring Session Information

To test the restoration of the app state information, use the same process as the one for testing the restoration of the navigation information:

1. Run the app.

2. Select one of the items in the list.

3. Go back to Visual Studio, and on the Suspend menu, click Suspend and Shutdown. When the app has completed termination, Visual Studio's menu bar returns to the nonrunning state.

4. Run the app again, and the app will load to the Main Page with the previous item selected once again.

5. Click Edit on the Main Page to navigate to the Details Page. The text box is filled in with the selected item. Make an edit to the text box.

6. Go back to Visual Studio, and repeat step 4—click Suspend and Shutdown. When the app has completed termination, Visual Studio's menu bar returns to the nonrunning state.

7. Run the app again, and the app will load to the Details Page with the text box restored to the previous value.

Summary

One of the major design considerations for Windows 8.1 is to maximize battery life and performance for tablets. One of the mechanisms utilized prevents background apps from stealing precious resources when the user isn't actively engaged. When an app isn't visible on the screen, it goes into a suspended state. While suspended, your app doesn't have access to any processor cycles. If system resources become low enough, Windows will terminate your app.

It is important for your app to gracefully handle app termination. If your app doesn't restore session data and state after a termination, then the user will believe (rightly so) that the app crashed and isn't stable. By saving the session data and state when an app is suspended (and subsequently restoring them when an app is started again after termination), the user experience will be seamless and the user will not have any cause for concern.

Using the `SuspensionManager` `SaveAsync` and `RestoreAsync` methods greatly simplifies the process by providing the plumbing to write the session data to disk during the suspend event in case of an eventual termination.

CHAPTER 11

Making Money

You've put a lot of hard work into developing your app. Now it's time to decide if you want to try and make money off of it. Before you say, "Of course I want to make money!" think about all of the options and reasons for having your app in the store.

Monetization Choices

There are many reasons you have written your app. Before you decide which monetization strategy to use, think about *why* you wrote your app. Did you want to try and hit the "app lottery"? Did you want to make a name for yourself? Or were you looking to provide software for coworkers? Once you know the goal for your app, the next step in the process is to determine your business model.

You have a lot of distribution options some of which maximize reach whereas others focus on direct financial gain. Options include apps that are totally free, purchased outright either through payment plans or an upfront payment, offered through free trials with the option to upgrade, supported through in-app purchases, and supported through in-app advertising. Regardless of the option you choose, Microsoft takes a cut of any revenue your app generates. The percentage is around 30 percent. All of the details are listed in your Windows Store agreement.

Neither this book nor the authors can help you decide which option to select. That would be like a recipe book telling its readers how much to charge for pancakes. Which option you choose is up to you and should be carefully considered.

If you decide to go with a revenue-generating model, you will need to set up a payout account before you finish submitting your app, as discussed in Chapter 12.

Free

This model is exactly what it sounds like. Your app is totally free to all users without restriction. By far the simplest option, you just need to get your app through the certification process, and viola, it's available for download.

Why would you make your app free after all the hard work that you did to build it? There are many reasons, but the most common is when your Windows app is an extension of your business, as opposed to being the core of your business. Prime examples are hotels and car rental companies. Users aren't necessarily paying for rooms or cars through your app, and certainly providing a mechanism to easily reserve them can drive more business to your company. And if you were to charge for your app in those cases, you would drive customers to the competition.

Free apps can also use in-app purchasing and ads to generate revenue. In fact, this has become a very common model.

Selling Your App

When you select a price tier other than free, the user downloading your app is presented with a choice to buy the app when they attempt to download it from the store. The price for your app can be as low as $0.99 and as high as $999.99. The pricing is configured through a drop-down list and not free form, so you have to pick one of the preset prices. The initial price increments are $0.50 (e.g. $1.49, $1.99) and then become larger as the price rises (eg $949.99 and then $999.99).

Purchased Upfront (No Trial)

If you select a price tier and do not offer a trial, the only options presented to your potential user is to buy or cancel the download. Whereas making your customers buy the app before they can download it is the simplest financial model to adopt, it might not bring you a lot of customers. Most users want to try before they buy. That is not to say that upfront purchase isn't a valid option. Just make sure you think through to potential ramifications.

Offered Through Free Trials

If you select a price tier (in other words, you have decided to sell your app), you are presented with the option to provide a free trial. The default option is no trial, which is the scenario just discussed. There are five trial scenarios, ranging from one to thirty days as well as never expiring. The entire list of options (including the default no trial option) is included here:

- No trial
- Trial never expires
- 1 day
- 7 days
- 15 days
- 30 days

The length of the trial is important. You want it to be long enough that your users get a chance to know your app and make it part of their routine. Too long and they might get what they need and never purchase it. What is the right decision? That depends entirely on your app.

Supported Through In-App Purchases

In-app purchases are becoming a more-and-more-popular mechanism for generating revenue. They allow your users to use a certain feature set and then purchase premium features without having to download a new version of the app. They also allow your users to add "consumables" to their installation of your app. In a game, this might be extra lifes. In a music app, it would be songs.

Supported Through In-App Advertising

Another common model is to provide a free trial without any expiration but to include advertising in it. If the user wants, she can remove the advertising by buying the app. For the Microsoft App certification requirements for in-app advertising, see this link on MSDN: http://bit.ly/1k9UN39.

Implementing Your Choice(s)

Once you've decided how (or if) you want to monetize your app, you need to implement your decisions. As a developer, how do you know whether an app is still under trial? Is the trial expired? How do you add in-app purchasing? Or advertising? The good news is that Microsoft has made these tasks very straightforward.

Programmtically Checking the Licensing Status

For determining licensing status, the `CurrentApp` object in the `Windows.ApplicationModel.Store` namespace has the information you need. The following steps demonstrate how to check the licensing status:

1. Create a new Blank App and replace the default `MainPage.xaml` (and `MainPage.xaml.cs`) with a Basic Page (as we've done throughout this book).

2. Open up `MainPage.xaml` and add the following XAML just before the final closing `</Grid>`:

```
<Grid Grid.Column="0" Grid.Row="1" Margin="120,0,0,0">
  <Grid.RowDefinitions>
    <RowDefinition Height="auto"/>
    <RowDefinition Height="auto"/>
  </Grid.RowDefinitions>
  <Grid.ColumnDefinitions>
    <ColumnDefinition Width="Auto"/>
    <ColumnDefinition Width="15"/>
    <ColumnDefinition Width="Auto"/>
  </Grid.ColumnDefinitions>
  <Button Grid.Row="0" Grid.Column="0" Content="Working Button"></Button>
  <TextBlock Grid.Row="0" Grid.Column="2" VerticalAlignment="Center">This is a button
  that always works</TextBlock>
  <Button Name="PremiumButton" Grid.Row="1" Grid.Column="0" Content="Trial Button"
  IsEnabled="False"></Button>
  <TextBlock Grid.Row="1" Grid.Column="2" VerticalAlignment="Center">This is a button
  only works when trial is active or app is purchased</TextBlock>
</Grid>
```

The view is simple—it has two buttons and two text blocks. One button is always enabled, and the other button is enabled if the app is in trial mode or if it has been purchased and disabled if the trial has expired. Figures 11-1 and 11-2 illustrate this.

Figure 11-1. *Software in trial/purchase mode*

Figure 11-2. *Software with trial expired*

3. Open MainPage.xaml.cs and add a using for Windows.ApplicationModel.Store:

    ```
    using Windows.ApplicationModel.Store;
    ```

4. Add a variable to hold the license information:

    ```
    private LicenseInformation _licenseInformation;
    ```

5. In the constructor, add the following code:

    ```
    //For testing use the following line
    _licenseInformation = CurrentAppSimulator.LicenseInformation;
    // For production use the following line
    //_licenseInformation = CurrentApp.LicenseInformation;
    CheckLicense();
    ```

For testing, we use the CurrentAppSimulator to get the license information for an app. When you are ready to move your app into production, remember to change all of those calls to use CurrentApp, as any calls to CurrentAppSimulator will result in an automatic rejection during the certification process.

6. Then, call to a method that checks the current license information:

    ```
    void CheckLicense()
    {
      if (_licenseInformation.IsActive)
      {
        if (!_licenseInformation.IsTrial ||
            (_licenseInformation.IsTrial &&
            _licenseInformation.ExpirationDate > DateTime.Now))
        {
          PremiumButton.IsEnabled = true;
        }
      }
    }
    ```

The CheckLicense method first checks whether the license is active. An inactive license can mean an error condition, but in any case, you should interpret it as the app isn't licensed. If IsTrial is false, the app was purchased, and you can proceed to enable any of the features that were disabled because of the trial. Likewise, if IsTrial is true (meaning the app has not been purchased) and the expiration date for the trial is in the future, the app is still running in trial mode, and you can enable/disable controls and pages accordingly.

When you run your app, calls to CurrentAppSimulator reference an XML file named WindowsStoreProxy.xml. This file can be found in the directory <installation_folder>\LocalState\Microsoft\Windows Store\ApiData.

■ **Note** The easiest way to find the installation folder is to open up the package app manifest, navigate to the Packaging tab, copy the package name to the clipboard, and then search your Users folder structure for the package name. On my machine, the location was C:\Users\Japikse\AppData\Local\Packages\{guid for sample app}. If you don't see the WindowsStoreProxy.xml file, deploy the app and then run it to have Visual Studio create the file.

7. Open that file in your favorite XML editor, and navigate to the bottom of the file where you will see something similar to the following snippet. Don't worry if you don't see the ExpirationDate, as it isn't added by default, but we need to add it in.

```
<LicenseInformation>
  <App>
    <IsActive>true</IsActive>
    <IsTrial>true</IsTrial>
    <ExpirationDate>2014-04-09T12:00:00.00Z</ExpirationDate>
  </App>
  <Product ProductId="1">
    <IsActive>true</IsActive>
  </Product>
</LicenseInformation>
```

8. To test the different states, modify the XML under the App node. If IsActive is set to false, the IsTrial and ExpirationDate nodes are ignored. If IsActive is true and IsTrial is false, then the app has been purchased. If IsActive and IsTrial are both true, then you need to add the ExpirationDate node. If it isn't found, the app is on a never-ending trial. If it is found, and is in the past, the license will respond as InActive.

While this example barely scratches the surface of what is contained in the licensing XML file, it gives you the information you need to respond to the licensing state of your app that appears on the user's machine. It's up to you how you want to enable/disable functions, pages, or the app itself.

Setting Up In-App Purchases

The first step to create an in-app offer is to make a meaningful offer token. This token can be anything you want, and only has to be unique to your app. For my awesome app, I've selected the token "MyCoolNewFeature".

Adding the Token to WindowsStoreProxy.xml

Once you've decided on the token, open up the WindowsStoreProxy.xml file (same location as listed in the previous steps) and replace the default <Product> element in the <LicenseInformation> node with the following:

```
<Product ProductId="MyCoolNewFeature">
  <IsActive>false</IsActive>
</Product>
```

You also need to update the `<ListingInformation>` to contain a product with the same token. To do so, add the following XML to the ListingInformation:

```xml
<Product ProductId="MyCoolNewFeature">
  <MarketData xml:lang="en-us">
    <Name>MyCoolNewFeature</Name>
    <Price>1.99</Price>
    <CurrencySymbol>$</CurrencySymbol>
    <CurrencyCode>USD</CurrencyCode>
  </MarketData>
</Product>
```

The entire WindowsStoreProxy.xml file looks like this:

```xml
<?xml version="1.0" encoding="utf-16" ?>
<CurrentApp>
  <ListingInformation>
    <App>
      <AppId>00000000-0000-0000-0000-000000000000</AppId>
      <LinkUri>http://apps.microsoft.com/webpdp/app/00000000-0000-0000-0000-000000000000</LinkUri>
      <CurrentMarket>en-US</CurrentMarket>
      <AgeRating>3</AgeRating>
      <MarketData xml:lang="en-us">
        <Name>AppName</Name>
        <Description>AppDescription</Description>
        <Price>1.00</Price>
        <CurrencySymbol>$</CurrencySymbol>
        <CurrencyCode>USD</CurrencyCode>
      </MarketData>
    </App>
    <Product ProductId="MyCoolNewFeature">
      <MarketData xml:lang="en-us">
        <Name>MyCoolNewFeature</Name>
        <Price>1.99</Price>
        <CurrencySymbol>$</CurrencySymbol>
        <CurrencyCode>USD</CurrencyCode>
      </MarketData>
    </Product>
  </ListingInformation>
  <LicenseInformation>
    <App>
      <IsActive>true</IsActive>
      <IsTrial>true</IsTrial>
      <ExpirationDate>2014-05-09T12:00:00.00Z</ExpirationDate>
    </App>
    <Product ProductId="MyCoolNewFeature">
      <IsActive>false</IsActive>
    </Product>
  </LicenseInformation>
</CurrentApp>
```

Checking the Status of Your Feature

To test the in-app purchase feature, we need to update our sample to include a feature that is only enabled through in-app purchases. Open up `MainPage.xaml` and add a new row definition, button, and text block. The entire XAML is shown here, with the new words in bold:

```xml
<Grid Grid.Column="0" Grid.Row="1" Margin="120,0,0,0">
  <Grid.RowDefinitions>
    <RowDefinition Height="auto"/>
    <RowDefinition Height="auto"/>
    <RowDefinition Height="auto"/>
  </Grid.RowDefinitions>
  <Grid.ColumnDefinitions>
    <ColumnDefinition Width="Auto"/>
    <ColumnDefinition Width="15"/>
    <ColumnDefinition Width="Auto"/>
  </Grid.ColumnDefinitions>
  <Button Grid.Row="0" Grid.Column="0" Content="Working Button"></Button>
  <TextBlock Grid.Row="0" Grid.Column="2" VerticalAlignment="Center">
    This is a button that always works</TextBlock>
  <Button Name="PremiumButton" Grid.Row="1" Grid.Column="0"
    Content="Trial Button" IsEnabled="False"></Button>
  <TextBlock Grid.Row="1" Grid.Column="2" VerticalAlignment="Center">
    This is a button only works when trial is active or app is purchased</TextBlock>
  <Button Name="FeatureButton" Grid.Row="2" Grid.Column="0"
    Content="Feature Button" IsEnabled="False"></Button>
  <TextBlock Grid.Row="2" Grid.Column="2" VerticalAlignment="Center">
    This is a button only works when in-app purchase is
    purchased</TextBlock>
</Grid>
```

Now, open `MainPage.xaml.cs` and navigate to the `CheckLicense` method. Then, add a new `if` block that checks the status of the product license as shown here:

```csharp
if (_licenseInformation.ProductLicenses["MyCoolNewFeature"].IsActive)
{
  FeatureButton.IsEnabled = true;
}
```

This checks the license for the token that we set up in the XML file. Run the app, and you will see that the button is disabled, as in Figure 11-3.

Figure 11-3. *In-app purchase button disabled*

Edit the XML file and change the IsActive flag to true for our cool new feature.

```
<Product ProductId="MyCoolNewFeature">
  <IsActive>true</IsActive>
</Product>
```

Now, run the app again, and you will see that the Feature Button is now active, as in Figure 11-4.

Figure 11-4. *Feature button activated after in-app purchase*

Adding the In-App Purchase UI

Users can't simply edit an XML file to turn features on or off. If they could, it wouldn't really be a purchase! Fortunately, from a developer's perspective, the process is very straightforward.

First, we need to add another button and text block to our main page. Open up MainPage.xaml and update the XAML to match the following (changes in bold):

```
<Grid Grid.Column="0" Grid.Row="1" Margin="120,0,0,0">
  <Grid.RowDefinitions>
    <RowDefinition Height="auto"/>
    <RowDefinition Height="auto"/>
    <RowDefinition Height="auto"/>
    <RowDefinition Height="auto"/>
  </Grid.RowDefinitions>
  <Grid.ColumnDefinitions>
    <ColumnDefinition Width="Auto"/>
    <ColumnDefinition Width="15"/>
    <ColumnDefinition Width="Auto"/>
  </Grid.ColumnDefinitions>
  <Button Grid.Row="0" Grid.Column="0" Content="Working Button"></Button>
  <TextBlock Grid.Row="0" Grid.Column="2" VerticalAlignment="Center">
     This is a button that always works</TextBlock>
  <Button Name="PremiumButton" Grid.Row="1" Grid.Column="0" Content="Trial Button"
IsEnabled="False"></Button>
  <TextBlock Grid.Row="1" Grid.Column="2" VerticalAlignment="Center">
     This is a button only works when trial is active or app is purchased</TextBlock>
  <Button Name="FeatureButton" Grid.Row="2" Grid.Column="0"
    Content="Feature Button" IsEnabled="False"></Button>
  <TextBlock Grid.Row="2" Grid.Column="2" VerticalAlignment="Center">
     This is a button only works when in-app purchase is purchased</TextBlock>
```

```
    <Button Name="BuyFeatureButton" Grid.Row="3" Grid.Column="0"
        Content="Buy the Feature" Click="BuyFeatureButton_Click"></Button>
    <TextBlock Grid.Row="3" Grid.Column="2" VerticalAlignment="Center">
        Buy the really cool feature</TextBlock>
</Grid>
```

We now have a button that can be used to buy the feature, so create a new click event handler for the button and add the following code:

```
private async void BuyFeatureButton_Click(object sender, Windows.UI.Xaml.RoutedEventArgs e)
{
    string myCoolNewFeature = "MyCoolNewFeature";
    if (!_licenseInformation.ProductLicenses[myCoolNewFeature].IsActive)
    {
        try
        {
            await CurrentAppSimulator.RequestProductPurchaseAsync(myCoolNewFeature);
            CheckLicense();
        }
        catch (Exception ex)
        {
            //Handle failure gracefully
        }
    }
    else
    {
        //Already purchased
    }
}
```

Edit the XML file and change the IsActive flag to true for our cool new feature.

```
<Product ProductId="MyCoolNewFeature">
    <IsActive>false</IsActive>
</Product>
```

We again use the CurrentAppSimulator to simulate going to the store to purchase the feature. Before you submit you app to the store, remember to change the code to use CurrentApp instead. The code is very simple: user get presented with a dialog (handled by the store) to allow them to purchase the app. If the purchase is successful, the return code is an empty string. If the purchase does not succeed, and an exception is thrown, you must handle it in an appropriate manner. That manner, of course, depends on your business rules. The simulated dialog is presented in Figure 11-5.

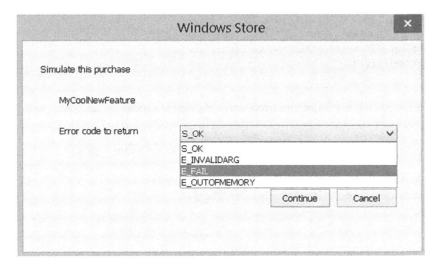

Figure 11-5. *Simulated in-app purchase dialog*

The final step in allowing a user to change the license while the app is running is to handle the LicenseChanged event. Open MainPage.xaml.cs and navigate to the constructor. Add the following line to the constructor just before the end of the method:

```
_licenseInformation.LicenseChanged +=
    licenseInformation_LicenseChanged;
```

Then, create the method handler, and call CheckLicense() in the event handler as follows:

```
void licenseInformation_LicenseChanged()
{
  CheckLicense();
}
```

Converting Trials to Purchased Apps

The process for allowing a user to purchase your app from within the app is a process very similar to in-app purchases. To see how this is done, open up MainPage.xaml and add another row, button, and text block as shown here (new code is in bold):

```
<Grid Grid.Column="0" Grid.Row="1" Margin="120,0,0,0">
  <Grid.RowDefinitions>
    <RowDefinition Height="auto"/>
    <RowDefinition Height="auto"/>
    <RowDefinition Height="auto"/>
    <RowDefinition Height="auto"/>
    <RowDefinition Height="auto"/>
  </Grid.RowDefinitions>
  <Grid.ColumnDefinitions>
    <ColumnDefinition Width="Auto"/>
```

```
  <ColumnDefinition Width="15"/>
  <ColumnDefinition Width="Auto"/>
</Grid.ColumnDefinitions>
<Button Grid.Row="0" Grid.Column="0" Content="Working Button"></Button>
<TextBlock Grid.Row="0" Grid.Column="2"
  VerticalAlignment="Center">
  This is a button that always works</TextBlock>
<Button Name="PremiumButton" Grid.Row="1" Grid.Column="0"
  Content="Trial Button" IsEnabled="False"></Button>
<TextBlock Grid.Row="1" Grid.Column="2"
  VerticalAlignment="Center">
  This is a button only works when trial is active or
  app is purchased</TextBlock>
<Button Name="FeatureButton" Grid.Row="2" Grid.Column="0"
  Content="Feature Button" IsEnabled="False"></Button>
<TextBlock Grid.Row="2" Grid.Column="2" VerticalAlignment="Center">
  This is a button only works when in-app purchase is
  purchased</TextBlock>
<Button Name="BuyFeatureButton" Grid.Row="3" Grid.Column="0"
  Content="Buy the Feature" Click="BuyFeatureButton_Click"></Button>
<TextBlock Grid.Row="3" Grid.Column="2" VerticalAlignment="Center">
  Buy the really cool feature</TextBlock>
<Button Name="BuyAppButton" Grid.Row="4" Grid.Column="0"
  Content="Buy the app" Click="BuyAppButton_Click"></Button>
<TextBlock Grid.Row="4" Grid.Column="2"
  VerticalAlignment="Center">Buy the app</TextBlock>
</Grid>
```

Open up MainPage.xaml.cs and create the BuyAppButton_Click event handler:

```
private async void BuyAppButton_Click(object sender, Windows.UI.Xaml.RoutedEventArgs e)
{
  if (_licenseInformation.IsTrial)
  {
    try
    {
      await CurrentAppSimulator.RequestAppPurchaseAsync(false);
      CheckLicense();
    }
    catch (Exception ex)
    {
      //Handle failure gracefully
    }
  }
  else
  {
    //Already purchased
  }
}
```

You'll see the code is almost exactly the same as that for the in-app purchase process. The purchase process will also trigger the LicenseChanged event, so you don't have to change any code for your app to recognize that the app is now a purchase instead of a trial.

In-App Advertising

For Windows 8.1 and Visual Studio 2013, the Microsoft Advertising SDK is in the box. With nothing extra to download and no versioning concerns, it has become even easier to add advertising into your app. To start (and to make sure the extension is present, select Tools ➤ Extensions and Updates. In the left rail, select Installed ➤ SDKs, and look for the Microsoft Advertising SDK for Windows 8.1 (as in Figure 11-6). Note that in this image, I already have the SDK installed, so the Uninstall button is visible. When you do not have the SDK installed, the button caption will say Install.

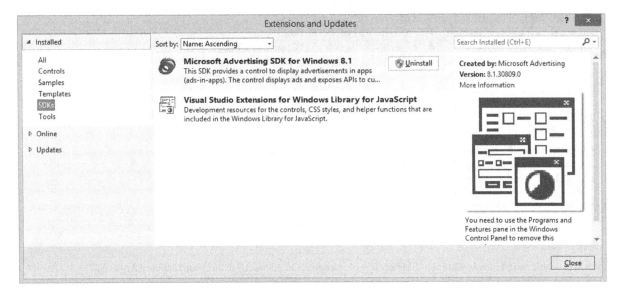

Figure 11-6. Ensuring the Advertising SDK is present in Visual Studio 2013

Registering with Microsoft pubCenter

Before you can start displaying ads in your app, you must register with the Microsoft pubCenter. To register, go to http://pubcenter.microsoft.com and follow the instructions there. You will need to add your demographic information, payment information, and tax profile (W-9 for the United States).

Once registered, you need to create a new app in the pubCenter. This (unfortunately) isn't tied into any apps that you have in the store, as it would be nice to have pubCenter pull up all of your apps from Dev Center. From the dashboard, select Monetize New App, and you will see a screen like the one presented in Figure 11-7.

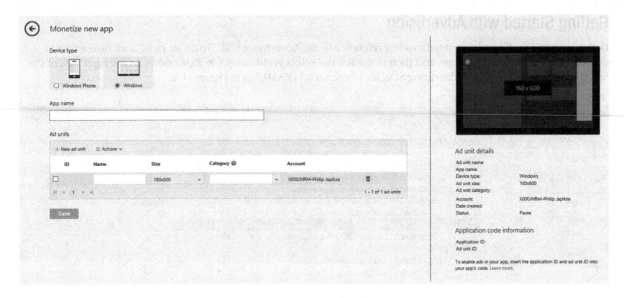

Figure 11-7. Creating a new app in pubCenter

Select Windows Store, enter in your name (note this does not have to match anything you already have), and then enter information into the first ad unit. You will need to name your ad unit, and select a size and category. Your account is automatically filled in. My example can be seen in Figure 11-8.

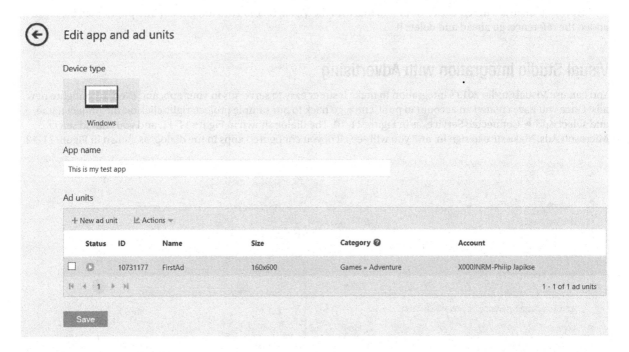

Figure 11-8. An example ad unit

Getting Started with Advertising

Before we begin coding ads, we need to add a reference to the Advertising SDK. To do so, right-click References in our sample, select Add Reference, and then in the left rail select Windows 8.1 ➤ Extensions. In the right side of the window, select the Microsoft Advertising SDK for Windows 8.1 (XAML) as in Figure 11-9.

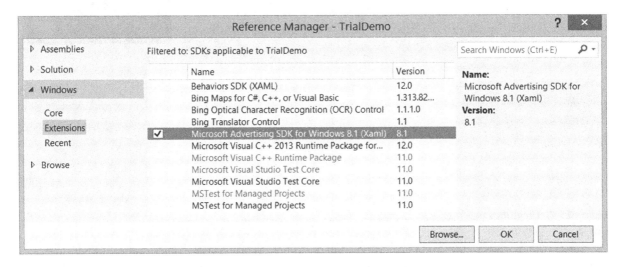

Figure 11-9. *Adding the Advertising SDK reference*

However, there is a much-easier way to do this with the Visual Studio 2013 integration into pubCenter. So, if you added the reference, go ahead and delete it.

Visual Studio Integration with Advertising

You can use Visual Studio 2013's integration to make it super easy to serve ads in your app, and even to configure new ads! Once you have created an account in pubCenter, go back to our sample project, right-click on the project name, and select Add ➤ Connected Service, as in Figure 11-10. The dialog shown in Figure 11-11, and you should select Microsoft Ads. Make sure to sign in, and you will see all of you configured apps in the dialog, as shown in Figure 11-12.

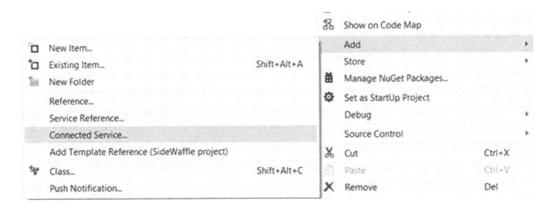

Figure 11-10. *Adding the Connected Service*

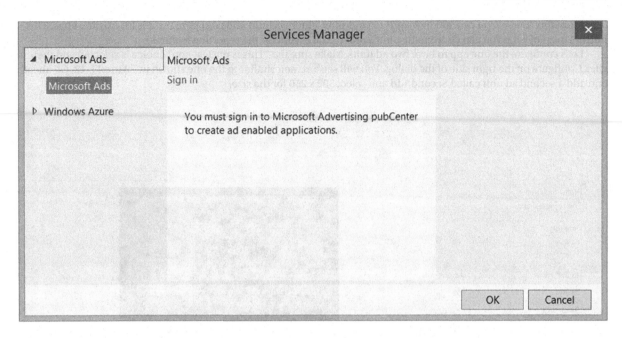

Figure 11-11. *Selecting Microsoft Ads*

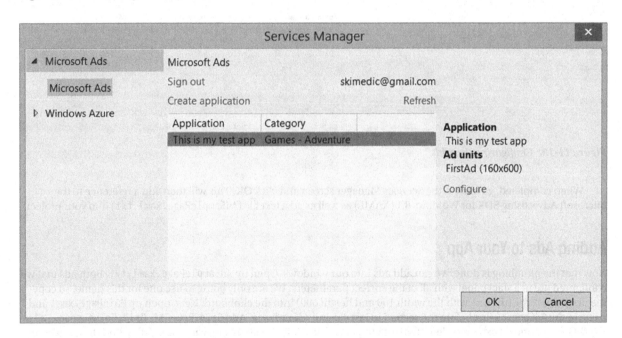

Figure 11-12. *Listing all of the configured apps*

From this screen, you can add new apps to your pubCenter account and configure the ads for existing apps. This mirrors most of what you can do from the pubCenter portal except for the reporting features).

Let's configure the one app to have two ad units. Make sure the "This is my test app" choice is selected and then click Configure on the right side of the dialog. You will see a screen similar to the one shown in Figure 11-13. Go ahead and add a second ad unit called SecondAdd and select 300 x 250 for the size.

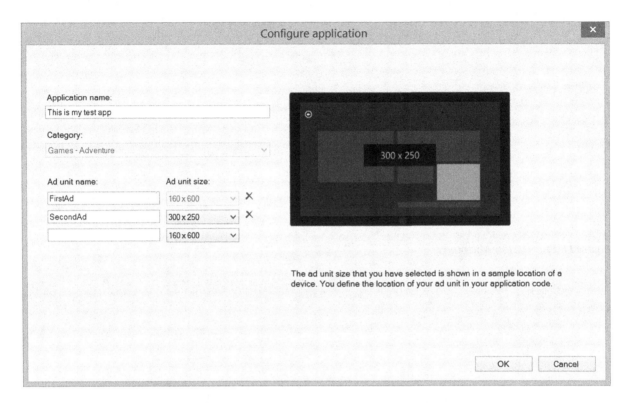

Figure 11-13. *Configuring the adds*

When completed, go back to the Services Manager screen and click OK. This will then add a reference to the Microsoft Advertising SDK for Windows 8.1 (XAML) as well as ad a text file (AdSamplePage.xaml.txt) into your project.

Adding Ads to Your App

Now that the plumbing is done, we can add ads into our windows. Open up AdSamplePage.xaml.txt. Both ads that we configured are in a stackpanel with all of the correct parameters. We are only going to use one for this demo, so copy the first AdControl (the one with the width 160 and height 600) into the clipboard. Next, open up MainPage.xaml and paste in the AdControl just before the second to last closing </Grid> tag. Add Grid.Row="5" Grid.Columnspan="2" to the AdControl and an extra row definition into the grid. The XAML is listed here, with the existing lines from previous examples omitted for brevity:

```
<Grid Grid.Column="0" Grid.Row="1" Margin="120,0,0,0">
  <Grid.RowDefinitions>
    <RowDefinition Height="auto"/>
    <RowDefinition Height="auto"/>
```

```
    <RowDefinition Height="auto"/>
    <RowDefinition Height="auto"/>
    <RowDefinition Height="auto"/>
    <RowDefinition Height="auto"/>
    <RowDefinition Height="auto"/>
  </Grid.RowDefinitions>
  <Grid.ColumnDefinitions>
    <ColumnDefinition Width="Auto"/>
    <ColumnDefinition Width="15"/>
    <ColumnDefinition Width="Auto"/>
  </Grid.ColumnDefinitions>
<!--Omitted for brevity -->
    <UI:AdControl Grid.Row="5" Grid.ColumnSpan="3"
      <!--The ApplicationId will be different for every app -->
      ApplicationId="0e42ce72-d233-4563-b91b-4a179a4d76f6"
      AdUnitId="10731177"
      Width="160"
      Height="600"
      Margin="0,0,0,0"
      HorizontalAlignment="Left"
      VerticalAlignment="Top"/>
</Grid>
```

The ad controls are created with all of the correct parameters entered in by using the Visual Studio 2013 integration. You can certainly create an AdControl by hand and then enter in all of these properties, but why would you need to? The integration does a great job of this for you. But if you need to update it, log into pubCentral, open up your app, and for each ad unit, the application code information is on the right side of the screen, as shown in Figure 11-14.

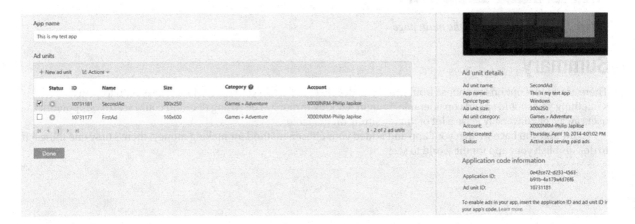

Figure 11-14. *Application code information*

The final step is to add the correct usings to the XAML. At the top of the page (in the page directive), add:

```
xmlns:UI="using:Microsoft.Advertising.WinRT.UI"
```

Now, run the app, and you will see your ad prominently placed on the screen, as shown in Figure 11-15.

Figure 11-15. Ad in place on the main page

Summary

There are a lot of options to choose from when you decide to monetize your app. Which one is right for you is something you should spend considerable thought working through. The wrong decision could scare your potential users away, or conversely leave a lot of money sitting on the table.

Now that you have written your app and added your chosen method for making money, there's only one thing left to do—publish your app for the world to see!

CHAPTER 12

■ ■ ■

Publishing Your App

You've written your app. It's tested locally. You've decided if (and how) you will try and make money from it. Now you are ready to publish it for the world to see. In this chapter, we show you how to do just that, from choosing the business model for your app to the many steps involved in publishing. But first, you need a developer account.

Signing Up for a Developer Account

Before submitting your app to the Windows Store, you must have a developer account. There are two types of developer accounts: individual accounts and company accounts. If you are a solo developer, you will want to select the individual account ($19 US at the time of this writing). If you are a corporate developer submitting apps on behalf of your organization, you may want to create a company account (US$99 at the time of this writing). For more information on the account types, please see this link on MSDN: `http://bit.ly/1hoUcLo`.

To get started, navigate to `http://dev.Windows.com`, click on Get Started, and then Sign Up. You will have to sign in with your Windows Live ID (and complete the two-factor authentication if that is how your account is set up). Once logged in, you will be presented with the Getting Started screen. This screen reminds you of the different developer accounts and what is required for each. Select the type carefully, as you can't change it later.

After selecting the type, you need to enter your demographic information. Once you've completed the registration process, you can't change your country either, so make sure to choose that as carefully as the type of developer account.

Setting Up Your Payout Account and Tax Information

If you plan on generating revenue from your app(s) (as discussed in Chapter 11), you need to fill out a payout account and complete the required tax information. To create your payout account, select Payout (under Profile) from the left rail for the Dev Center home page (shown in Figure 12-1). The forms walk you through setting up the account where any payouts will be deposited. Microsoft verifies that the account is correct before any payouts are sent. This means that if you change your account, payments might be delayed, so keep that in mind when setting up your payout account.

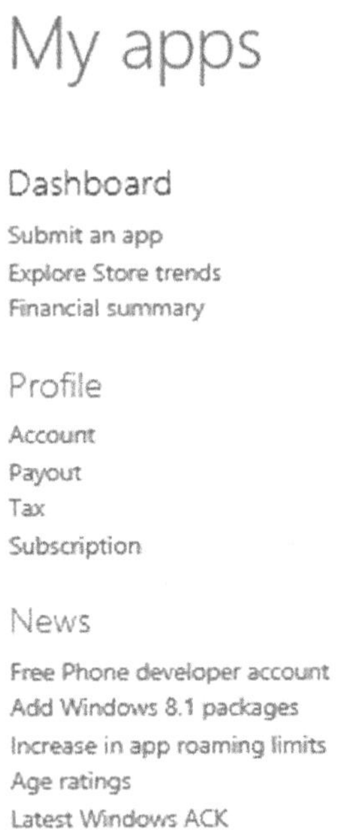

My apps

Dashboard

Submit an app
Explore Store trends
Financial summary

Profile

Account
Payout
Tax
Subscription

News

Free Phone developer account
Add Windows 8.1 packages
Increase in app roaming limits
Age ratings
Latest Windows ACK

Figure 12-1. *Windows Dev Center options*

Next, you need to configure your tax information by selecting Tax (under Profile) in the left rail of the home page of the Dev Center. The type of tax information is automatically selected for you by the wizard based on where your account is registered.

Now that you are a registered store developer complete with payout and tax information, you are ready to submit your app.

The App Submission Checklist

All of the following steps are under the Dashboard menu in Windows Dev Center on `http://dev.windows.com`. After logging in, select Dashboard, and then in the left rail, select Submit an App, as shown previously in Figure 12-1.

All of the steps are lined up in a series of buttons, as shown in Figure 12-2. The process if very linear, and at the end of it, you can submit your app for certification. If it passes, you will be a published app author! The rest of this chapter will walk you through the various steps in the process and discuss your various options.

Submit an app

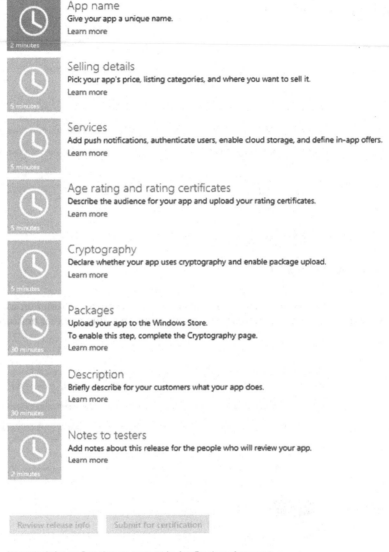

App name
Give your app a unique name.
Learn more

Selling details
Pick your app's price, listing categories, and where you want to sell it.
Learn more

Services
Add push notifications, authenticate users, enable cloud storage, and define in-app offers.
Learn more

Age rating and rating certificates
Describe the audience for your app and upload your rating certificates.
Learn more

Cryptography
Declare whether your app uses cryptography and enable package upload.
Learn more

Packages
Upload your app to the Windows Store.
To enable this step, complete the Cryptography page.
Learn more

Description
Briefly describe for your customers what your app does.
Learn more

Notes to testers
Add notes about this release for the people who will review your app.
Learn more

Review release info   Submit for certification

Your submission confirms that you agree to the App Developer Agreement.

Figure 12-2. *The submission workflow*

Picking an App Name

The name of your app is very important. Be creative, but not crazy. Catchy, but not quirky. Make sure it's representative of what your app does. "Phils Awesome App" might stroke your ego if your name is Phil but probably won't lead to downloads (except maybe by other people named Phil).

App names have to be unique. Spend some time coming up with choices, and then try them out in the dashboard. The good news is that you can reserve your name as soon as you come up with it. Once you have a unique name, you have one year to publish it before the name gets released back into the wild.

Click on the App Name button (shown earlier, in Figure 12-2). You are presented with a screen that explains the process pretty clearly (see Figure 12-3).

Submit an app

App name
Selling details
Services
Age rating
Cryptography
Packages
Description
Notes to testers

App name

Reserve the name under which we will list this app in the Windows Store. You must use this name as the DisplayName in the app's manifest.

Only this app can use the name you reserve here. Make sure that you have the rights to use the name that you reserve.

After you reserve a name, you must submit the app to the store within one year, or you lose your reservation. Learn more

App name

Phils Awesome App ☒

Reserve app name

Figure 12-3. *Submitting an app name*

If your name passes the uniqueness test, you will be presented with a confirmation screen explaining that your name is reserved and that you have to successfully submit your app within one year or lose the name, as shown in Figure 12-4.

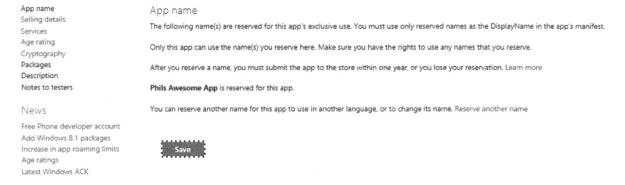

App name
Selling details
Services
Age rating
Cryptography
Packages
Description
Notes to testers

News

Free Phone developer account
Add Windows 8.1 packages
Increase in app roaming limits
Age ratings
Latest Windows ACK

App name

The following name(s) are reserved for this app's exclusive use. You must use only reserved names as the DisplayName in the app's manifest.

Only this app can use the name(s) you reserve here. Make sure you have the rights to use any names that you reserve.

After you reserve a name, you must submit the app to the store within one year, or you lose your reservation. Learn more

Phils Awesome App is reserved for this app.

You can reserve another name for this app to use in another language, or to change its name. Reserve another name

Save

Figure 12-4. *Confirmation dialog for reserved name*

If everything looks the way you want it to, click on Save. Now that you have a name reserved, we can associate our app with the store. Instead of doing that now, we are going to do that later in the process.

Setting Selling Details

To set the pricing and selling options for your app, click the Selling Details option in the workflow. On the Selling Details page, you set the selling price, whether there will be a trial period (and if so, how long), as well as many other options.

Price Tiers

As we mentioned in Chapter 11, the app's prices can be as low as US$0.99 and then go up from there. The lower tiers are shown in Figure 12-5.

Figure 12-5. Price tiers

Paid Upfront (No Trial)

To create a paid-upfront app without a trial option, select a price tier and set the free trial period to No Trial.

Paid Upfront (with Trial Option)

If you select a price tier, the free-trial-period combo box becomes available. The trial period can be one of a number of choices, as shown in Figure 12-6.

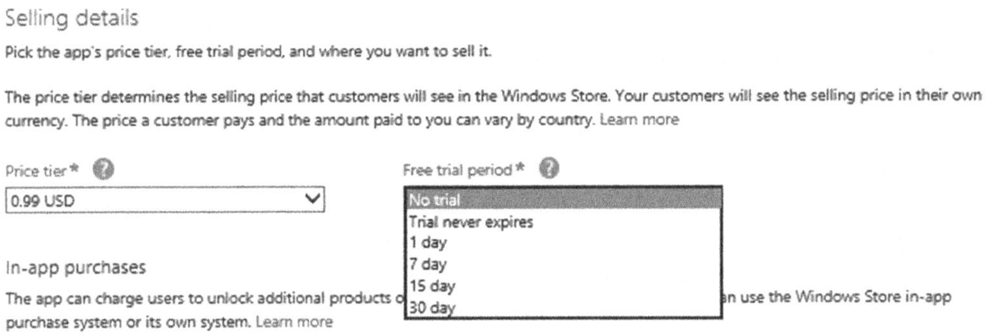

Selling details

Pick the app's price tier, free trial period, and where you want to sell it.

The price tier determines the selling price that customers will see in the Windows Store. Your customers will see the selling price in their own currency. The price a customer pays and the amount paid to you can vary by country. Learn more

Price tier * ❓
```
0.99 USD                        ⌄
```

Free trial period * ❓
```
No trial
Trial never expires
1 day
7 day
15 day
30 day
```

In-app purchases

The app can charge users to unlock additional products o[...]n use the Windows Store in-app purchase system or its own system. Learn more

Figure 12-6. *Trial options*

Configuring In-App Purchases

As we discussed in Chapter 11, in-app purchases are becoming a more-and-more-popular mechanism for generating revenue. They allow your users to use a certain feature set and then purchase premium features without having to download a new version of the app.

▪ **Note**   You must set up the in-app purchase tokens and features prior to submitting your app to the store. If you decide to change the offers in any way, you must resubmit a new version of your app.

As shown in Figure 12-7, just below the Price Tier and Free Trial Period selections is the In-App Purchases section.

Selling details

Pick the app's price tier, free trial period, and where you want to sell it.

The price tier determines the selling price that customers will see in the Windows Store. Your customers will see the selling price in their own currency. The price a customer pays and the amount paid to you can vary by country. Learn more

Price tier * ❓
```
0.99 USD                        ⌄
```

Free trial period * ❓
```
30 day                          ⌄
```

In-app purchases

The app can charge users to unlock additional products or features using in-app purchases. Your app can use the Windows Store in-app purchase system or its own system. Learn more

Use the Windows Store in-app purchase system

☐ My app uses a third-party commerce system for in-app purchases.

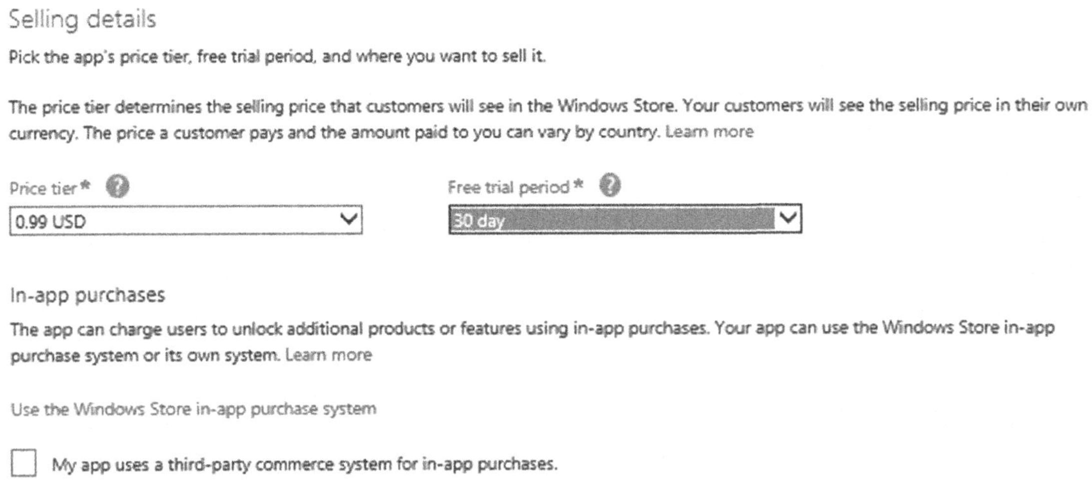

Figure 12-7. *The In-App Purchases section*

Click the link Use the Windows Store In-App Purchase System. You will see the screen shown in Figure 12-8. In the figure shown, I have already manually entered the data for MyCoolNewFeature. The screen will load with nothing selected. You can also use a third-party commerce system in your app, which we don't cover in this book.

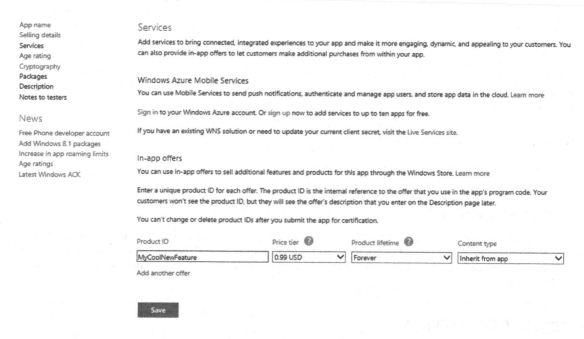

Figure 12-8. *Adding the CoolNewFeature as an in-app purchase*

The Product ID is the in-app purchase token that we created in Chapter 11. Select the Price Tier, the Product Lifetime, and the Content Type. The price tiers are the same as we previously discussed. The Product Lifetime can be set to a range from one day up to a year, forever, or marked as consumable (such as increasing the number of lives a user has in a game). You can also select a variety of options for Content Type, from in-app content, music, videos, books, or software as a service. Once you have all of the entries configured, click Save.

Markets

The next section on the Selling Details page allows you to pick the markets that you want to make your app available to. If you have selected a price tier, it will show the amount that will be charged in the local currency for that market. Of course, international pricing is subject to change based on current currency-conversion rates, so I would recommend considering those "suggestions" as opposed to the actual exact price in those markets.

Release Date

Next, you can set the release date. The earliest your app can be released is after passing certification, and that timing is, of course, variable. But you can also set the app to be released on a specific date and time if you want to hold up the release for some reason.

App Categories and Subcategories

Categorization is very important to the visibility of your app. Select a wrong category and it might never be found! So, choose from the available list and pick a subcategory if your main category allows you to choose any further distinctions (most of them don't). For example, the Music & Video category has a subcategory option (shown in Figure 12-9), but Productivity does not.

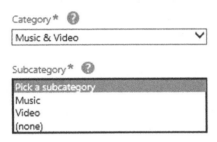

***Figure 12-9.** Music & Video list with Subcategory list showing*

Hardware Requirements

You can also specify that your app will only be available to certain hardware. The two choices are Minimum DirectX Feature Level and Minimum System RAM. For most applications (except games), the default value of "Available to all systems" is probably fine for each of these options. Of course, it is up to you and the nature of your app to determine how to fill this out.

Accessibility Requirements

Finally, you can assert that your app meets the accessibility requirements. More information is available on this MSDN page: `http://bit.ly/1n9jLzw`.

Services

The next step in the process is to determine if your app will tie into any services. We are already subscribing to one: in-app purchases. Additional examples of services are in Chapter 9 in the discussion of notifications, where we use Push notifications from Azure Mobile Services.

Age Rating and Rating Certificates

The section lets you select the ratings for your app, from being accessible to young children all the way to adults only. Read the ratings carefully. If you select one that is too low, your app can be removed from the store, and once that happens, it's a lot more work to get it back in.

Games might require additional documentation that is beyond the scope of this book.

Cryptography

Here, you are required to declare if your app uses any type of cryptography. This is important to get correct since the export laws of many countries forbid exporting tech that uses certain types of cryptography. For more information on the restrictions see this MSDN article: `http://bit.ly/1gfyWCA`.

Packages

This is the place where you upload your packages to the store. It is also a great time to associate your project with the store in Visual Studio 2013. For step-by-step instructions, see "Updating Your App's Identity (Associating Your App with the Store)" in Chapter 9.

Once you have your project associated with the store, you can create and test-certify your packages directly from Visual Studio by following these steps:

1. Right-click on the project name, select Store ➤ Create App Packages, as in Figure 12-10.

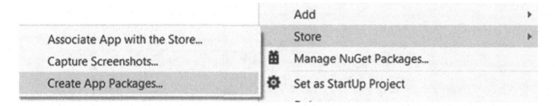

Figure 12-10. *Creating app packages*

2. After logging into your store account, you will be prompted with the following dialog (as shown in Figure 12-11). If you select Yes, the packages will be uploaded to the store for you.

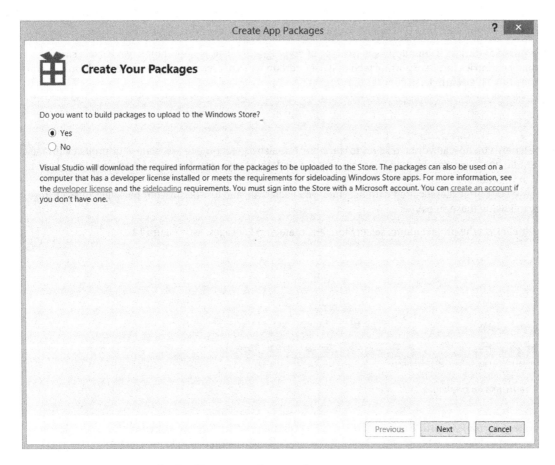

Figure 12-11. *Creating and uploading your packages to the store*

3.   The next screen confirms your identity (if you have more than one store account, you can select another account than the one you are currently signed in with). After confirming your identity, the wizard asks you to select the correct app. This needs to be the same app that you associated with your project, as in Figure 12-12.

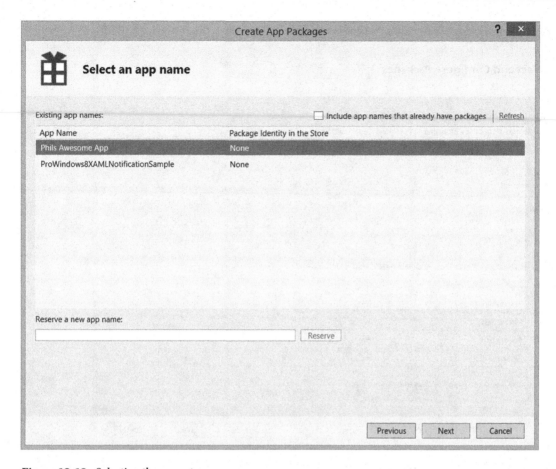

Figure 12-12. *Selecting the correct app*

4. The Select and Configure Packages screen, shown in Figure 12-13, allows you to choose your options for creating your app package(s).

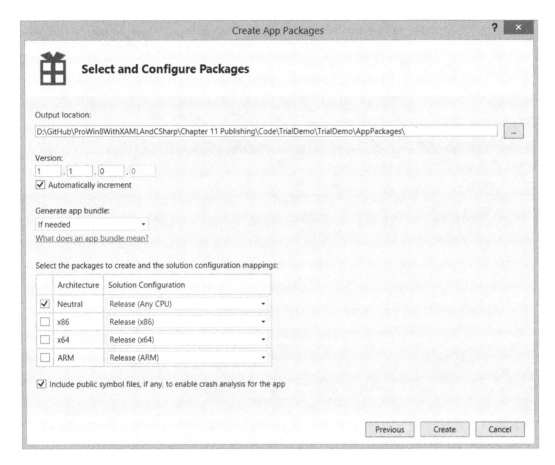

Figure 12-13. *Configuring the app package(s)*

App bundling allows you to package your app in smaller increments. This is beneficial if you utilize localization, image scales, or other options that result in users not needing to download the entire package all at once.

5. The Package Creation Completed screen, shown in Figure 12-14, shows the success/failure of the package creation and allows you to run the certification tests on either the local machine or a remote machine. This is helpful if you want to do tests on an ARM device such as a Surface RT. To run the tests, select the Launch Windows App Certification Kit button.

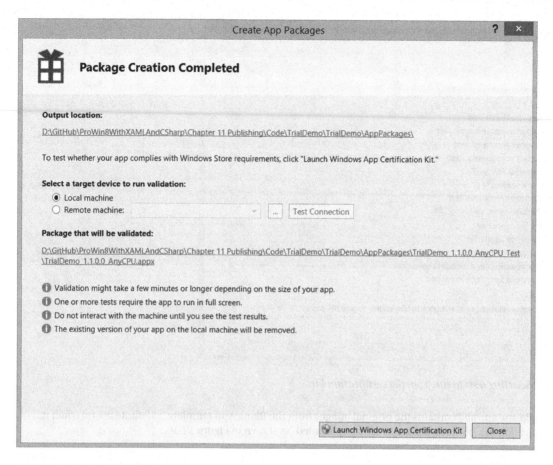

Figure 12-14. *Test certification screen*

6. The certification kit process isn't exhaustive testing but it is a good way to catch common mistakes. Select all of the tests offered, as in Figure 12-15. Your app will restart several times, and if it's installed on your machine, it will be uninstalled.

Figure 12-15. *Selecting tests to run from the certification kit*

For example, my app still contains the original images from the Blank App template, a definite no-no when it comes to certification. It's not surprising that my sample failed, as shown in Figure 12-16.

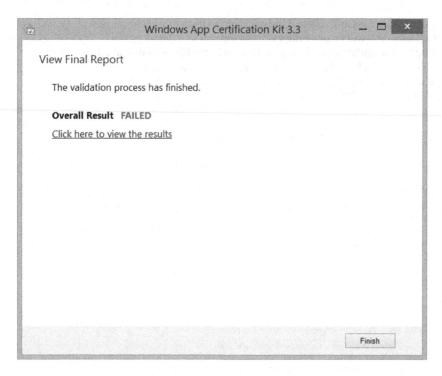

Figure 12-16. *Local certification test failure*

7. Clicking on the button to view the results proves that the app failed because of the images, as shown in Figure 12-17. It *didn't* fail because of the use of CurrentAppSimulator. It will fail the real certification process if you leave the calls to CurrentAppSimulator. But it's still a good first test to run the certification kit process. As of this writing, it's been updated to version 3.3, and with every release it gets better.

App manifest resources test

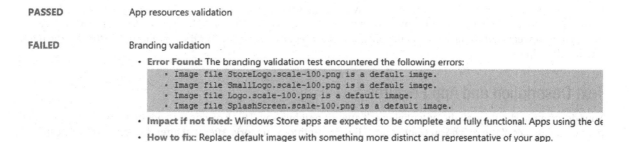

Figure 12-17. *Failure due to using template images*

8. When you fix the issues and you are ready to upload the package, go back to your dashboard and select Packages. You will be presented with the option to either drag the appxupload file created by Visual Studio onto the page or browse to the file to be uploaded. As a reminder, the location of the package file is shown in Figure 12-14 (as part of the building process). Once you upload the file, if it's successful, it will be listed under the correct version (either Windows 8.1 or Windows 8.0), as shown in Figure 12-18.

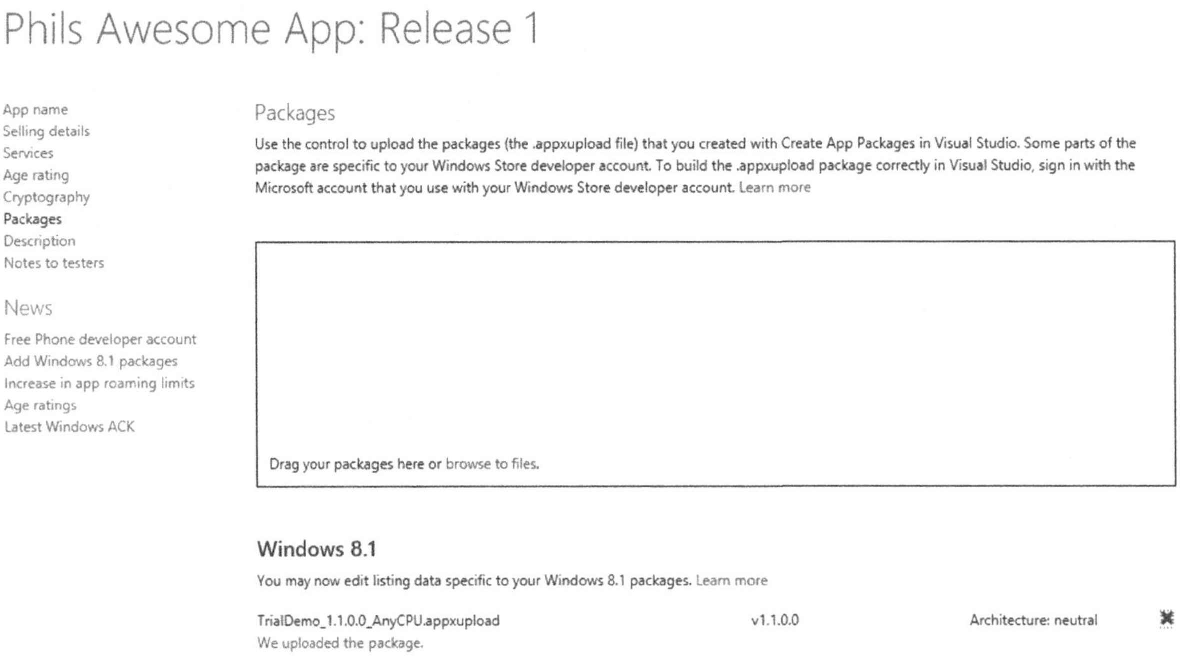

Phils Awesome App: Release 1

App name
Selling details
Services
Age rating
Cryptography
Packages
Description
Notes to testers

News

Free Phone developer account
Add Windows 8.1 packages
Increase in app roaming limits
Age ratings
Latest Windows ACK

Packages

Use the control to upload the packages (the .appxupload file) that you created with Create App Packages in Visual Studio. Some parts of the package are specific to your Windows Store developer account. To build the .appxupload package correctly in Visual Studio, sign in with the Microsoft account that you use with your Windows Store developer account. Learn more

Drag your packages here or browse to files.

Windows 8.1

You may now edit listing data specific to your Windows 8.1 packages. Learn more

TrialDemo_1.1.0.0_AnyCPU.appxupload We uploaded the package.	v1.1.0.0	Architecture: neutral	✖

Figure 12-18. *Package upload screen after successful upload*

Description

Once you have uploaded packages, you can start working on the description entries. There is a lot of work to do here, so dig in and prepare to spend significant time on it. And really, that is as it should be. You've done a lot of hard work to get your app ready for publishing and the only thing that separates it from all of the other apps out there is the name and the description.

Text Description and App Features

Your description should grab the potential user's attention right away. Think of a newspaper headline and the first few sentences of the story. You want to draw the viewer into your story. After that attention-grabbing intro, be concise. Short paragraphs and lists are recommended by Microsoft. Not recommended are dry language and detailed descriptions of every feature. Consider this: you probably only have one chance to entice a user to download and install your app. You want the description and feature list to get him to go ahead and click the Install button. A great description and a free trial are a great combination! To see all of the Microsoft guidelines, go to this MSDN page: http://bit.ly/1hy8HMS.

What types of packages you uploaded (Windows 8.1 or Windows 8.0) will determine which descriptions and app features will be available to be filled out. In my example, since I only uploaded 8.1 bits, the 8.0-specific content isn't available for me to fill out (see Figures 12-19 and 12-20).

Figure 12-19. *Adding a description and app features for the Windows 8.1 package*

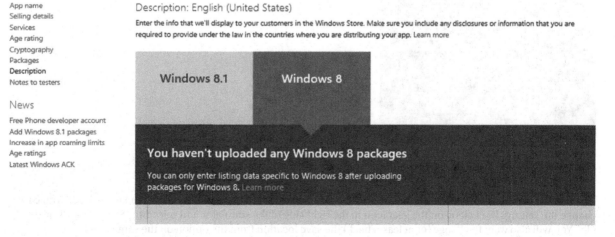

Figure 12-20. *Windows 8.0 description options disabled without a Windows 8.0 package*

The app features will appear as a bulleted list underneath your description (the bullets are supplied automatically; no need to add them yourself).

Screenshots

There are a variety of images already used by your app such as tile images, the splash screen, and so on. In addition to those, you also need to upload screenshots that will be used by the store. The first image can be custom-made (such as a promotional image), but the rest must be actual screenshots. Each image must be at least 1366 x 768 pixels (or 768 x 1366 if in portrait view), in PNG format, and smaller than 2 MB. Before we get into adding the images, let's talk about how to create all of the screenshots that are needed for submission.

Creating Screenshots with the Simulator

To create a screenshot, open up your project in Visual Studio and change the target run location to the Simulator, as shown in Figure 12-21. Once running, you can change the screen resolution by clicking on the image of the monitor in the right corner of the simulator (see Figure 12-22).

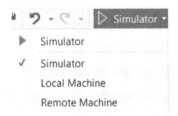

Figure 12-21. Configuring Visual Studio 2013 to run app in the simulator

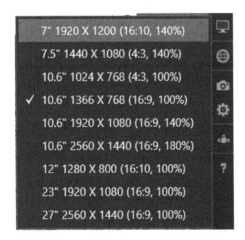

Figure 12-22. Changing the screen resolution

Prior to capturing images, you will want to know where they are being saved. As shown in Figure 12-23, you can change the settings by clicking on the gear icon in the right side of the simulator and selecting "Save screenshot as file." You will also want to change (or at least check) the save location from the option on the same menu.

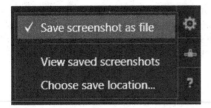

Figure 12-23. Changing the screenshot settings

Once you have the settings correct, run the app and click on the camera on the side of the simulator to take a screenshot. Rotate the simulator (if your app supports a portrait) and take another screenshot. You can also change the resolution of the simulator and take more screenshots. At least one is required, but you can add up to eight in total.

Adding App Images

For the first image, we need to select something that represents our app. What is more fitting than taking a screenshot of the book cover on the Apress site? It is important to note that the image must be 1366 x 768 pixels, or 768 x 1366. The dimensions 1365 x 768 will not upload (believe me, I've tried!). For the promotional image, I selected the one shown in Figure 12-24.

Pro Windows 8.1 Development with XAML and C#
By **Jesse Liberty**, **Jon Galloway**, **Philip Japikse**

Learn to develop feature-rich Windows 8.1 apps using the proven C# language.

v Full Description v

ISBN13: 978-1-4302-4047-1
325 Pages
User Level: Beginner to Advanced

Figure 12-24. Promotional image

Click on Add Image in the first box in the Screenshots area of the description page (shown in Figure 12-25) and add an image of your choice. It's important to select the first box for the promotional image because the rest of the choices are for actual application screenshots. Next, add to the app settings the screenshots you created with the simulator. For each image, you need to provide a description (up to 200 characters). My final image settings are shown in Figure 12-25, although you probably want to include better descriptions when you're doing a real app!

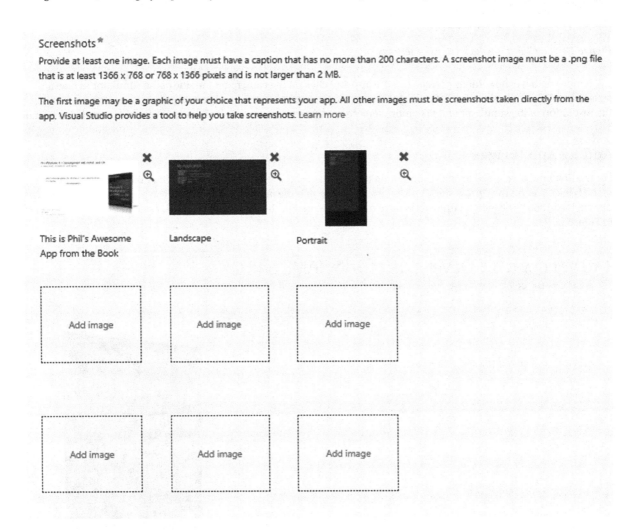

Figure 12-25. *Promotional image and screenshots added*

Adding Notes and Recommended Hardware

The last section of the platform-specific entries is for notes as well as hardware recommendations. The notes field is a great place to add update information (telling users what's new in this release) or any other information that doesn't belong in the general description.

If your app needs a certain level of hardware, you can list the requirements in a bulleted list (the store will add the actual bullets for you) in this section.

Keywords

The Keywords section is the same across all versions of Windows. It's important to use keywords that apply to your app. It might seem like a good idea to put the name of the latest wildly popular game in the list of keywords to drive traffic to your app. However, if your app isn't anything like that game, you will get a reputation for trolling, and it will hurt your reputation as a publisher. You can add up to seven keywords, so choose carefully.

Copyright and Trademark Info and Additional License Terms

Copyright and trademark information is required. You can optionally add additional license terms if they apply to your app.

Promotional Images

If your app gets featured in the store, you will need to have promotional images included with your submission. If you don't supply the images, your app won't qualify to be selected as a featured app in the Microsoft Store. However, even if you add the correct image sizes, it doesn't mean your app *will* get featured. It's recommended to supply the images just in case the stars align and your app is selected to be a featured app in the store.

Web Site and Contact Info

The support contact information is required. This can be an e-mail address or a web page. The web site is optional, but having a site with links to your other apps is a great cross-promotional tool.

Privacy Policy

While the privacy policy is not marked as required, I know plenty of app developers who have had their submissions rejected because they didn't include a privacy policy. If your app collects any personal information, connects to a service, or in any way makes it possible for a user to accidentally share her personal information, a policy is required.

In-App Offers Description

If your app offers in-app purchasing, you need to supply a description for each offer in your app. This is another reason that all in-app offers must be defined prior to final submission to the store.

Notes to Testers

This section allows you to leave instructions for the people who will be testing your app. For example, if they need to log into a service, provide them with a user ID and password to fully test the features.

Submitting for Certification

Once you have entered everything to your satisfaction, you can review your release info and submit your app for certification, as shown in Figure 12-26. If it passes, then you are in the store!

Phils Awesome App: Release 1

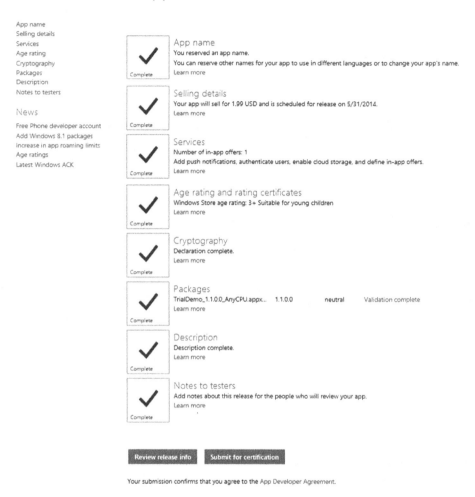

App name
Selling details
Services
Age rating
Cryptography
Packages
Description
Notes to testers

News

Free Phone developer account
Add Windows 8.1 packages
Increase in app roaming limits
Age ratings
Latest Windows ACK

App name
You reserved an app name.
You can reserve other names for your app to use in different languages or to change your app's name.
Learn more
Complete

Selling details
Your app will sell for 1.99 USD and is scheduled for release on 5/31/2014.
Learn more
Complete

Services
Number of in-app offers: 1
Add push notifications, authenticate users, enable cloud storage, and define in-app offers.
Learn more
Complete

Age rating and rating certificates
Windows Store age rating: 3+ Suitable for young children
Learn more
Complete

Cryptography
Declaration complete.
Learn more
Complete

Packages
TrialDemo_1.1.0.0_AnyCPU.appx...   1.1.0.0   neutral   Validation complete
Learn more
Complete

Description
Description complete.
Learn more
Complete

Notes to testers
Add notes about this release for the people who will review your app.
Learn more
Complete

Review release info   **Submit for certification**

Your submission confirms that you agree to the App Developer Agreement.

Figure 12-26. *Ready for submission!*

Certification Requirements

The certification process is a combination of automated and manual testing. The process begins when you upload your package. During the package upload, your app is tested for technical compliance based on the following rules, documented on MSDN: `http://bit.ly/0QYsGD`.

Submitting the app for certification queues the app for automated testing. The first round checks for viruses or other malware. If your app is clean, the next step is technical compliance, which amounts to almost the same test as the one in the certification kit provided. I say "almost" because the downloadable software always lags somewhat behind what is being used in production. This is simply a fact of life, since it takes time and resources to package up software.

If the technical compliance test passes, then certification testers (and yes, I mean real live people) will test it for content compliance. Make sure you include notes to the testers (as previously described) so that they can effectively test your app. They will *not* sign up for your really cool service themselves. You must provide them with a user ID and password that they can use to do the test.

Finally, after all that, you get a report indicating if your app passed or failed, and if it failed, why. Keep in mind that any failure along to pipeline will stop the process. So if your package includes a virus or the app fails the technical specifications, don't expect a certification tester to test your app.

If your app passes, it will be published for the store. Either as soon as your place in the queue gets processed, or the date that you specify, whichever is later. While your apps listing page will appear as soon as your app is published, your app might need a little time before it starts showing up in searches, as indexes have to be rebuilt, caches flushed, and so on.

Summary

As you can see from the length of this chapter, there are a lot of steps involved in publishing your app. I believe this is by design to help minimize the amount of frivolous apps getting submitted to the store. While many analysts and some media outlets seem to be focused on the raw numbers of apps, users care about the quality.

The combination of automated testing and manual review helps keep the quality high, improving user experiences. It also helps to reduce the risk of malware and other malignant software, increasing users' trust in software from the store. Both of these factors help you to increase your reach and potential revenue.

Index

■ X, Y, Z

Get the eBook for only $10!

Now you can take the weightless companion with you anywhere, anytime. Your purchase of this book entitles you to 3 electronic versions for only $10.

This Apress title will prove so indispensible that you'll want to carry it with you everywhere, which is why we are offering the eBook in 3 formats for only $10 if you have already purchased the print book.

Convenient and fully searchable, the PDF version enables you to easily find and copy code—or perform examples by quickly toggling between instructions and applications. The MOBI format is ideal for your Kindle, while the ePUB can be utilized on a variety of mobile devices.

Go to www.apress.com/promo/tendollars to purchase your companion eBook.